10/96

WITHDRAWN

 St. Louis Community College

Forest Park
Florissant Valley
Meramec

Instructional Resources
St. Louis, Missouri

GA

Dandies and Desert Saints

Dandies and Desert Saints

Styles of Victorian Masculinity

JAMES ELI ADAMS

Cornell University Press

Ithaca and London

First published 1995 by Cornell University Press.

Printed in the United States of America

Library of Congress Cataloging-in-Publication Data
Adams, James Eli.
    Dandies and desert saints : styles of Victorian masculinity / James
Eli Adams.
        p.   cm.
    Includes bibliographical references and index.
    ISBN 0-8014-3017-8 (alk. paper).—ISBN 0-8014-8208-9 (pbk. : alk.
paper)
        1. English literature—19th century—History and criticism.
2. English literature—Men authors—History and criticism.   3. Great
Britain—Intellectual life—19th century.   4. Masculinity
(Psychology) in literature.   5. Gender identity in literature.
6. Aestheticism (Literature)   7. Patriarchy in literature.   8. Sex
role in literature.   9. Dandies in literature.   10. Men in
literature.   I. Title.
PR468.M38A33   1995
820.9'353—dc20   95-11320

⊗ The paper in this book meets the minimum requirements of the American National Standard for Information Sciences—Permanence of Paper for Printed Library Materials, ANSI Z39.48-1984.

For Michele
and
In Memoriam
E. P. A. 1922–1983
J. E. A. 1913–1979

Contents

Acknowledgments

In a book much concerned with the solitude of intellectual labor, it is a special pleasure to acknowledge so much intellectual exchange and support. This project began to stir at Cornell University, where M. H. Abrams, Jonathan Culler, Dorothy Mermin, and Paul Sawyer were especially helpful. I was able to begin writing during a junior faculty research leave at the University of Rochester, for which I owe special thanks to Morris Eaves and Cyrus Hoy. I am also grateful to Indiana University for a summer faculty fellowship and a junior research semester, which greatly assisted me in completing the book.

The English department at Indiana University, Bloomington has been such a stimulating and supportive environment that it seems invidious to single out particular colleagues. But I am especially grateful to Patrick Brantlinger, who helped to make room for yet another Victorianist and read much of the book in draft, and to my colleagues at *Victorian Studies*, Andrew Miller, whose exacting criticism is too little in evidence here, and Donald Gray, whose generosity made possible additional course relief, and whose editorial genius is an inspiration. For sympathetic and painstaking readings of particular chapters, I am greatly indebted to Amanda Anderson, Mary Burgan, David DeLaura, Richard Dellamora, Lee Sterrenburg, Herbert Sussman, Steve Watt, and Paul Zietlow, as well as the readers for Cornell University Press. At an early stage of the project I was prodded by conversations with Herb Sussman, who along with Linda Dowling generously shared unpublished material. John Kucich, whose rich and provocative work on the Victorian novel was a crucial stimulus to this project, has helped in more ways than he knows. George Ford and Gerhard Joseph have provided wonderfully steadfast encouragement and guidance through the years; every young scholar should have the good fortune of such mentors. Bernhard Kendler of Cornell University Press has been an extremely supportive and patient editor. For a wealth of other forms of advice, criticism, and encouragement, my thanks to Sharon Bassett, Joe Bizup, Bill Burgan, Carol Christ, Evan Davis, Regenia Gagnier, Donald E. Hall, Donald L. Hill, Billie Andrew Inman, Kenneth Johnston, John Jordan, John Maynard, John McGowan, Thais Morgan, Russell Peck, John Reed, Matthew Rowlinson, Linda Shires, William Shuter, Sandra Siegel, Herbert F. Tucker Jr., Hayden Ward, Robyn Wiegman, and Lisa Wilson.

Portions of this book were delivered as talks at the Northeast Victorian Studies Association meetings at NYU and Princeton, the Victorians Institute, the University of Illinois at Urbana-Champaign, and the Dickens Project conferences at the University of California at Santa Cruz; I am grateful to all those audiences.

My greatest debt is to Michele Moody-Adams, who has taken time out from the truly ascetic regimen of philosophical argument to read and quarrel with this less-disciplined project, and whose remarkable life I have had the great joy of sharing. I dedicate this book to her and to the memory of those whose devotion outlives them.

The excerpts from Walter Pater's unpublished essay "The Aesthetic Life" are reprinted with the kind permission of the Houghton Library, Harvard University, and Sharon Bassett, who is editing the Pater manuscripts for publication. Portions of Chapter 5 have appeared in an earlier version as "Gentleman, Dandy, Priest: Manliness and Social Authority in Pater's Aestheticism," *ELH* 59 (1992): 441–66; portions of Chapter 4 were published as "Pater's Muscular Aestheticism," in *Muscular Christianity: Embodying the Victorian Age*, ed. Donald E. Hall (Cambridge: Cambridge University Press, 1994); and a portion of Chapter 1 appears as "The Hero as Spectacle: Carlyle and the Persistence of Dandyism," in *Victorian Literature and the Victorian Visual Imagination*, ed. John Jordan and Carol Christ (Berkeley and Los Angeles: University of California Press, in press). I am grateful to the publishers, Johns Hopkins University Press, Cambridge University Press, and the University of California Press, for permission to use the material here.

J. E. A.

Dandies and Desert Saints

Introduction

The old ideal of Manhood has grown obsolete, and the new is still invisible to us, and we grope after it in darkness, one clutching this phantom, another that; Werterism, Byronism, even Brummelism, each has its day.

> Thomas Carlyle, "Characteristics" (1831)

To be bold against the enemy is the prerogative of brutes; but the prerogative of a man is to be bold against himself.

> Charles Kingsley, *Westward Ho!* (1857)

In this book I explore a contradiction within Victorian patriarchy, by which the same gender system that underwrote male dominance also called into question the "manliness" of intellectual labor. Under the gendered logics of domestic ideology, a wide array of Victorian intellectual vocations—Tennysonian poetry, Tractarian faith, Arnoldian culture, Paterian aestheticism, even Carlylean prophecy—came to resemble models of feminine activity and authority, particularly the "influence" assigned to the domestic woman. From this perspective, the exclusionary force of Carlyle's "hero as man of letters" is charged with the energies and anxieties of masculine self-legitimation; it represents one especially vehement effort to claim for those engaged in the work of Coleridge's "clerisy" the status of normative manhood. The convergence of domestic and intellectual labor has been noted in recent feminist analyses of Victorian gender and culture; typically, however, those analyses concentrate on the work of gender in marginalizing women and mystifying class hierarchies. Most notably, Mary Poovey's influential account of *David Copperfield* interprets Dickens's representation of a male writer's life as an exemplary "feminization of authorship" that occludes "the iniquities and hypocrisies of class society" (78). But the feminization of intellectual labor may also be turned against the male writer through the social leverage attached to such epithets as "unmanly" or "effeminate." As male intellectual labor is susceptible to such labels—and to the varieties of powerful, sometimes violent stigma they convey—that labor becomes an especially revealing focus of the shifting contours and internal stresses in Victorian discourses of gender.

Dandies and Desert Saints examines the various ways in which male Victorian writers represent intellectual vocations as affirmations of masculine identity. The middle-class male authors I analyze—Carlyle, Tennyson, Thomas Arnold, Newman, Dickens, Kingsley, Pater, and Wilde—depict their own intellectual labors in markedly varied rhetorics, but those rhetorics are persistently related in their appeal to a small number of models of masculine identity: the gentleman, the prophet, the dandy, the priest, and the soldier. Each of these models is typically understood as the incarnation of an ascetic regimen, an elaborately articulated program of self-discipline. As such, they lay claim to the capacity for self-discipline as a distinctly masculine attribute and in their different ways embody masculinity as a virtuoso asceticism. Such discipline is familiar enough in accounts of Victorian repression, where Victorian "manliness" often figures as one more mechanism for enforcing continence.[1] But regimens of masculinity regulate more than erotic desire; they are many-faceted constructions of identity and social authority that inevitably situate the private self in relation to an imagined audience. In this light, what I call Victorian "styles of masculinity" exemplify Judith Butler's claim that "gender is always a doing" (25), although I approach that practice along the lines Foucault urges in studying Greek *askesis*: "not as an expression of, or commentary on, deep and essential prohibitions, but as the elaboration and stylization of an activity" (*Uses of Pleasure* 23). Analyzing the representation of masculine identity as an ascetic discipline, variously conceived, brings to light a wealth of neglected affinities among widely disparate writers, and thus reshapes some of the familiar outlines of Victorian literary history. The rhetorics of Carlylean heroism and of John Henry New-

---

1. Cohen, *Talk on the Wilde Side*, and Mosse, *Nationalism and Sexuality*, are two recent studies that understand "manliness" primarily as a mechanism of sexual regulation.

man's Tractarian priest, for example, can be seen to shape the narrative strategies of high modernism in James and Conrad through the crucial mediating rhetoric of Paterian aestheticism. Through such connections, I hope to elicit a complex and largely unexplored interplay between Victorian literary forms and the social logics of masculine self-fashioning, and to underscore the importance of masculinity as a central problematic in literary and cultural change.

That masculine identities are multiple, complex, and unstable constructions, even within the framework of a particular culture, has been a long-standing emphasis in the social sciences, and has been implicit in much feminist analysis of gender over the past quarter of a century. Explicit and sustained articulation of this emphasis within literary and cultural studies, however, has been resisted by those concerned that dwelling on the complexities and burdens of masculine identity would serve to obscure, and thereby to reinforce, the brute realities of male domination against which feminist analyses were and are in the first place directed.[2] To take issue with large generalizations about "patriarchy," for example, by stressing "the fragility of masculinity at the psychic level, rather than elaborating on its role as a foundation for man's social power" (Roper and Tosh 15), may seem to buttress the masculine hegemony that it claims to analyze—or, less charitably, to participate in what Eve Kosofsky Sedgwick has called a "vast national wash of masculine self-pity" (*Epistemology* 145). That possibility is a recurrent subject of this book, inasmuch as the possibility can be seen as an eminently Victorian logic. But the formulation in question is misleading not in its emphasis on psychic fragility, but in its construction of an apparent dichotomy between that fragility and "social power." The articulation of social power works through as well as against the fragility of masculine identities. Not only may that fragility reflect objective social and economic stresses, but it may powerfully inform both the domination of women and exclusionary logics directed against men.

Homophobia is the most obvious and violent of such logics, and recent work in gay studies and queer theory has been especially pow-

2. Taking aim at that possibility, Stephen Heath opened his influential essay, "Male Feminism" (1987), with the flat assertion, "Men's relation to feminism is an impossible one" because "we are always also in a male position which brings with it all the implications of domination and appropriation, everything precisely that is being challenged, that has to be altered" (1). Wiegman, "Feminism and Its Mal(e)contents," offers a recent, lucid overview of feminist studies of masculinity.

erful in challenging the assumption that "a male position" is always unitary, and always a position of dominance.[3] The argument of this book, however, focuses on the complexities and internal tensions of gender rather than sexuality—of gender understood as a system of social authority frequently articulated across apparent divides of normative and transgressive sexualities. The dichotomy of hetero- and homosexuality that emerges from late Victorian discourse has often distorted earlier Victorian constructions of "manliness" by being unreflectively read back on them. To use the Foucauldian terms that dominate much recent study of sexuality, Victorian men are "marked" not simply by medico-juridical regulation of the body, but by assignments of gendered identity that circulate outside that discourse, and are shaped through comparatively occasional, informal, even haphazard rhetorical engagements (as in Kingsley's notorious passing slur against "Romish priests," which called forth Newman's *Apologia Pro Vita Sua*).[4] Certainly this is true, for example, of the increasingly pointed and violent social leverage inherent in the authority to designate a man or an idea "effeminate"—a label that in early Victorian usage has no clear bearing on sexuality. This is a norm that was being contested well before the taxonomies of Nordau or Krafft-Ebing, and largely apart from legal and medical discourse, in a great variety of discursive forms—from novels to scholarly treatises to biographies to newspaper editorials to lyric poems to private correspondence.

Self-discipline is of course a fabled Victorian attribute, whose extraordinary prominence in nineteenth-century culture historians have explained as a function of the conjoint rise of Evangelicalism and an increasingly pervasive market economy, as well as the Malthusian logics common to both arenas.[5] In emphasizing the economic utility of self-discipline, however, historians have devoted less attention to the forms of symbolic capital it might afford. The passing of "the old ideal of Manhood," in Carlyle's phrase, points to the broadly European phe-

---

3. The extraordinary growth of gay studies may be gauged from the 1987 collection *Men in Feminism* (edited by Alice Jardine and Paul Smith), in which only one essay, by the late Craig Owens, called attention to the exclusionary force of constructions of "men" deployed by both men and women in feminism.

4. Even recent studies of sexuality have suggested that the Foucauldian model gives too much weight to the authority of medical discourse. Maynard, *Victorian Discourses of Sexuality and Religion*, makes this point in reference to heterosexual identities; Chauncey, "Christian Brotherhoods," draws the conclusion from his study of homosexual subcultures in early-twentieth-century America.

5. Christopher Herbert's *Culture and Anomie* offers a recent and richly textured account of this interrelation as it shapes the notion of "culture."

nomenon that Peter Stearns has called "the unseating of patriarchal manhood" (51), which is but one facet of the profound transformation of English culture in the wake of industrialism. The English, Samuel Johnson confidently asserted in 1755, were effectively governed by "the fixed, invariable, external rules of distinction of rank" (Perkin 25). A century later, those rules and the security they afforded had largely disintegrated as "rank" gave way to structures of class, yet social hierarchy was a more urgent preoccupation than before—largely as a consequence of its new flexibility. What had intervened, notoriously, was a momentous transformation of economic possibility that incited increasingly complicated and anxious efforts to claim new forms of status and to construct new hierarchies of authority—and hence new means of marking or delineating one's membership in particular groups. In this context, the energetic self-discipline that distinguished manly "character" offered not only economic utility but also a claim to new forms of status and privilege within an increasingly secular and industrialized society.

At the same time, however, reconfigurations of masculinity frequently compensated for the loss of traditional, more assured forms of masculine identity and authority; they endeavored to restore the prerogatives of a "manhood"—as distinct from mere "maleness"—that had been severely eroded by the pressures of modernity. The separation of home and workplace, and the increasingly rigorous gendering of that division, led to a growing isolation of middle-class fathers from their sons, who in their early years were immersed in a sphere increasingly designated "feminine," and then—in a phenomenon unparalleled elsewhere in Europe—transported to the all-male environment of boarding schools, which tended to become surrogate family structures. The expanding social mobility available to young men in an industrial society also strained relations between generations and unsettled customary genderings of male labor, as traditional continuities between the "places" of father and son were disrupted by participation in that new and more volatile social structure, the career. Even traditional associations of manhood with sexual prowess were weakened by the pursuit of middle-class standards of living, which led men increasingly to delay marriage in pursuit of adequate income; tributes to economic "abstinence" were thus increasingly associated with, and energized by, a regimen of specifically sexual restraint. Long-standing associations of manhood with independence were likewise undermined, as men increasingly bequeathed their sons education (or simply the middle-class status signified by schooling) rather than property, and as newly

demanding divisions of time and labor gave rise to daily routines that
were more intricately regimented than ever before (E. P. Thompson).[6]

The passing of "the old ideal of manhood" thus marked the loss of
a central point of identity and social reference for large numbers of
men across the class spectrum. The consoling power of gender to bol-
ster or bestow status and security is reflected in the reception of Carlyle's own famous coinage, "Captains of Industry," perhaps the most
widely echoed Victorian reconfiguration of masculinity. The phrase was
quickly separated from Carlyle's furious attack on the economic rationality of his age, but it gained wide currency because it attached to the
economic power of the entrepreneur the status of a traditional martial
ideal and thereby solidified the social authority of what had been at
best a fragile norm of manhood under an aristocratic ethos contemp-
tuous of "trade." Such an ideal, however, was predicated on brute economic power, and hence had little to offer middle-class men who were
not themselves masters of capital. Carlyle's vision of "the hero as man
of letters" is largely a response to this dilemma: it attempts to redeem
the "manfulness" of intellectual labor by arguing that the writer is a
latter-day priest, a vocation for which priesthood was the historical prototype.

As this association claimed new status for the male writer, it would
prove a powerful model for another form of emergent masculine identity, the "professional man." Like the Carlylean sage, the professional
professes to disdain narrowly economic interests; as a result, his authority, like that of the writer, depends crucially on strategies of persuasion or charismatic self-presentation designed to convince an
audience that it ought to value (and to pay for) entertainment or expertise whose worth cannot be measured by the market (Perkin 170;
Larson 215–31). But the Carlylean model of the writer as prophet was
typically modified in the interests of less eccentric, and more stable,
relations with an imagined audience. Increasingly, middle-class professionals (including male writers) legitimated their masculinity by identifying it with that of the gentleman—a norm that was the subject of
protracted contention throughout Victorian culture, because the concept served so effectively to regulate social mobility and its attendant
privileges. It is an ideal that is famously resistant to the incursions of
entrepreneurial manhood (Wiener), but throughout the first half of

---

6. This brief overview is indebted to Stearns, *Be A Man!*, which offers the best social
historical survey of European and American masculine identity in the wake of industrialism.

the nineteenth century it was reshaped as an incarnation of ascetic discipline and infused with the fabled Victorian earnestness. The gentleman was thereby rendered compatible with a masculinity understood as a strenuous psychic regimen, which could be affirmed outside the economic arena, but nonetheless would be embodied as a charismatic self-mastery akin to that of the daring yet disciplined entrepreneur. Charles Kingsley's injunction in *Westward Ho!*, one of the most popular of all Victorian novels, is exemplary in transferring the burden of manhood from martial courage to inner struggle: "The prerogative of a man is to be bold against himself" (*Life and Works* 5:19).

By founding the manliness of intellectual labor on self-discipline, however, male writers laid claim to an ideal whose authority in Victorian culture derived in large part from its apparently egalitarian character. Self-discipline seemed a virtue open to all; hence efforts to claim it as a gendered activity are unusually revealing of the complexity and internal strain that characterize gendered identity. In Nancy Armstrong's influential account, self-discipline figures centrally in the construction of a distinctly modern subjectivity in the late eighteenth century, in the form of a putatively classless yet emphatically gendered being, the domestic woman. While assigning to man the work of accumulation, this scheme reserved for women "a form of labor that was superior to labor"—the labor of self-regulation, on which the success of the husband's accumulation would depend (81). By the 1830s, however, particularly in the discourse of political economy, self-discipline is increasingly claimed as the special province and distinguishing attribute of middle-class men, as both manhood and masculine labor are constructed in increasingly agonistic forms. In Victorian tributes to self-discipline, men take over the work of both accumulation and self-regulation, and women are relegated to the netherland that Nancy Cott has called "passionlessness." That state marks a reductio ad absurdum of an ongoing struggle to appropriate the very real authority attached to the power of self-discipline. Although the purported passionlessness of women exempted them from the traditional, degrading stereotype of the sexual temptress, it also excluded them from the ascetic regimen that authorized participation in economic life. Only men could acquire the self-discipline that functioned as the governor (in both a political and a technological sense) of political economy, since that regimen required an energizing struggle with wayward desires that women allegedly did not experience (Cott). Thus in 1839, for example, Archibald Alison argued against an extension of the franchise on the grounds that the fundamental virtue of civic life, self-discipline, is the

distinguishing feature of professional men: "Existence to them is an
incessant scene of toilsome exertion and virtuous self-denial . . . their
whole life is a sacrifice of the present to the future" (296).

The more emphatically this gendered distinction is affirmed, however, the more overtly problematic it becomes. Because self-discipline
perplexes the binaries of active and passive, of self-assertion and self-
denial, tributes to it frequently confound traditional assignments of
gender. This is particularly marked in appeals to the religious paradigm
of Victorian self-regulation: Sarah Ellis in 1837 eagerly claimed Christ
as an exemplar of distinctly feminine virtues, as the only man ever to
have displayed the "self-sacrifice and pure devotion" of women (Nelson 10), and forty years later Thomas Hughes was still struggling
against those associations in affirming, as he put it, "the manliness of
Christ." The vastly popular writings of Samuel Smiles reflect a more
general confusion. They urge that the crowning virtue of "character"
owes less to "head-power" than to "heart-power," which (Smiles concedes) women possess in greater abundance than men; but Smiles
nonetheless insists that character is a mode of energetic self-discipline
most fully realized by men (140).

Such contradictions are more subtly inscribed throughout Victorian
representations of womanhood. Dickens's *Hard Times* offers an especially vivid instance of what seems a universal discipline when Sissy Jupe
confounds the cynical, feckless Harthouse with her announcement that
he will never again see Louisa Gradgrind: "Her modest fearlessness,
her truthfulness which put all artifice aside, her entire forgetfulness of
herself in her earnest quiet holding to the object with which she had
come; all this, together with her reliance on his easily-given promise—
which in itself shamed him—presented something in which he was so
inexperienced, and against which he knew any of his usual weapons
would fall so powerless, that not a word could he rally to his relief"
(171). Were one to alter the pronouns, it is easy to imagine this passage
describing young Arthur of *Tom Brown's Schooldays*, or Dobbin in *Vanity
Fair*, because what Dickens attributes to Sissy is also the quiet, fervent,
self-forgetful integrity of the early Victorian gentleman, most memorably evoked by Newman in *The Idea of a University*. We glimpse in these
characters something of the moral androgyny informing early-
nineteenth-century children's literature, where "manly" is an honorific term applied to boys and girls alike, as denoting moral maturity
generally (Nelson 7–10). Over the course of the century, however,
commentators increasingly distinguished between a masculine self-
discipline, which they represented as an ongoing regimen of aggressive

self-mastery, and a feminine self-denial, which they represented as a spontaneous and essentially static surrender of the will to external authority. John Stuart Mill summed up this distinction in attacking it in *The Subjection of Women*: "All women are brought up from their very earliest years in the belief that their ideal of character is the very opposite to that of men; not self-will, and government by self-control, but submission, and yielding to the control of others" (21:271). As "government by self-control," self-discipline secures the most fundamental attribute of traditional manhood, autonomy. Women are not allowed to be the masters of their own repression, Mill argued, because such mastery is inseparable from self-determination. This shadowy but powerful boundary frequently structures the careers of heroines in Victorian novels, who often lay claim to productive agency by transforming submission into a virtuoso ascetic regimen, only to be stigmatized when that self-discipline is recognized as an assertion of independent will. Whereas the commanding earnestness of Sissy Jupe (as of so many of Dickens's female characters) expresses a "child-like ingenuousness," George Eliot's heroines typically provoke suspicion by channeling their earnestness into a calculated and concerted—and hence unsettlingly aggressive—regimen of self-mastery. In their different ways, Maggie Tulliver and Dorothea Brooke claim to participate in a decidedly masculine self-fashioning that is vividly captured by Tennyson, in a passage widely cited by Victorian proponents of heroic masculinity:

> . . . life is not as idle ore,
>
> But iron dug from central gloom,
>   And heated hot with burning fears,
>   And dipt with baths of hissing tears,
> And batter'd with the shocks of doom
>
> To shape and use.
>   (*In Memoriam* 118:20–25)

This fierce technology of masculine selfhood similarly informs that ne plus ultra of Victorian gendered binaries, Ruskin's *Sesame and Lilies*: "You may chisel a boy into shape . . . But you cannot hammer a girl into anything. She grows as a flower does" (*Collected Works* 18:108).
The very familiarity of these passages may have dulled us to their potentially subversive implications. To begin with, they point to a self-fashioning not easily accommodated by domestic ideology. If masculinity defines a fundamentally ascetic regimen, if manhood must be forged through being "batter'd with the shocks of doom," then the feminine

balms of home may seem to enervate rather than support men. This logic is one important, albeit largely tacit, rationale for the Victorian public school: the "manliness" of a Charles Kingsley is a virtue that cannot be acquired at home. Less often observed is the more subversive possibility that manhood cannot be *sustained* within domesticity, since the ideal is incompatible with ease. Moreover, insofar as regimens of manhood embody an active self-mastery rather than a mere capitulation to circumstance, they reproduce within masculinity a paradox central to what Weber calls inner-worldly asceticism. Virtuoso asceticism, in Weber's account, always incorporates an element of the mediated, performing selfhood against which it defines itself. The ascetic who wishes to annihilate worldly selfhood, to construct a subjectivity that flows directly from God, nonetheless concedes a persistent authority to "the world" as the theater in which to prove his otherworldly distinction: "It is imperative for the virtuoso that he 'prove' himself before God, as being called solely through the ethical quality of his conduct in this world. This actually means that he must 'prove' himself to himself as well. No matter how much the 'world' as such is religiously devalued and rejected as being creatural and a vessel of sin, yet psychologically the world is all the more affirmed as the theatre of God-willed activity in one's worldly calling" (*From Max Weber* 290–91).

This paradox is recast in a variety of secular forms within the classical sociological tradition—perhaps most provocatively in Hegel's construction of the master-slave paradox, which has a profound bearing on the anxious self-fashioning of Victorian masculinities. Under the conjoint authority of Evangelical faith and romantic subjectivity, early and mid-Victorian norms of manhood construct an ideal of essential selfhood that repudiates self-consciousness as a mark of theatricality. In attacks on the dandy or "swell," for example, a theatricality readily accommodated in earlier constructions of aristocratic manhood is disavowed as the sign of a socially mediated identity, which betrays both religious integrity and the social autonomy fundamental to manhood. But a manhood that ostensibly transcends self-interest and the gratifications of social regard must nonetheless be proved in the theater of the world. Like the Hegelian master, the Victorian gentleman—in common with the Carlylean hero, the Tractarian priest, and the Tennysonian poet—invariably depends on forms of recognition that he professes to disdain, and is thus implicated in the logic of the dandy.

The title of this book, *Dandies and Desert Saints*, points to the importance of this anxious conjunction of discipline and performance in middle-class Victorian constructions of masculinity. More generally, the title hints at the intractable element of theatricality in all masculine self-fashioning, which inevitably makes appeal to an audience, real or imagined. I associate those appeals with "styles" of masculinity (rather than "representations" or "forms") in order to emphasize the inter-relatedness of literary and social logics in constructions of masculine identity. By approaching masculinity as a rhetorical transaction, one acknowledges not only the embeddedness of gender in discursive struc-tures but also the very personal urgencies informing the human en-gagements that shape gendered identity. Such dynamics readily lend themselves to analysis in the broadly Lacanian terms that have domi-nated much recent discussion of gender and sexuality. In early and mid-Victorian discourses of masculinity, norms of manhood consistently work to resist the possibility that human identity is inevitably mediated and self-estranged. They thus confirm the view, in Kaja Silverman's for-mulation, that "classic male subjectivity rests on the denial of castra-tion"—the "castration" of severance from integral, self-sufficient identity, which every subject experiences in entering the order of lan-guage (44). Yet the very ideality of this formulation—which is captured in the phrase "classic male subjectivity" (or, alternatively, "traditional masculinity" [51])—makes it of limited use for discriminating among historical variations in "male subjectivity," or (more important for my purposes) of analyzing competing constructions of normative masculin-ity within a single historical moment. The challenge is to move beyond the deconstruction of gender, to move beyond perpetually rediscover-ing that "the feminine" conceived in terms of "lack" is always already at the heart of masculinity. This dynamic is a truism in anthropology: as David Gilmore's recent cross-cultural survey of norms of masculinity argues, "manhood" almost universally assumes the form of "a pose that is deeply conflicted, pressured, and forced, a mask of omnicom-petence and almost obsessive independence" (209). As the theatrical tropes imply, even normative masculinity is typically asserted as an unending performance, in which, in the words of Pierre Bourdieu, a man must "offer himself to be seen, constantly put himself in the gaze of others" (Gilmore 51).

The masculine, in short, is as much a spectacle as the feminine.[7] This book in effect explores the varied ways middle-class Victorian male

7. So powerful is this gendered paradigm that a 1993 article in *PMLA* urges the novelty of contending that masculinity might also assume the form of a spectacle (London). As most work in this vein derives from Laura Mulvey's seminal 1975 essay, "Visual Pleasure and Narrative Cinema," it is worth recalling that Mulvey explicitly confines her analysis to "the cinematic apparatus."

writers represent masculinity—and hence themselves—as spectacle.
More precisely, it focuses, first, on constructions of gendered identity
as forms of intellectual and social authority that are established through
ascetic self-presentation to an audience; and, second, on the connections between the literary and social logics informing those constructions—as well as the frequent disjunctions between the rhetorical
self-construction and the historical reception of the author. I concentrate on authors and works explicitly concerned to legitimate vocations
devoted to intellectual labor, because such projects represent with special clarity the perplexities that follow from the Victorian "feminizing"
of such labor. Moreover, as these writers typically construct such labor
as a world apart from women, their works throw into especially sharp
relief the ascetic, and often misogynistic, logics informing Victorian
constructions of manhood. As Herbert Sussman has powerfully argued,
the pervasive Victorian preoccupation with male brotherhoods recognizes that the monk or celibate priest marks one logical limit to manliness understood as self-control. This book, by contrast, adopts a more
external perspective on the figures it analyzes, focusing on masculine
identity as a social logic, a strategy of self-presentation, to the compar-
ative neglect of libidinal investments. As such the argument is vulnerable to Richard Sennett's objection to the work of Erving Goffman and
its dramaturgic paradigms: that his people behave, but they do not have
experiences (35–36). I run that risk, however, in an effort to recover
the nuances of gender as an emphatically social discourse, and with it
the historical particularity too often obscured in categorizations of desire.

   This book follows a number of recent studies that have finally begun
to treat disciplinary regimens as productive dynamics, as something
other than examples of a repression understood to deform some elemental or essential selfhood—a view that in large part reproduces the
frequent complaints of the Victorians themselves. The constitutive powers of an ascetic regimen—its function, in Foucault's phrase, as a technology of the self—have been suggestively demonstrated in Geoffrey
Galt Harpham's *Ascetic Imperative in Culture and Criticism*, in which asceticism is explored as the agency that gives aesthetic form to human
life. A more precisely historicized account of the productive effects of
self-discipline has been offered by John Kucich, who, in *Repression in
Victorian Fiction*, analyzes Victorian novelists' representation of repression as a production of eroticized internal conflict, a "luxuriously self-
disruptive" libidinal energy, in pursuit of self-negation as the ultimate

end of desire. As novelists invoke repression to create this richly eroticized interiority, Kucich argues, they produce a subject that values
silenced or negated feeling above open expression, and thereby separate selfhood from collective life, subjectivity from social identity. In a
displacement very similar to that which Armstrong describes, the capacity for repression is invoked as "a sign of deeper resources of subjectivity," a claim to "libidinal distinction" offered in place of social
hierarchies structured around economic and political power (31).

Kucich's analysis is particularly helpful as it prompts an understanding of repression in relation to an imagined audience, an "external
regard" whose pressures are registered with special force in the label-
ing of deviance. Gender deviance in Victorian culture, I have suggested,
is a social category more inclusive, and more complex, than the assign-
ment of transgressive sexuality. That complexity is especially important,
I argue in Chapters 2 and 5, in understanding Victorian constructions
of secrecy between men. It is of course the case that male-male desire
throughout the Christian West has tended to be cloaked in secrecy, but
this does not entail—as a good deal of recent literary and cultural
criticism tends to assume—that secrecy always speaks of homoerotic
desire. Victorian obsessions with secrecy are manifold and powerfully
overdetermined. They are animated by pervasive fears of economic and
political dislocations, as well as by the development of a recognizably
modern information culture, in which an explosion of new technolo-
gies of information, along with increasingly extensive and intricate webs
of commercial relationships, seemed everywhere to compromise traditional forms of autonomy, and thus prompted an often desperate with-
drawal into the shelters of private space. In what Richard Sennett has
called "the fall of public man," individuals tend to pursue autonomy
not through action but through an increasingly exacting regulation of
personality, through "a constant effort to formulate what it is that one
feels" (152). The writer's vocation, which is centrally preoccupied with
varieties of self-representation and problematics of audience, condenses with special clarity this more diffuse and encompassing social
pursuit of mastery through self-definition. But the sense of vulnerability
that prompts increasingly elaborate and guarded forms of self-
presentation to an imagined audience also animates a deep mistrust of
such strategies in others. Hence the increasingly acute Victorian unease
with strangers—an anxiety vividly registered in etiquette books, in nov-
elistic treatments of blackmail, in paranoid preoccupation with secret
societies, and (most broadly) in a general devaluation of the public

sphere.[8] This complex of anxieties helped to solidify in England by
midcentury a norm of "manliness" identified above all with honest,
straightforward speech and action, shorn of any hint of subtlety or
equivocation.

But under the sway of this norm, the subjectivity inculcated by ascetic discipline—and by early Victorian rhetorics of masculinity—became suspect. The various rhetorics of masculinity explored in this
book all locate in the capacity for self-discipline a charisma that seems
to emanate from a rich interiority or "deep" subjectivity commonly associated with romantic selfhood. From the regimen of Foucault's "cal-
culable man" writers attempted to recover the individuality of the
"memorable man," who is distinguished not by the regularity of his
discipline but by the singular energies that sustain it (*Discipline and
Punish* 193). This is a subjectivity defined (at least in principle) apart
from, often in overt antagonism to, traditional economic and social
norms; hence its recurrent association with eager social mobility,
which Dickens so insistently caricatured in characters like Uriah Heep.
Yet Dickens's portraits suggest how powerfully programs of masculine
self-fashioning may arouse the pervasive suspicion of hidden designs.
That suspicion becomes especially pronounced when regimens of virtuoso masculine discipline assume collective forms, which are frequently denounced as priesthoods or masonic brotherhoods—social
forms always exposed to attack as "unmanly" because they seem to be
hiding something.

In emphasizing the overdetermination of gender, I am arguing that
what Eve Kosofsky Sedgwick has powerfully analyzed as "the homosocial continuum" is a structure subject to "double binds" from forces
other than homophobia. In this regard, the book sketches what one
might call a genealogy of the closet, which attempts to complicate Sedgwick's epistemology of the closet by placing it within a more fully articulated social and discursive history. Sedgwick's work is so suggestive that
most criticism of it seeems carping and pedantic by comparison; nonetheless, as she and a number of commentators have noted, her mar-

8. On the various pressures bound up with strangers becoming "more intractably a mystery" (Sennett 20), see Stearns (53), Welsh (60–109), and, most comprehensively,
Sennett's *Fall of Public Man*, which explores the nineteenth-century construction of a
"culture of intimacy" as a flight from the complexities of public life. Curtin (129–30)
notes the "chilling cast" of Victorian etiquette books in their "profound distrust of
the motives and intentions of strangers," which contrasts markedly with the sociability
emphasized in eighteenth-century courtesy books.

velous literary readings are relatively impoverished historically. This weakness reflects in part the origins of her ongoing project in her work on the gothic novel, a genre whose constructions of gender and sexuality have not been adequately historicized. The force of this juncture in Sedgwick's own intellectual genealogy is perhaps clearest in chapter 5 of *Between Men*, where she discovers in the rise of the Gothic what she calls "terrorism and homosexual panic." Early-nineteenth-century England, she argues, might be called "the age of Frankenstein," given the frequency with which novels of the period describe men who feel themselves persecuted by, or even transparent to, and often under the compulsion of, other men (91–92). If, she continues, "we follow Freud in hypothesizing that such a sense of persecution represents the fearful, phantasmic rejection by recasting of an original homosexual (or even homosocial) desire, then it would make sense to think of this group of novels as embodying strongly homophobic mechanisms" (92). But there is another avenue for considering these structures of male rivalry, which derives not from Freud but from a popular maxim of the late 1960s: "Just because you're paranoid doesn't mean they're *not* out to get you." That is to say, the remarkable prominence of male rivalries in gothic fiction, as in Victorian culture generally, should be seen as a response not only to private phantasms, but to the public, collective reality of middle-class social and political anxiety throughout the nineteenth century. Such rivalries need to be understood under the shadow of at least two revolutions, the French and the Industrial. Thus, for example, one can recognize in the religious demonology of gothic fiction an episode in the ongoing construction of a myth of Englishness, which addresses fears of working-class insurrection by displacing them onto a Continent infested with deranged priests fomenting terror— beings that Protestant England liked to think itself well rid of.[9] It is this aspect of the gothic tradition, I suggest in Chapter 2, that shapes contemporary hostility to the Oxford Movement, hostility that would have surprisingly far-reaching echoes in late-Victorian constructions of masculinity.

Throughout the book I speak to the interrelations among gentleman, dandy, priest, prophet, soldier, and professional as models of identity central to the rhetorical self-fashioning of Victorian intellectual men. But the argument is arranged in a roughly chronological sequence, so that individual styles in their complex particularity can also

9. Sage, *Horror Fiction*, offers a stimulating account of the force of Protestant theology in shaping gothic constructions of subjectivity.

be seen as engagements with an evolving, collective discourse of gendered identity. Each chapter focuses on a small group of authors of largely neglected (and sometimes unlikely) affinities in their construction of masculinity—Kingsley and Tennyson, Pater and Kingsley, Wilde and Newman, among others. In eliciting these affinities, I try to underscore not only the writers' participation in a collective discourse, but their elaboration and revision of other models in shaping their distinctive rhetorics. Chapter 1 implicitly sketches the historical trajectory of the book as a whole by examining the figure of Carlyle's prophet in the wilderness—probably the most familiar, and most influential, construction of Victorian intellectual patriarchy—less as a figure of neglected wisdom ("the Victorian sage") than as a paradigm of ascetic manhood. Carlyle's symbolic opposition of prophet and dandy in *Sartor Resartus* introduces the tensions between autonomous and ascribed identity that haunt Victorian constructions of masculinity, but also points to the dynamics of social authority informing reconfigurations of aristocratic Georgian masculinity. The Carlylean hero-prophet also exemplifies a widespread Victorian representation of masculinity as a virtuoso asceticism, a rigorous discipline staged before an imagined audience. The "parades of Pain" that Tennyson rehearses in *In Memoriam* and the martyrdom of Sydney Carton in Dickens's *Tale of Two Cities* are just two instances in which masculine identity is realized through a regimen of solitary but emphatically visible suffering, which claims the authority of manhood while estranging the hero from all forms of collective identity.

Chapter 2 examines early Victorian efforts to reconcile such discipline with forms of collective identity. The widespread Victorian fascination with brotherhoods, real or imagined, suggests a preoccupation with fellowship that cuts across ideological divides, yet the frequent demonizing of such groups also captures a pervasive uneasiness aroused by "closed corporations" of various kinds. This tension, I argue, shapes the reception of two extremely influential ascetic brotherhoods of the 1830s and 1840s, Thomas Arnold's Rugby School and the Tractarian movement at Oxford centered around John Henry Newman. As they attempt to realize an ascetic manhood through group membership, both of these societies resemble Carlyle's Abbey of St. Edmundsbury in *Past and Present*, which attempts to represent a social order compatible with the rigors of Carlylean discipline. But in the popular imagination both also came to resemble secret societies, whose social integrity and appeal were solidified by rhetorics of arcane experience that also incited widespread suspicion. The contemporary hostility aroused by the Tractarians has come to be read as an expression of homophobia, aroused by a social formation in which intense homosocial relations were not occluded by the exchange of women that typically facilitates bonds between men. But a comparison with the reception of Arnold's Rugby, both before and after A. P. Stanley's influential biography of Arnold, suggests that the primary anxieties were more overtly political. Secrecy was interpreted less as an index of sexual transgression than as a sign of conspiracy directed against the existing political order. What we do find in attacks on the Tractarians, however, is the emergence of a gendered rhetoric that facilitated the subsequent sexualizing of gender transgression, in which "effeminacy" was seen not as a public failure of forthright courage, but as the outward manifestation of a private, sexual deviance. The reception of early Victorian brotherhoods, that is, put in wide circulation a social semiotic that was to transform male secrecy into the sign of "the closet."

Charles Kingsley was perhaps the single most prominent figure in this momentous cultural transformation. Certainly his ideal of "muscular Christianity," formulated largely in antagonism to Newman's ascetic discipline, has long been seen to codify a crucial shift in Victorian conceptions of masculinity, through which an earlier paradigm of spiritual discipline gave way to a celebration of unreflective bodily vigor. In this regard Kingsley may seem the odd man out in my array of authors. In Chapter 3, however, I argue that Kingsley's "muscular" ideal of manhood is structured by the very asceticism he insistently attacked. His writings incorporate this tension in an especially violent oscillation of discipline and abandon, which magnifies an instability inherent in a notion of manhood as an incessant mastery of temptation. Much as in Tennyson's poetry, the potential loss of "manly" self-control confronts the heroes of Kingsley's novels in figures of liminal or divided identity—hysterical men, women of mixed race, men of uncertain class affiliation—whose sufferings frequently reach the pitch of utter abasement. As they insistently rehearse the burdens of masculinity, these figures bring home the powerfully equivocal significance in Victorian representations of male suffering. Although they may work to underscore the prerogatives of male dominance, those representations may also register objective strains in the psychic regimen of what Marx called the science of renunciation. In particular, Kingsley's writings expose the masochistic logic informing the embrace of self-discipline not merely as an instrumental virtue but as the basis of a fundamental autonomy: as "true manhood" inheres in conjoining self-mastery with the defiance of circumstance, it follows that the true man punishes himself.

In Chapters 4 and 5 I explore neglected continuities between late-Victorian rhetorics of "decadence" and earlier representations of masculine identity, which intersect with particular richness in the writings of Walter Pater. In his later works, Pater draws on early Victorian rhetorics of earnestness in implicit response to attacks on the "effeminacy" of *The Renaissance*. Yet this appropriation is possible only because Pater's writings are centrally structured by a psychic economy derived from Carlylean earnestness, under which the disciplined male body incarnates an exhilarating release from the burdens of self-consciousness. As a discourse of the male body, the aestheticism that Pater derives from German Hellenism has important points of contact with late-Victorian athleticism, as well as with Ruskin's widely echoed claim that the gentleman's authority derives from an innate, somatic sensibility. Pater, however, cannily elicits the homoerotic overtones informing these celebrations of the virile body and thereby anticipates the powerful continuum between the mystique of the Victorian public school and the emergent homosexual identity legitimated in the 1890s as (among other things) the "New Chivalry."

Pater's most important contribution to fin de siècle constructions of masculinity, however, was a rhetoric of dangerous enticement, of the "fascination" of art and the artist, which is the central concern of Chapter 5. This is the rhetoric that was to exert such a profound influence on Wilde—who repeatedly echoed Pater in evoking the fascinations of the double life—and on the more diffuse preoccupation with obliquity and obscurity that distinguishes the modernist narratives of Conrad and James. But if the genealogy of modernism thereby incorporates a rhetoric of transgressive male desire, as Sedgwick has powerfully argued, it also develops dynamics of social authority informing the rhetoric of Tractarian reserve, as well as early Victorian evocations of charismatic manhood, both of which figure centrally in the logics of Wilde's prose. Where Pater and Wilde departed from these earlier rhetorics is in more openly embracing the theatricality—the mediated, dandyistic identity—that attends programs of masculine self-fashioning. As the aesthete solicits a public gaze, which would acknowledge his very being as the consummation of "culture," his display of disciplined reserve marks an especially distinctive convergence of the Victorian gentleman, the dandy, and the priest.

A brief afterword, finally, points to the overlooked persistence in our late-twentieth-century sexual idiom of rhetorical preoccupations that animated early Victorian constructions of "manliness." This is in keeping with my emphasis throughout on unexpected points of continuity and contact between normative and transgressive masculinities. This emphasis, like the neglect of constructions of manhood by women writers, necessarily shapes a partial portrait. But both emphases will be seen, I hope, as an effort to stimulate more inclusive and historically specific studies, not merely of masculine identity, but of the particular and constantly changing ways in which gender shapes the texture of our lives. "Manliness" is exemplary of all gender norms in being always under pressure from the very social dynamics that authorize it, the changing consolidation of social authority through new varieties of suspicion, exclusion, and affirmation.

CHAPTER ONE

Dandies and Prophets: Spectacles of Victorian Masculinity

He looked very handsome then, with his black hair, fine Eyes, and a sort of crucified expression.
> Edward Fitzgerald, recalling Carlyle in 1840

> Who best
> Can suffer, best can do.
>> Milton, *Paradise Regained*

"The Dandiacal Body," Carlyle's savagely witty attack on dandyism in *Sartor Resartus* (1833), defines a manifold and richly suggestive juncture in the social history of early Victorian England. The caustic portrait of an England reduced to antithetical "sects" of Dandies and Drudges, which anticipates by more than a decade Disraeli's trumpeting of the "two nations," also heralds a distinctively middle-class ascendancy in British culture—and with it, a norm of middle-class manhood. In Carlyle's satire, the dandy becomes the grotesque icon of an outworn aristocratic order, a figure of self-absorbed, parasitic existence, against which Carlyle evokes a heroism founded on superbly self-forgetful devotion to productive labor—an ideal most famously celebrated as the reign of the "Captains of Industry" in *Past and Present*. This antagonism between the hero and the dandy not only organizes much of Carlyle's writing, but operates as one of the founding symbolic oppositions of Victorian discourse.

But the dandy and the Carlylean hero are far less securely opposed than this familiar account suggests. The dandy haunts the Carlylean hero less as an emblem of moral indolence or economic parasitism than as an image of the hero as spectacle, which arrestingly embodies a problematic of audience and authority—and hence of masculinity. Far from presenting an assured "nonchalance" (Buckley 37), the dandy Carlyle describes in "The Dandiacal Body" is an anxious, almost plaintive character, wholly lacking a secure sense of self. His sole desire, Teufelsdröckh mocks, is "that you would recognise his existence; would admit him to be a living object; or even failing this, a visual object. . . . Your silver or your gold . . . he solicits not; simply the glance of your eyes . . . do but look at him, and he is contented" (205). Carlyle thus seizes the paradox that Camus would echo more than a century later: for all the dandy's defiance of convention, in Camus's words, "He can only be sure of his own existence by finding it in the expression of others' faces" (51). The dandy is a fundamentally theatrical being, ab- jectly dependent on the recognition of the audience he professes to disdain.[1] As such, the dandy is antithetical to the Carlylean hero, whose essential selfhood is typically bodied forth in a "savage" disregard for social decorum and the public gaze. Yet the dandy's theatricality clearly figures a powerful impulse in Carlyle's own aspirations as a writer and prophet. Indeed, Carlyle tacitly acknowledges the affinity throughout his early writings, where he caricatures both himself and dandies as acolytes of an ascetic religious order. "They affect great purity and separatism," Teufelsdröckh remarks of the dandy "tribe," "distinguish themselves by a particular costume . . . likewise, so far as possible, by a particular speech . . . and, on the whole, strive to maintain a true Naz- arene deportment, and keep themselves unspotted from the world" (207). The trope develops Carlyle's belief that all human striving, wit- tingly or not, partakes of a quest for religious faith—even if the dandy's "sect" exemplifies such faith at its most enervated. But the conceit has a special application to Carlyle's own eccentric vocation, which he typ- ically imagines as just such a spectacle of estrangement from "the world." In early 1833, for example, as he pondered a permanent move to London, Carlyle wrote to a friend there in jocular prophecy of his arrival: "If I break forth some day in Cockney-land, like some John Baptist, girt about with a leathern girdle, proclaiming anew with fierce

---

1. The visual dependency complements the dandy's dependence on the economic sys- tem he also disdains—a dependence that Baudelaire readily acknowledges and that Zima analyzes at some length.

Annandale intonation: 'Repent ye, ye cursed scoundrels,' for &c &c you will not think it miraculous'' (*Collected Letters* 6:334).[2] While repudiating the dandy's coat in favor of the prophet's mantle, Carlyle nonetheless imagines his vocation as an ascetic project, within which he, too, will be making a spectacle of himself, outwardly distinguished from the dandy only by the particulars of his own idiosyncratic costume and idiom.

The dandy's anxious desire for a literal visibility thus figures an aspiration closely akin to Carlyle's longing for literary authority. To be sure, the literary careers of middle-class Victorian men frequently underscored the social affinities between the dandy and the man of letters. Disraeli, Dickens, and Matthew Arnold, to name just three very different figures, all made early claims to social distinction and dissent through a dandyism that would eventually be overshadowed—but not necessarily superseded—by the authority accorded to their writings as social criticism. Baudelaire, the dandy's greatest apologist, trenchantly grasped and idealized the social logic informing this connection. Dandyism, he contended in *The Painter of Modern Life* (1862), is a distinctly contemporary heroism, "the last spark of heroism amid decadence," which responds to the crisis of cultural authority that structures so much Victorian social discourse. Amid the transition from aristocracy to democracy, dandyism arises in a spirit of "opposition and revolt" to affirm "a new kind of aristocracy" anchored in intellectual distinction rather than economic or social status (28). Baudelaire's dandy thus incarnates, as "a kind of religion," a claim to cultural authority that would resist the ever more powerful reign of the marketplace and bourgeois respectability. This is an aspiration remarkably akin to that of the aspiring hero as man of letters, who is likewise engaged in an anxious self-construction, eager to claim and transfigure the space of cultural authority left vacant by the waning of traditional models.[3]

Carlyle's version of the dandy, however, brings home the dilemma of reconciling programs of masculine self-fashioning with an ideal of essential selfhood. The charismatic authority to which Carlyle aspired can only be confirmed by the submission of an audience; hero-worship is a fundamentally relational structure. Yet Carlyle also insists, in *Heroes and Hero-Worship* (1840), that the hero's self-forgetful integrity entails

2. This self-conception clearly shapes Teufelsdröckh, who is "a wild Seer, shaggy, unkempt, like a Baptist living on locusts and wild honey" (*Sartor Resartus* 21).
3. Ellen Moers's classic study of the dandy fails to note this affiliation with middle-class social aspirations, which is emphasized by Gagnier (*Idylls* 67–73).

a sublime disregard for any audience, any appeal to "the world's suffrage." The dandy epitomizes this corrosive predicament, since he incarnates the Carlylean demon of self-consciousness in an emphatically
public arena. Thus although Carlyle disdained the dandy's stance, his
writings are incessantly preoccupied with the dandy as a figure of masculine identity under stress. The dandy unsettles Carlyle, and the culture Carlyle helped to shape, as a conjunction of two forms of
emasculation: the failure to realize a life of "manful" action and the
radical failure of autonomy inherent in the dandy's abject appeal to an
audience for his very identity.

It may be, as anthropologists have argued, that an absolutely assured masculinity is a contradiction in terms. But for Carlyle and other
early Victorian male intellectuals, the burdens of manhood were exacerbated by a bewildering loss of clearly defined structures of initiation. The traditional "scripts" of masculinity no longer obtained, "the
old ideal of Manhood" was gone, as Carlyle remarks in "Characteristics." Inherent in Carlyle's quest for a "new Mythos" to lead his contemporaries out of the wilderness of unbelief is a corresponding
struggle to define and realize a new model of manhood. In this struggle, the figure of the prophet has a central place. Indeed, that figure
has in many respects presided over popular and scholarly reception of
Carlyle from the time of his earliest success. "He was a teacher and a
prophet in the Jewish sense of the word," wrote his first biographer,
James Anthony Froude (*Thomas Carlyle* 1:xv), and that notion, vary-
ingly understood, has continued to preoccupy his twentieth-century
admirers and critics. Long after the eclipse of Carlyle's reputation as
a guide to the perplexed, the idea of the writer as prophet has continued to inform academic analysis of Carlyle's stylistic and generic innovation. Indeed, in this regard the figure of the prophet has centrally
influenced the major revival of interest in Victorian cultural criticism
since World War II—particularly through the sustained and many-
faceted rhetorical analysis set in motion by John Holloway's book, *The
Victorian Sage* (1953). In such work, however, the situation of the
prophet has tended to be a powerfully disembodied one. As an emblem of a cultural vocation, the prophet has been understood almost
entirely as a voice of moral wisdom (or blindness) in a baffled and
self-mistrustful age, and hence in terms of the rhetorical challenges attendant on the prophet's necessarily marginal or eccentric intellectual
position.[4]

4. Geoffrey Hartman's *Criticism in the Wilderness* is an especially intriguing example, which

My own approach to Carlyle likewise stresses the central importance
of this Carlylean self-conception, but seeks to elicit what I hope will
seem a more comprehensive significance, by viewing the prophet not
only as a rhetorical and moral stance, but also as a model of masculine
identity under stress. Like the dandy and the gentleman, the prophet
is a figure of masculine vocation defined in antagonism to the marketplace, or (more broadly) the influence of "circumstances"—whether
those be physical constraints or the more subtle undermining of autonomy inherent in the pressures of respectability, that anxious middle-
class decorum that Carlyle contemptuously called "gigmanity." These
models of manhood locate authority not in action but in a rich, charismatic subjectivity, which is intimated in, and in turn reinforced by,
an individual's capacity for ascetic discipline. In representing such subjectivity, Carlyle's rhetorical strategies instantiate a central preoccupation of middle-class discourse. Yet the representation of such heroic
modes of subjectivity inevitably reinscribes their dependence on the
social mediation that they resist; in such representation, masculinity is
always a spectacle exposed to a public gaze. In this regard, "the epitaph
of the Regency dandy," as Ellen Moers has called "The Dandiacal
Body," also prefigures the persistent afterlife of the dandy in much
Victorian writing, and its unexpected affinities to its ostensible antagonist, the prophet. This shared preoccupation takes many forms, since
it articulates shifting relations of hero and audience, and the writers
on which I focus in this chapter—Carlyle, Tennyson, and Dickens—are
chosen in part to stress that variety, as well as to sketch a broad historical trajectory that will be fleshed out in later chapters. Carlyle represents the redemptive subjectivity of his heroes as a visual and linguistic
affront to bourgeois social decorum. In remarkably similar fashion,
Tennyson's early poetry represents the emotional integrity of the poet
in spectacles of exorbitantly ascetic self-discipline, staged before a baffled or openly hostile audience. In Dickens's *Tale of Two Cities*, the Carlylean association of heroic subjectivity with social opacity is developed
into an exploration of masculine self-discipline under hostile surveillance. In all of these models, however, the construction of heroic masculinity and its attendant discipline is represented as an ascetic project
offered up to an imagined public gaze. The persistence of the hero as
spectacle thus confirms persistent affinities among the prophet, the
dandy, and the gentleman, which in turn make plain that "the hero as

enlists the Carlylean prophet as a herald of poststructuralist rhetorics. George Landow, *Elegant Jeremiahs*, offers a more extended generic analysis of "sage writing."

man of letters" is a far more anxious, complex, and unstable norm of gendered identity than most recent criticism allows.

JOHN THE BAPTIST IN COCKNEY-LAND

Carlyle's self-mocking vision of himself as a Scottish John the Baptist confronting a bewildered London crowd offers an image of the prophet rather different from that which shapes most accounts of Carlyle. As he contemplates permanent settlement in London after years in the isolation of Craigenputtock—and a lifetime in Scotland—the figure of the prophet incorporates many facets of Carlylean self-consciousness under a single image of alienation. His foreign nationality; his uncertain class status; his vocation as a writer; his consequent economic marginality; his accompanying failure to achieve a satisfyingly "manful" competency; his lack of children; his imaginative estrangement from his wife; his pretensions to rare moral insight, with its attendant demands for an idiosyncratic vehicle of expression; and his frustration at being thus far unappreciated: all of these preoccupations are condensed in a sense of being on display before an alien and uncomprehending audience—an audience that he professes to hold in contempt, yet whose attention he eagerly seeks.

Carlyle's wry prophecy of his arrival in London suggests why the prophet had such widespread appeal as a model of masculine intellectual authority throughout early Victorian England. First, the passage emphasizes a profoundly *social* dimension in the prophet's estrangement—recalling us to the fact that the prophet's claims to moral authority frequently emanate from, and perhaps compensate for, positions of cultural marginality or exclusion, whether by class, nationality, or gender. "Gender" may seem a peculiar locus of tension in this context, but the priest or prophet has throughout history been associated with a model of masculinity in some way supplementary to or divergent from normative manhood. And the potential conflict among competing masculinities informs the second significance and attraction of the prophet: the many male writers who felt estranged from ascendant models of Victorian "manhood"—often by virtue of their occupation as writers—could find in the prophet (as in the priest) a masculine role exempted from some of the stresses associated with traditional masculine identity, such as sexual prowess, martial virtues, and wealth (Stearns). At the same time, however—and this is the third broad appeal—the prophet could form the model of an ascetic discipline, which would rival the strenuous (and more celebrated) psychic economies of the daring yet disciplined warrior-capitalist, Carlyle's own icon of early Victorian middle-class masculinity, whose manhood the male writer often seemed to have renounced, or simply failed to achieve. Fourth, the prophet exemplified a vocation entirely removed from the structures and demands of domestic life. It thus offered sanction for imagining masculinity as something to be realized entirely within all-male communities (a possibility to be explored in the next chapter) or in solitary projects of self-definition, which nonetheless (in keeping with the prophet's social function) were carried out either in the gaze of the "great Taskmaster's eye" or in the sometimes more demanding, because more capricious, eye of the British public.

Fifth, and finally, the prophet's vocation was an especially arresting vehicle for a problematics of audience, social as well as rhetorical, which was envisioned not only in stylistic or epistemological terms, but in terms of a more inchoate anxiety over masculine self-display. The increasing social and economic mobility brought about by the Industrial Revolution made the interpretation of strangers an increasingly frequent and significant challenge. As a result, men caught up in such mobility experienced with corresponding frequency and anxiety a sense of putting themselves on display, imagining themselves as spectacles offered up to an unfamiliar gaze. In the process they found themselves enacting rituals of manly self-display under intensified pressure, owing to a less secure sense of their audience and its expectations. One result of this preoccupation was a phenomenon to which we will return in Chapter 2, a widespread fascination with male secret societies, conceived both as imagined adversaries and as an idealized fellowship in a hostile world—a function increasingly taken up by public schools, whose growing authority during the period answered to an increasingly complex desire for secure delineation of male privilege. This experience of constant scrutiny exacerbated, or reanimated, a long-standing association of anxious self-display with effeminacy, as in the contemporary attacks on Keats (Carlyle's exact contemporary) and "Cockney poetry." Furthermore, Evangelical discipline—energized by widespread British recoil from the upheavals of the French Revolution—had identified ostentation with a corrupt and ungodly aristocratic ethos, against which Evangelicalism affirmed the countervailing authority of a more rigorous inner life, which made itself felt in public life as a renewed "seriousness." Under such hostility, the man on display was in a sense doubly unmanned. But the biblical prophet offered the precedent of a heroic manhood called on to make a spectacle of himself, to set an example for a bewildered public. Hence Carlyle's self-construction as a latter-day John the Baptist, in and out of Cockney-land.

Carlyle's long and arduous literary apprenticeship was shaped by a protracted wrestling with "the old ideal of manhood" and a search for models who might enable him to formulate a new one. "The old ideal" was powerfully incarnated in his father, James Carlyle, whose life of humble but pious and exacting labor as a stonemason, and stern, un-questioned paternal authority, was untroubled (at least in his son's retrospective idealization) by baffled ambition or self-doubt. Measuring himself against this paragon of self-sufficient masculinity, Norma Clarke has recently argued, the young Carlyle could not help but feel less than a man; indeed, the portrait of his father in his *Reminiscences* is obviously shaped by contrast with Carlyle's own sense of failure. But Carlyle's sense of frustrated manhood was also responsive to larger historical forces. He set out to become a clergyman, the traditional path for young men of intellectual promise, which made allowance for a less "worldly" manhood that was affirmed through—and not in spite of—seemingly passive absorption in intellectual labor, rather than eco-nomic or political struggle. From this path, however, Carlyle was turned aside by a crisis of faith, a crisis that his own writings would help to make virtually a defining attribute of intellectual modernity in Victorian England. Half-hearted study in other professions gradually gave way to a new career: that of the man of letters. Yet though a writer's life of-fered an outlet for Carlyle's intellectual ambitions, it failed to offer an assured sense of manhood that would rival his father's. In effect, Carlyle had internalized the aristocratic contempt of the professional writer's lack of independence, to which he joined the disdain of an increasingly utilitarian society for the literary world as a realm of unprofitable, and thus unmanly, intellectual exchange. It was out of this frustration, Clarke concludes, that Carlyle constructed "a social role for himself that corresponded more to Calvinist notions of the priesthood than to contemporary expectations about writers": the hero as man of letters (Clarke 39–40). This most famous construction of Victorian intellectual patriarchy can thus be seen as a direct outgrowth of the profound gen-der anxiety of Carlyle's early life; it was a model of manhood in which he finally seemed to reconcile the conflicting models of masculine vo-cation represented by his father, the world of letters, and a traditional religious calling.

The hero as man of letters thus secularizes the self-fashioning of the ascetic prophet or desert wanderer, for whom trials of belief are always trials of vocation, and hence of gendered identity. If, as Teufelsdröckh puts it, "Our Wilderness is the wide World in an Atheistic Century" (*Sartor Resartus*, 139), then the Carlylean prophet incarnates an exemplary renunciation in the pursuit of renewed faith—and with it, a new identity. In this light, Carlyle's writings reproduce the central imperative of Western asceticism, as that has recently been analyzed by Geoffrey Galt Harpham. The reader is exhorted to repress, ideally to destroy, an existing but adventitious and degraded self, that "Shadow of Ourselves," as Teufelsdröckh calls it (144–45), in order to discover or release a more essential, ultimately transcendent selfhood animated by divine necessity. Thus the act of "Selbst-tödtung" that Teufelsdröckh celebrates is also a "new birth"; the "death" of self precipitates a radical reinvention of one's identity, through which the aspiring saint or hero struggles to become "the total stranger," an alien to all human customs and ties, responsive instead solely to divine imperatives. The ascetic program aims at a mortification of the body that would purge not only the flesh and its desires but all that is merely circumstantial in one's identity, thereby discovering an integral selfhood removed from social life, even from human genealogy. Thus the ascetic hero aims to submerge personal identity in what Harpham calls "the sensation of necessity" (25).

Carlyle clearly imagined his own early life in such terms and recast that self-conception in *Sartor Resartus* and subsequent writings. During the 1820s, as Carlyle struggled to find expression (and audience) for a "new mythos," he was laboring in the remote "wilderness" of Craigenputtock—a solitude he mockingly called his Patmos (*Collected Letters* 5:109). In the course of this ordeal, Carlyle found imaginative coherence and consolation by recasting himself as a latter-day prophet crying in the wilderness—in the process too often losing sight of the suffering he caused his wife through his frequent confusion of the drawing room with the desert.[5] Those years, John Rosenberg observes, mark Carlyle's "self-creation as a prophet" (4); that persona was eagerly embraced by Carlyle's admirers, and sealed by James A. Froude's controversial biography, in which Carlyle became a figure "tempted in his hermitage, like another Saint Anthony, by the spirit of the world"—in this instance, by the prospect of editing the *Edinburgh Review* (*Thomas Carlyle* 2:56–57). The central preoccupations of that long ordeal of self-

5. As Clarke points out, Carlyle's preoccupation with domesticity in the 1820s represented an effort to construct an eminently traditional patriarchal household that would rival and displace the authority of his father's—a project that frequently reduced the brilliant Jane Welsh Carlyle to little more than a drudge.

definition would of course be represented in *Sartor Resartus*, whose distinctive rhetorical strategies and generic complications can be seen as a sustained, semiparodic recasting not only of early Christian asceticism, but of its hagiography. In other words, *Sartor Resartus* represents an ascetic technology of both selfhood and literary representation that Carlyle idiosyncratically refracted through the structures of the Goethean *Bildungsroman*. Teufelsdröckh's protracted crisis of faith in *Sartor Resartus* is represented as "some purifying 'Temptation in the Wilderness,' before his Apostolic work (such as it was) could begin" (140). And after Carlyle had resolved his own protracted crisis, he in effect perpetually exhorted his audience to recognize that his writing *was* "Apostolic work"—thereby acting, in effect, as John the Baptist to his own gospel, proclaiming the renewed ascendancy of hero-worship, and with it his own heroism.

Teufelsdröckh's alienation begins as a fact of birth, in his status as an orphan of unknown parentage (63)—an obvious parody of the myth of the Christ child, whose struggles are the paradigm for Carlylean aspiration. Even in the lap of his adoptive parents, the young Diogenes experiences estrangement, out of which blossoms a "strange scientific freedom" from human ties and affections, and a habit of contemplating the world "like a man dropped hither from the moon" (21). Subsequently, that isolation is confirmed when Teufelsdröckh, on the verge of manhood, is jilted by the faithless Blumine—an episode in which Carlyle's comic refusal of the consolations of romance also redirects the journey to masculine identity. In exploding the marriage plot, as Herbert Sussman points out, Carlyle reconfigures masculinity by setting his hero on a celibate, ascetic path to fulfillment (45–47). The subsequent isolation he endures will be a harrowing ordeal, "the sum total of wretchedness to man," as Carlyle describes isolation in *Past and Present* (271). But that ordeal is essential to a self-annihilation that makes way for the construction of a new identity, in the recognition of his divine parentage, which brings with it a sense of selfhood inseparable from the sensation of necessity. As Teufelsdröckh phrases it, "Obedience is our universal duty and destiny . . . too early and too thoroughly we cannot be trained to know that Would, in this world of ours, is as mere zero to Should" (75). "I can do no other": Luther's proclamation, Carlyle contends in *Heroes and Hero-Worship*, is "the greatest moment in the Modern History of Men" (365).

The imperative of that divinely ordained "necessity," which overrides all merely human imperatives, informs Carlyle's prose as a remarkably consistent rhetorical strategy, within which heroic demeanor is evoked as a perpetual affront to social decorum (DeLaura, "Ishmael as Prophet"). Thus Carlyle's Cromwell, for example, intimates his heroic stature by his very uncouthness, which confounds the elegance that surrounds him: "Rude, confused, struggling to utter himself, with his savage depth, with his wild sincerity; and he looked so strange, among the elegant Euphemisms, dainty little Falklands, didactic Chillingworths, diplomatic Clarendons!" (*Heroes* 442). The resistance to civility stressed by the leading adjectives—"wild," "strange," "rude," "savage"—affirms an elemental social autonomy, and thus an essential manhood. "Virtue, *Vir-tus*, manhood, *hero*-hood, is not fairspoken immaculate regularity" (443). Luther, similarly, displays "a rugged honesty, homeliness, simplicity; a rugged sterling sense and strength"—attributes which, not surprisingly, carry over to his countenance: "a rude plebeian face; with its huge crag-like brows and bones, the emblem of rugged energy; at first, almost a repulsive face" (369, 372). There may well be an element of self-portraiture in this emphasis, but it instantiates a more programmatic logic, which drives a wedge between heroism and popular favor. The identity and mission of the Carlylean hero lie elsewhere, in a divine imperative that overwhelms all human claims. Thus Carlyle's account of Dante, for example, focuses on his "rigour, earnestness, and depth," which finds expression in "a kind of godlike disdain of the thing that is eating out his heart" (319).

Ultimately, such disdain extends to language itself. Language is not simply incapable of capturing the ineffable force that impels heroic selfhood; it actively enmeshes the hero in a web of compromising social relations. The Carlylean hero finds it impossible to articulate his identity, which is to say his relationship to divinity, except in action; hence speech becomes at best a distracting social expedient, at worst sheer inanity. "Words dilute and brutalize," as Nietzsche would later put it (*Will to Power* 810). When the hero does speak, his words invariably disrupt the regimen of linguistic decorum, whether through a "rude" sincerity bordering on incoherence, or through an economy of speech whose very terseness does violence to polite form. A redemptive subjectivity cannot be directly expressed in language; it can only be intimated as an ironic disjunction of surface and depth. Thus in *Past and Present*, for example, in contrast to "some light adroit man of Theory," "the cloudy-browed, thick-soled opaque Practicality, with no logic-utterance, in silence mainly, with here and there a low grunt or growl, has in him what transcends all logic-utterance: a Congruity with the Unuttered!" (161). The tension between theory and practice, between the abstract and the concrete, is largely obscured by celebration of an otherworldly integrity.

The ascetic character of Carlylean heroism thus shapes Carlyle's insistent oppositions between the real and the sham; the hero and the quack; silent, "savage depths" and polished, theatrical surfaces. Idiosyncratic as this prose may seem, its rhetorical oppositions pervade middle-class Victorian discourse, where moral and cultural authority is typically bodied forth as a visual or verbal disruption of a world of cultivated superficiality—a "savage depth" or "wild sincerity," to use Carlyle's account of Cromwell. Ruskin in *The Stones of Venice* (1853), for example, celebrates the "savagery" of Gothic architecture as an index of imaginative and moral integrity; Brontë in *Jane Eyre* similarly attributes irresistible moral force to her heroine's quiet but tenacious affronts to decorum. As in Carlyle's prose, the disruption of social forms bodies forth an interiorized, putatively classless selfhood, whose authority challenges traditional political hierarchies and the decorums they enforce.[6] "The Dandiacal Body," in this light, encapsulates with remarkable clarity the momentous historical displacement analyzed by Nancy Armstrong in *Desire and Domestic Fiction*, under which an interiorized selfhood is constructed as a dismantling of what Armstrong calls "the aristocratic body" (77–79). In Armstrong's account, this reconstruction of cultural authority is developed in the work of women writers, whose paradigm of the new subjectivity is the domestic woman. But Carlyle's writing clearly attempts to claim and reconfigure the moral authority of such subjectivity for male heroism. Thus Teufelsdröckh is constructed as a disembodied subjectivity defined in emphatic antagonism to "the dandiacal body" as depth to surface: his is "the gravity as of some silent, high-encircled mountain-pool, perhaps the crater of an extinct volcano; into whose black deeps you fear to gaze" (23). And that same construction of cultural authority would come to shape contemporary reception of Carlyle, not only in such grandiloquent labels as "the Sage of Chelsea," but through visual representations as well. Thus Julia Margaret Cameron's haunting photograph of Carlyle in 1867, for example, turns the sage of Chelsea into an icon of Thought, removed from any distracting signs of social affiliation, by isolating the

---

6. In Joseph Litvak's terms, *Jane Eyre* thereby reinforces a convention "that dissociates rhetorical (and ontological) power from social power, producing a chiasmus in which the inferiority of oppressed or marginalised groups virtually guarantees their latent, but all the more disruptive, 'eloquence' " (56). Litvak's valuable study explores the tension between textuality and theatricality as a constitutive feature of the Victorian novel.

famous countenance in soft focus in an enveloping space of darkness. The strategy is tellingly analogous to the "chiaroscuro" that Carlyle deployed in creating the analogously disembodied and socially deracinated Teufelsdröckh (140). Both representations locate authority in a charismatic subjectivity defined apart from all structures of social identity.

All these constructions, in short, invoke a force closely akin to Weberian charisma: moral and social authority is recast as an ineffable personal influence, which would disrupt, and ultimately reconfigure, existing economies of power and gender. But the Carlylean prophet brings to light the internal contradictions that beset this appeal, contradictions that emerge when the figure in represented in a densely specified public context. For example, Ford Madox Brown's panorama of Victorian labor, "Work," probably the best-known visual tribute to Carlyle's "gospel of work," inadvertently raises an awkward question about Carlyle's vocation: as Carlyle slouches against a railing at one edge of the canvas, apparently in casual conversation with the theologian and Christian socialist F. D. Maurice, just what sort of work is he engaged in? The catalog of Brown's exhibition in 1865 anticipated just this concern, describing Carlyle and Maurice as those who, "seeming to be idle, work, and are the cause of well-ordained work and happiness in others" (Bowness 164). Yet this apology explains the prophet's work—an outwardly passive but profoundly efficacious labor of guidance—as a function strikingly akin to the "influence" of the domestic woman.[7] And when Carlyle's own authority seemed to wane, this unstated congruence eventually became a focal point of contemporary attacks. Thus W. J. Courthope complained in 1874 that Carlyle's influence (like that of his master, Goethe) had been an enervating, effeminizing force—that his attacks on "present action of every kind" had in fact given rise to a "gospel of inaction" closely akin to the "culture" of Arnold and Pater ("Modern Culture" 207).

Courthope's impatience registers the increasing tension between traditions of Christian heroism and shifting Victorian gender norms. Carlylean models of heroism are deeply indebted to the discourse of Protestant martyrdom, in which, as John Knott puts it, "the highest form of action is the apparent inaction of enduring, with patience and

7. The congruence is implicit in Armstrong's argument, and is noted by Deirdre David (14), but in both instances the concentration on women's claims to authority neglects the effects that this gendering of "influence" would have had on the careers of Victorian men of letters.

composure, any physical and spiritual torment that may be imposed"
(35). They also serve who only stand and wait. Milton's apology is recast
not only in Brown's defense of Carlyle and Maurice, but in Thomas
Hughes's 1878 response to Holman Hunt's painting, *The Finding of the
Saviour in the Temple* (exhibited 1860), which appeals to the archetype
of Christian heroism. It may seem that the young Jesus was "unmanly,"
Hughes observes, in defying his parents to enjoy a seeming idleness,
but in fact he was all the while engaged in the patient, eminently manly
labor of self-reflection, which culminates in the keen awareness captured in Holman Hunt's canvas (*Manliness* 33–37). Yet the very fact
that Hughes would feel obliged to defend the "manliness" of Christ
points to the increasing friction between Victorian manhood and traditional Christian virtues.

Ironically, such defenses of intellectual labor reflect more than the
growing secularism of Victorian life; they drew much of their urgency
from Carlyle's own rhetoric of heroism as a life of self-denying labor.
How does one attach a normative masculinity to a vocation that inheres
less in action than in a mode of being—or, more precisely, that makes
being itself a mode of action, much along the lines of the dramatic
monologue? Carlyle anticipates this crucial challenge in *Sartor Resartus*:
"For the shallow-sighted, Teufelsdröckh is oftenest a man without Activity of any kind, a No-man; for the deep-sighted, again, a man with
Activity almost superabundant, yet so spiritual, close-hidden, enigmatic,
that no mortal can yet foresee its explosions, or even when it has ex-
ploded, so much as ascertain its significance" (76). Here the fundamental contrast of surface and depth sustains the more complex
distinction we have been tracing all along: is the outwardly idle Teufelsdröckh truly a seer, or merely another form of dandy, a "No-man"?
The model of the prophet, with its attendant rhetoric of "wild" and
"savage" integrity, speaks directly to this anxiety, by claiming exemption from customary norms of masculine activity. Carlyle's prophet,
however, must base his claim to authority on something close to unalloyed charisma. As a result, the prophet remains uneasily akin to that
other figure of the self-made man, the dandy, not only in his detachment from conventional forms of action, but in his insistent specularity.
Like the dandy, the Carlylean prophet can only manifest his inspired
selfhood by presenting himself as a spectacle to an uncomprehending
world. But Carlyle's onslaught against the dandy as a "No-man" left his
own vocation exposed to similar attack.

Carlyle's presentation of himself as John the Baptist in Cockney-land
acknowledges the energies of self-invention at work in the prophet's

role. Yet this ironic self-portraiture is sustained by the faith of the ascetic—that one's agency is in fact authorized by divine will, and hence
that the self one fashions is grounded in some transcendent reality. As
Weber reminds us, this is a faith that unites the prophet with a more familiar version of the "self-made man," the capitalist. In this regard,
Carlyle's portrait of Teufelsdröckh points to that conjunction of economic discipline and imaginative self-creation which Dickens so deftly
captured in his portrait of Bounderby in *Hard Times*. But the persistence of the dandy as a shadow of both prophet and capitalist reflects a
paradox within the regime of what Weber called inner-worldly asceticism. Carlyle's hero always works (in the Miltonic phrase that Carlyle
frequently echoes) in his "great Taskmaster's eye"; like the desert eremite, the Carlylean hero is constantly on display even in the midst of
solitude. In the words of Paul, "We are made a spectacle to the world,
and to angels, and to men. We are fools for Christ's sake" (I Corinthi-
ans 4:9–10). Ascetic discipline dictates the presence of an audience;
hence the paradox that the focal point of the ascetic's desire for self-
transcendence, the flesh that he seeks to mortify, becomes the palpable,
visual index of spiritual excellence. The ascetic self is an observable self.
But from this point of view, dandyism is an exemplary asceticism, shorn
of any claims to transcendent selfhood. In Baudelaire's canny description, it is "a kind of religion" governed by discipline "strict as any monastic rule," but one that openly acknowledges a public gaze. (In Max
Beerbohm's more cynical rendering, the dandy mortifies his soul that
his body might be perfect.) And it is for this reason that the dandy is
such a tenacious and central presence in Carlyle's writings—as in so
many Victorian discourses of middle-class masculine self-fashioning.
The dandy shadows the Carlylean hero as the mark of the theatricality
from which Carlyle anxiously sought to dissociate his heroes, but which
seems inseparably bound up with their vocation.[8]

In his representation of the dandy, then, Carlyle embodies the pressures of self-consciousness as an emphatically social dynamic, which is
responsive not only to religious anxiety and romantic models of subjectivity, but to trials of masculine identity. In most accounts of Carlyle,
self-consciousness is a private, solitary dynamic, one aspect of all-
devouring "speculation" that entices the seeker into a bottomless "vor-
tex" of introspection in which all belief is drowned. This emphasis is

8. In this regard, as Jessica Feldman urges, the dandy is not merely a figure of deviant
masculinity, a "No-man," but an emblem of the essentially relational character of
gender, who "moves beyond dichotomous gender itself" (11–13).

in keeping with the traditional approach to Carlyle as a religious thinker, whose attack on self-consciousness represents, broadly construed, a repudiation of Cartesianism. But Carlyle's presentation of the dandy teases out the complex tropes inherent in "self-reflexion" to figure self-consciousness as the awareness of oneself in the mirror of an audience's gaze—a mirror that in Carlyle's accounts has a seemingly irresistible power to compromise the autonomy of heroic selfhood. Instead of experiencing only "the sensation of necessity," the aspiring hero who presents himself to the gaze of an audience is always liable to submit to its desires, and thereby subvert the integrity of his mission. The "great Taskmaster's eye" will be usurped by the eye of the British public, and the prophet will assume the theatrical, emasculating posture of the dandy.

Of course Carlyle's suspicion of theatricality is deeply embedded in Western culture (Barish). Most notably, as an important model for Carlyle's career, Samuel Johnson frequently represents the professional author's exposure to the marketplace as a demeaning theatricality associated with prostitution (Adams, "Economies of Authorship"). But Carlyle is distinctive in his tendency to push this mistrust to its logical extreme: at points in his writings, *any* utterance that finds a receptive audience is suspect, because the audience itself is presumed to be debased. "Thought will not work except in Silence; neither will Virtue work except in Secrecy," Teufelsdröckh proclaims (164). Once again "the great Empire of *Silence*," as Carlyle puts it in *Heroes and Hero-Worship*, enjoins fidelity to the ineffable by repudiating socially mediated identity. "If he cannot dispense with the world's suffrage, and make his own suffrage serve, he is a poor eye-servant; the work committed to him will be *mis*done" (*Heroes* 350). The appeal to an audience marks a poverty of faith, a lack of confidence in one's "own suffrage," which ushers in a pervasive theatricality: "Genuine Acting ceases in all departments of the world's work; dextrous Similitude of Acting begins. . . . Heroes have gone out; quacks have come in" (402).

In this resistance to theatricality, the ascetic impulses of Carlyle's puritanism are further energized by the legacy of romantic fidelity to a transcendent, personal vision. This congruence may support Harpham's suggestion that the figure of the romantic poet is itself indebted to the model of the desert eremite (31). But it also helps to explain why Carlyle's attacks on the dandy so strikingly parallel Mill's exactly contemporary insistence in "What is Poetry?" that the true poet is oblivious to any audience: "No trace of consciousness that any eyes are upon us must be visible in the work itself" (56). Mill's lyric poet shares

with the Carlylean hero the challenge of affirming integral, autonomous selfhood in modern life; poetry that fails to achieve the requisite
authenticity is deprecated as a form of theatricality, mere "oratory." In
this light, the problematic of audience and spectacle implicit in the
Carlylean resistance to speech anticipates the late-century demand that
poetry be purged of what Yeats would call "rhetoric." The logic of
poetic innovation in the nineteenth century, that is, can be usefully
understood as an increasingly emphatic asceticism of style. Certainly
Carlyle anticipates a central development in lyric form in his account
of Dante in *Heroes and Hero-Worship*, where he describes poetry as "melody" or "song" unalloyed by separable discursive content, "a kind of
inarticulate unfathomable speech" (316). Thus Carlyle can claim even
of Dante, "his silence is more eloquent than words" (325). In this
mistrust of language, Carlyle gestures toward Mallarmé's dream of
"poesie pur," "une poème dégagé de tout appareil du scribe," thereby
suggesting a continuum between personal and poetic asceticism that
will be powerfully confirmed in the writings of Pater.[9] Remote as Carlyle
might seem from such figures, he shares with them an asceticism
founded on allegiance to an essential spirit or form that must be ex-
tracted from the crudities of language and the wayward flux of emotion
and desire by means of a consummate discipline that is at once literary
and experiential.

Carlyle's preoccupation with heroic spectacle, idiosyncratic as it
might seem, thus suggests a momentous point of intersection between
the logics of romanticism and anxieties over masculine self-display. Indeed, as a literary production Carlyle's heroes are strikingly akin to the
subjects of an exactly contemporary literary development, the dramatic
monologue. It is not coincidental that what Herbert Tucker has called
the first dramatic monologue, Tennyson's "St. Simeon Stylites," likewise centers on a figure of early Christian ascetic self-discipline. Like
the Carlylean prophet and his shadow, the dandy, Tennyson's aspiring
saint longs for a self-transcendence that can only be conceived, paradoxically, in a form that subverts it—as an appeal to an audience. Although this preoccupation with the relation of self and circumstance
arises out of the imaginative dynamics of romanticism, the striking convergence of Tennyson's lyric strategies with Carlyle's expository ones
suggests that the energies that shaped the dramatic monologue assumed added force in the early 1830s from a preoccupation with the

9. Kermode's *Romantic Image* remains the classic literary treatment of the widespread
   aspiration to purge poetry of "rhetoric," in Yeats's disparaging phrase.

transgressive dynamics of masculine self-definition understood as a form of self-display. For Tennyson as for Carlyle, a crisis of authority is figured as a moment of self-conscious theatricality, in which the poet's or prophet's claim to divine inspiration, and the transcendent selfhood that derives from it, would be exposed as a vain, calculated appeal to an earthly audience, and the aspiring hero be judged instead a monomaniac or "quack." (Carlyle himself suggests the parallel in *Past and Present*, where he attacks the histrionics of failed "liturgies": "Stylitisms, eremite fanaticisms and fakeerisms; spasmodic agonistic posture-makings . . ." [230].) I have argued that the distinctive rhetorical strategies of Carlyle's writings embody a perpetual resistance to this seduction, which at the same time works to reinforce the sense of essential selfhood that is undermined by the pressures of the audience and social convention. Carlyle's ascetic stylistics, that is, enact an unceasing struggle between, on the one hand, an ideal of transcendent, heroic selfhood and, on the other hand, capitulation to the identity enforced by an audience—a surrender most vividly figured in the image of the dandy.

Carlyle frequently represents this conflict as a dichotomy, which allows no middle ground between the hero, who lives "direct from the Inner Fact of things," and an empty simulacrum, "an Inanity and Theatricality, a poor conscious ambitious schemer" (*Heroes* 281). As the hero participates in an eternal divine Idea, he becomes a force of Nature, and as such always appears as the "wild," "savage" outcast, variously typified as Orson or Ishmael or John the Baptist. This logic is played out in the increasingly violent and rebarbative rhetorics of Carlyle's later career, which seem designed in part to preserve the integrity of the prophet by distancing an increasingly eager public embrace of the sage of Chelsea. In this respect, Carlyle is faithful to a potent logic in his writings: the prophet whose claims are readily acknowledged is typically a quack in disguise. For the prophet, in this sense, nothing succeeds like failure. Yet such resistance preserves the integrity of the prophet at the expense of the social reciprocity on which Carlylean hero-worship is ostensibly founded.[10] The construction of heroism as pure charisma undermines any effort to institutionalize the prophet's

10. Carlyle's mesmerized preoccupation with the "unspeakably deplorable" decline of his friend Edward Irving to the brink of madness may reflect a fear that his own mode of utterance could become just as incomprehensible as Irving's congregation, speaking in tongues. "Come, they are prophesying," Irving hauntingly remarked to Carlyle in one of their last meetings (*Collected Letters* 6:25).

example in new social forms. "Savage" purity, in short, offers no answers to "the Condition of England question."

Carlyle's asceticism thus underscores the tensions between personal
identity and collective life that were endemic to Victorian individual-
ism. Those tensions become especially pointed in *Past and Present*, Carlyle's most sustained effort to imagine forms of collective heroism, in
which he tellingly envisions social renewal on the model of two great
ascetic institutions: the military and the monastery. In the process, the
eremitic model of asceticism yields to the cenobitic, a collective and
more stable form of rigor. Whereas the eremite, whose archetype is the
desert solitary, renounces worldly order and uniformity, the cenobite
of the great monastic establishments resists the very eccentricity that
distinguishes the Carlylean prophet, instead gradually submerging the
self in perfect obedience to a collective discipline. In *Past and Present*,
then, Carlyle envisions social renewal as, in Weber's terms, the insti-
tutionalization of prophetic charisma. This same structure informed
the widespread Victorian preoccupation with brotherhoods or secret
societies, whose vitality in the popular imagination registered many of
the tensions between masculine identity and collective life that structure Carlyle's writings. These all-male societies—whether Abbot Samson's monastery, Thomas Arnold's Rugby School, or Newman's Oxford
Movement—depended on not one but two models of heroism: that of
the charismatic leader, and that of the devoted followers who strive to
embody his imperatives in a systematic discipline.[11] Carlyle of course
envisioned himself in the former role, but the two positions, and their
rhetorics, formed mutually dependent models of heroism, which cor-
respond to eremitism and cenobitism as "necessary and intrinsic
double[s]" within the encompassing unity of ascetic discipline (Harpham 28).

Ultimately, Carlyle acknowledges the interdependence of these two
heroisms at just those moments when his prose concedes the impossibility of the prophet's ideal of perfect social autonomy. Diogenes Teufelsdröckh, "like a man dropped thither from the Moon," is obviously
modeled on the extravagantly deracinated young Carlyle, who in October 1820 wrote to a friend, "I am like a being thrown from another
planet on this dark terrestrial ball, an alien, a pilgrim among its pos-

11. Philip Rosenberg, *The Seventh Hero*, is especially helpful on this reciprocity, under
which hero-worship is itself a form of heroism, and on the charismatic structures of
the relation (194–98).

sessors; I have no share in their pursuits; and life is to me like a pathless, waste, and howling wilderness" (*Collected Letters* 1:286). The ironic contexts of *Sartor Resartus*, however, remind us that such autonomy would arise only with the entire extinction of self-consciousness, any residue of which (as the dandy brings home) would betray the persistence of a socially mediated identity. And Carlyle readily concedes—even in "Characteristics" (1831), the essay that most fully enunciates the ideal—that a perfectly unself-conscious, charismatic vitality is "an ideal, impossible state of being" (351). As he restates the predicament in *Sartor Resartus*, the silence that would manifest heroic autonomy is "nearly related to the impossible talent of Forgetting" (37). Like saintliness itself, such integrity can be realized only by a repression that destroys selfhood. Carlyle wishes to distinguish "Genuine Acting" from its "dextrous Similitude," to purge *action* of the theatrical associations of *acting*, and thereby present heroism as pure, unmediated self-presence. Yet the impossibility of self-forgetfulness ensures that the distinction can never be rigorously maintained. *Heroes and Hero-Worship* deftly evokes the predicament in recounting an anecdote of Chatham, who, forgetting in the heat of Parliamentary debate that he is acting the role of a sick man, "snatches his arm from the sling, and oratorically swings and brandishes it!" (402–3). The irony is unexpectedly complex. Carlyle may seem to claim that Chatham inadvertently exposes his own theatricality when the "fire" of commitment burns away self-consciousness, and he forgets the demands of his role. But in fact the passage describes the exchange of one role for another: the flourish of Chatham's arm does not express some essential self, but answers to the conventions of oratory. And Carlyle goes on to suggest that such a condition is paradigmatic of struggling heroism. "Chatham himself lives the strangest mimetic life, half hero, half quack, all along. For indeed the world is full of dupes; and you have to gain the *world's* suffrage!" (403).

One must both dispense with and gain the world's suffrage. In these contradictory imperatives Carlyle concedes a fundamental paradox in ascetic masculinity. The prophet depends on an audience, every bit as much as the audience depends on the prophet's guidance. This paradox is inscribed throughout the elaborate, sometimes self-baffling ironic structures of Carlyle's writing. In his later writings—and this is one way to define the often-reiterated distinction between early and late Carlyle—Carlyle grew increasingly impatient with such compromised autonomy, and increasingly imagined answering the world's claim to suffrage with violent repression. But much of the satisfaction

of Carlyle's early works comes from their incessant exploration and
dramatization of the social and rhetorical construction of masculine
identity. These pleasures are a commonplace in discussions of Carlyle's
"romantic irony," but it is important to recognize the emphatically
social dynamics at play in that irony. The dazzling rhetorical structures
of *Sartor Resartus* are perhaps the most striking Victorian anticipation
of postmodernist conceptions of subjectivity, intimating as they do that
whatever divinity the self possesses is ultimately that of language itself,
since Teufelsdröckh's identity is quite emphatically created out of a
tissue of writing.

In this respect, Carlyle's preoccupation with heroism as spectacle
leads him to a canny representation of the fundamental dynamic of
Lacanian psychology, under which language itself is understood as a
self-estranging specularity, in which every human being constantly and
vainly looks to discover an impossible unity of selfhood.[12] "The thing
we call 'bits of paper with traces of black ink,'" Carlyle remarks in "The
Hero as Man of Letters," "is the *purest* embodiment a Thought of man
can have"; writing is the mode of labor most faithful to "the true thau-
maturgic virtue" of man, the least distorted or contaminated by mediating forces (*Heroes* 393). And if, in the credo from *Sartor Resartus,*
"Our Works are the mirror wherein the spirit first sees its natural lineaments" (124), writing is the truest mirror. It is important to give that
trope its due weight: as an escape from disabling self-consciousness,
work also (ideally) displaces the literal mirror that figures so powerfully
in the mock-aristocratic ethos of the dandy and reflects to the beholder
not the corporeal body but the "natural lineaments" of spirit. But even
the Carlylean hero must find something more than his own image in
the glass: he, too, requires an observer to acknowledge his achievement.
Hence Carlyle's incessant preoccupation in his early correspondence
with trying to imagine what audience, if any, his works might find. As
he wrote to Mill, pondering that "dangerous instrument," irony, "I
cannot justify, yet can too well explain what sets me so often on it of
late; it is my singularly anomalous position to the world. . . . I never
know or can even guess what or who my audience is, or whether I have
any audience: thus too naturally I adjust myself on the Devil-may-care
principle" (*Collected Letters* 6:449). Like so many of Carlyle's accounts
of his own writing, this seems to disclaim any suggestion of concern for
his audience; yet "the Devil-may-care principle" mockingly signals the

---

12. Viscusi (23–28) offers some helpful suggestions on continuities between the dandy
    and Lacan.

self-reflective calculation informing even what are ostensibly the most spontaneous or impulsive features of Carlyle's prose. As in his self-portrait as John the Baptist in Cockney-land, Carlylean irony perpetually stages "a singularly anomalous position to the world." One's book, like one's self, is never wholly one's own, but is constructed as an ongoing transaction with an audience, real or imagined.

PARADES OF PAIN

Carlyle's rhetoric of heroism, I have suggested, undermines the apparently secure distinction between dandy and prophet by eliciting the force of social mediation common to both identities. In this regard, Carlyle's writings vividly represent a logic likewise central to the Victorian dramatic monologue, a form that, as Herbert Tucker points out in a provocative essay, "disintegrates the implicit claim of self-presence in lyric into a rhetorical fabric of self-presentation" ("From Monomania to Monologue" 125). In Carlylean terms, heroic selfhood is lost in the dandy's performing self. Thus we might profitably read "The Dandiacal Body" alongside Tennyson's early dramatic monologue, "St. Simeon Stylites"—which Tucker calls the "prototype" of the form—as satiric portraits of a self-baffling pursuit of essential selfhood. But reading the two works in this way unsettles the ironic mastery that most critics accord them. The object of Tennyson's satire, Tucker urges, is the absurdity of Simeon's "premeditated saintdom," in which the pursuit of sanctity is reduced to "the holding of a pose" (129–30). In this construction, Tennyson's irony, like Carlyle's, rests on the ability to separate a genuine vocation from debased, because theatrical, imitations—to separate the true prophet or saint from the dandy. But this distinction can be securely drawn only by God; this is the somber, unstated implication of the Calvinist logic that underwrites Tennyson's mockery of Simeon. That same logic also informs the paradox noted by Weber, that all asceticism contains an intractable element of theatricality; every program of ascetic discipline requires holding a pose. Hence Simeon's agonies only magnify a conflict that is endemic to more mundane norms of Victorian masculinity—indeed, to any norm of "manhood" that is regarded as both an essential selfhood and an object of deliberate striving. The Victorian gentleman represents in this context a secular sainthood: the gentleman is celebrated as a moral ideal open to all who prove themselves worthy, yet the true gentleman, apologists agree, is distinguished by his lack of self-consciousness.

Hence arises a conflict that will be a recurrent theme of this work: the aspiring gentleman is as much a contradiction in terms as the aspiring saint. He stands condemned of what Tucker calls Simeon's "paradoxically wilful striving after a goal that lies beyond the will" (129).[13]

If "St. Simeon Stylites" is a prototype of the Victorian dramatic monologue, then its congruence with Carlyle's prose suggests that the development of the literary form is energized by anxieties of masculine self-fashioning. Simeon's asceticism, as Tucker points out, is an especially apt vehicle for exploring the gaps between mind and physical nature, and between consciousness and history, that are a central legacy of romanticism. But asceticism also fascinates Carlyle and Tennyson as a regimen of self-definition that foregrounds the forces of social mediation at work in the formation of masculine identity. And the rigors of Simeon's discipline have an especially pointed bearing on the situation of the lyric poet, who also insistently offers up his sufferings to an imagined audience. Critical response to Tennyson's monologue has uncannily reproduced the hostility anticipated by the poet of *In Memoriam*, who imagines a hostile audience disparaging his own display of grief: "He loves to make parade of pain" (21:10). Pathological as Tennyson's aspiring saint may seem, he rehearses with surprising exactitude a central emotional structure and rhetorical strategy of *In Memoriam*. In that poem, the poet repeatedly stages his exorbitant grief as a spectacle for a hostile audience, yet claims moral authority for his suffering even as, and in part because, it seems to emasculate the sufferer.

The suggestion that "St. Simeon Stylites" was obliquely aimed at Charles Simeon, vicar of Trinity Church, Cambridge (Buckley 26), captures a suggestive affinity between Tennyson's monologue and one particularly influential scheme of early Victorian discipline. The poem of course exploits a traditional suspicion of virtuoso religion as a hypocritical guise for eminently worldly interests, in which hypocrisy is figured as theatricality: thus Shakespeare's Malvolio, for example, as well as Browning's many variations on the theme. But as "the old Apostle of Evangelicalism" (Bradley 22), Simeon was especially vulnerable to this suspicion, owing not only to the extremity of Evangelical discipline, but to its undoubted success in meeting the worldly demands of an emergent industrial economy. Thus a Baptist minister in 1805, for ex-

13. Tucker's canny analysis captures the hint of social mobility in referring to Simeon's preoccupation with "the rigor vitae of his sanctimonious careerism" and his "unsaintly concern with public image" ("From Monomania to Monologue" 128).

ample, exploited such suspicion by mocking a characteristic Evangelical demeanor as "solemn uplifting of the eyes, artificial impulses of the breath, grotesque and regulated gestures and postures in religious exercises, and an affected faltering of the voice" (27). The description, Ian Bradley notes, anticipates Dickens's portrait of Chadband, but it equally looks forward to Tennyson's aspiring saint.

The Evangelical believer in this respect occupies a predicament strikingly akin to that of the poet on the threshold of the Victorian era. In well-known debates about "the place of poetry," early Victorian responses to the legacy of romanticism left lyric poetry divided between often conflicting imperatives: the gratification of a large audience—whether for instruction or pleasure—and fidelity to a unique selfhood, whose integrity was increasingly understood as a radical social autonomy, as in Mill's "What is Poetry?" Tributes to the influence of early Evangelicals often reflect the familiar Christian tension between salvation and renown—the "fame" of Wilberforce's noble influence, contemporaries urged, should lead us to emulate his devotion to God's will. In a parallel tension, Victorian poets are asked to be faithful to an idiosyncratic vision yet at the same time offer wisdom for the times—to be, in the terms of Hallam's review of Tennyson's *Poems* of 1830, at once poets of sensation and poets of reflection. And the burden of this divided allegiance is exacerbated by the distinctive character of Tennyson's poetry, which is so powerfully (and notoriously) absorbed in loss and frustrated longing.

"St. Simeon Stylites" is thus a surprisingly apt vehicle for exploring the suspicions that dogged Tennyson's early sense of his vocation as a poet. Those suspicions are suggestively captured by invoking a central term in his poetry, which conjoins explorations of personal intention, social value, cosmic design, schemes of progress, and sheer temporality. What is the *end* of Simeon's self-inflicted torment, or of the overwhelming grief of *In Memoriam*? The speaker of *In Memoriam* poses this question throughout the poem—perhaps most notably in section 21, when he imagines a hostile audience commenting on his display of grief:

> Another answers, "Let him be,
> > He loves to make parade of pain,
> > That with his piping he may gain,
> > The praise that comes to constancy."
> > (21:9–12)

This imagined comment rehearses two distinct but closely related ap-
prehensions. The first, widely recognized by commentators, is a fear
that the poet's expression of his sorrow might seem indecorous or "unmanly." But the imagined interrogation also links this anxiety to the
fear that the speaker's grief will seem not spontaneous utterance—in
this case, the irresistible outpouring of his devotion to Hallam—but
calculated performance, an exorbitant, theatrical "parade of pain." For
Tennyson as for Carlyle, a crisis of heroic vocation is figured as an
emasculating moment of self-conscious theatricality, in which the poet-
hero's professed fidelity to a transcendent, divinely authorized selfhood
is exposed as a vain, calculated appeal to an earthly audience.

"He loves to make parade of pain" is one of a catalog of imagined
taunts that charge the speaker with a failure of manliness: "this fellow
would make weakness weak / And melt the waxen hearts of men" (7–
8); to represent such sorrow is little more than "to sicken and to
swoon" (17); it is to embrace "private sorrow's barren song" rather
than engage the pressing, masculine demands of political life, "when
more and more the people throng / The chairs and thrones of civil
power" (15–16). In effect, the speaker thus rehearses a series of imagined interpellations, in Althusser's term, in which the voice of social
authority hails him as a feminized subject. Ostensibly, the speaker does
so in order to resist that ascription, to claim instead his participation
in a normative manhood. Yet his *defense* against these objections turns
unexpectedly into an embrace of a feminine role:

> I do but sing because I must,
> And pipe but as the linnets sing:
>
> And one is glad; her note is gay,
> For now her little ones have ranged;
> And one is sad: her note is changed,
> Because her brood is stolen away.
>
> (23–28)

In response to the suspicions cast on his masculinity, the speaker likens
himself to a female bird. It is an urgent imperative indeed that would
lead Tennyson to risk such bathos. But the lines claim for his own
utterance the character and moral authority of maternal devotion, his
culture's most powerful emblem of absolute emotional integrity. The
model of authentic, unmediated feeling that romantic poets similarly
discover in the bird's song is here reshaped as a distinctively feminine

ideal, which incarnates a devotion that is entirely instinctive, and hence unself-conscious. As Mill looks to an idealized poet for a Carlylean psychic integrity, *In Memoriam* looks to an idealization of domestic femininity for much the same reason: the poet's maternal attributes declare the authority of his sorrow as arising from an integral (albeit simple and fixed) selfhood.

The poet's identification with a femininity that he seems to disown is reinforced by a further paradox in the apologia of section 21: the poet as mother linnet sings in the conventions of Greek pastoral. Again, Tennyson is drawing on a familiar tension in romantic poetry, the clash of nature and artifice, but his version is striking in the emphasis and apparent deliberation with which it foregrounds the conflict. Against the suspicion that "he loves to make parade of pain," Tennyson defends himself in perhaps the most self-conscious posture available to the poet: this is one of the rare moments when Tennyson calls on the pastoral trope of the poet blowing on his grass pipe at the grave of his fellow shepherd. He resists accusations of artifice, paradoxically, by recourse to the most obviously artificial of poetic conventions, and within that convention he proclaims the authority of instinctive, unself-conscious expression by imagining himself as a spectacle before an audience. The paradox is a repeated phenomenon in the poem, but it does not simply affirm an inescapable conflict of nature and artifice; instead, it is elaborates a crisis of masculine identity, through which Tennyson repeatedly stages his grief as a conscious resistance to norms of manhood. The poet affirms his integrity by embracing a traditionally feminine position of unrestrained public sorrow, which will indeed bring with it "the praise that comes to constancy." That constancy is understood, however, not simply as fidelity, but (as in Mill's account of the poet) as a subjective capacity that the masculine subject lacks.

Tennyson would thus seem to confirm the suspicions of his imagined observers: he loves to make parade of pain precisely in order to win the praise that comes of constancy to Hallam—a constancy that reflects the poet's capacity for both devotion and suffering. Over against a masculine discipline that would repress and sublimate grief, Tennyson's speaker indulges instead an utterly unregulated suffering, which seems to dissolve the structures of masculine identity. The very first section of the poem, for example, contrasts a structure of regulated progress with the static indulgence in seemingly inexhaustible "Grief." Under the rationalizing discipline of romantic *Bildung*, "men may rise on stepping stones / Of their dead selves to higher things," finding "in loss a gain to match . . . the far-off interest of tears" (1–2; 6, 8). This normative economy is multivalent, grounding schemes of personal and cultural development in a capacity for sublimation that likewise energizes the disciplines of more narrowly economic "interest," the accumulation of capital. In opposition, however, to this manifold structure of regulated development and deferred gratification—"emotional capitalism," in Herbert Tucker's deft phrase (*Tennyson* 358)—the poet abandons himself (at least for the moment) to an ecstatic "loss":

> Let Love clasp Grief lest both be drowned,
>> Let darkness keep her raven gloss:
>> Ah, sweeter to be drunk with loss,
> To dance with death, to beat the ground . . .
>> (1:9–12)

The integrity of the poet's devotion, and the persistence of his very identity—"all he was"—are affirmed through a grief so exorbitant it entirely overthrows masculine self-regulation. Suffering becomes a mode of ecstasy, a perpetual intoxication of "loss," whose only regulating principle is the tenacity with which the poet clings to it. What, then, is the end of such suffering? It may seem to have no end—to be without object, intention, goal, or cessation. But of course such extremity does have a specular logic, which clearly informs the personification of "Sorrow" as a grieving widow. Only through an extravagant, ecstatic suffering can the speaker forestall the possibility

> . . . that the victor Hours should scorn
>> The long result of love, and boast,
>> "Behold the man who loved and lost,
> But all he was is overworn."
>> (1:13–16)

Thus, despite the disclaimer of section 21, the poet does indeed solicit "the praise that comes of constancy": he configures his grief as a spectacle under an imagined gaze—those of "the victor Hours"—whose "scorn" he forestalls by refusing to cease grieving.

In the opening section of the poem, then, the speaker has already occupied the position of the grieving widow, thereby establishing a many-faceted identification that structures much of the elegy. This feminine identification is affirmed in varieties of abasement defined in opposition not only to change—no "stepping stones to higher things" here—but to rational comprehension of the subject's predicament.

These qualities, and the poet's identification with them, are developed
more explicitly and expansively in section 97, for example:

> She keeps the gift of years before,
>   A wither'd violet is her bliss:
>   She knows not what his greatness is,
> For that, for all, she loves him more.
>
> Her faith is fixt and cannot move,
>   She darkly feels him great and wise,
>   She dwells on him with faithful eyes,
> "I cannot understand: I love."
>   (97:25–28, 33–36)

So extreme is the abasement here that one cannot easily tell whether
Tennyson is describing marriage or widowhood: "the praise that comes
of constancy" can only be affirmed through deprivation, whether the
object of one's devotion be living or dead. But the feminine pronoun
clearly identifies the subject position of the poet, who throughout the
poem lays claim to the very praise he disclaims: the poem itself, after
all, is a monument to his constancy. Hence the basic congruence between *In Memoriam* and the project of Simeon Stylites: just as Simeon
cannot disentangle his self-mortifying devotion to God from the solicitation of worldly "fame," so the suffering of Tennyson's ostensibly self-
transcendent devotion nonetheless requires "the praise that comes of
constancy" in order to affirm its authenticity. At least initially, moreover, that praise can be claimed only in profound antagonism to the
masculine economies of rationality and progress evoked at the opening
of the poem. So long as "Love clasps Grief," and the poet's bliss is
fixed on a wither'd violet, his lament resists the most fundamental burdens of masculine self-discipline and identity.

So extreme is the sorrow that, as Benjamin Jowett put it, "it would
not have been manly or natural to have lived in it always" (Craft 86).
Recent commentators concerned to stress the prominence of homoerotic desire in the poem frequently point to such responses, along with
the emphatically gendered character of Tennyson's sorrow, as contemporary recognition of homoerotic desire. Thus Christopher Craft's
canny analysis appeals to Jowett's remark in support of his claim that
the speaker's "desperate erotic distress" is "indistinguishable from his
grief" (89). But "manly" was a more ambiguously sexualized term in
1893 (when Jowett made his comment) than it was in 1850. The early
reception of the poem suggests that the erotic valence of the poet's

grief was of less moment than the sheer extremity of his suffering, which is what shatters his masculine self-discipline. Tennyson, that is, defines masculinity against femininity more than against homoerotic desire. The logic of the poem of course demands the ultimate repair of the masculine economies ruptured by the poet's suffering. In this regard, Tennyson poses for himself a challenge that is at once psychic, formal, and theological—that recuperation of coherence announced perhaps most suggestively in section 128:

> I see in part
> That all, as in some piece of art,
> Is toil cooperant to an end.
>   (22–24)

"Toil cooperant to an end" is precisely what is called into question in the poem's opening stanza; yet this teleology is essential to Tennyson's schemes of cosmic order, human progress, and poetic design—as well as masculine identity. Thus the threat to patriarchal stability posed by the demonic "wild Pallas" of stanza 114, an incarnation of a masculine knowledge loosed from the feminine "wisdom" of sympathy, is present in inverted form in the "wild poet" of section 34, who "works / Without a conscience or an aim" (7–8)—who, that is, embodies feminine feeling disjoined from masculine foresight and self-restraint (M. Shaw 84). Manhood itself is for Tennyson "toil cooperant to an end": it is rational—which is to say, moral—self-discipline governed by "a conscience or an aim." Ultimately, the poem affirms the recuperation of a governing moral design, and with it a manifold coherence in the poem's multiple structures. The emblematic reparation of the concluding marriage affirms an enduring biological continuity, which is also a social and moral "ascent," which in turn confirms the ongoing rule of a beneficent divinity. And the poet's capacity to affirm these orders confirms in turn that he has achieved the function of a truly masculine poet, whose works participate in these multiple structures of order.

The poem would have us regard this crowning achievement not merely as restoration, but as sublimation—as a *transcendence* of loss that reaffirms the pattern of ascent sketched in the opening stanza, whereby men would "rise on stepping-stones / Of their dead selves." And this design has a special bearing on the poet's own self-construction. "Parades of pain" and other feminizing postures have apparently been discarded, but they have been incorporated tacitly into a more comprehensive ideal of masculinity, which seems to complicate the binary

disjunction of masculine/feminine. The poem effects this not only in
the poet's insistence on the exorbitance of his grief but also in Tennyson's staging of that grief as a public spectacle—a representation that
of course also addresses the social situation of poetry. Thus, for example, section 77 echoes section 21 in its profoundly equivocal representation of the poet's suffering as poetic utterance. On the one
hand, the speaker disparages the previous sections of the poem as
"these mortal lullabies of pain" (77:5)—thereby relegating them, as
Marion Shaw notes, to the realm of the feminine or infantile. But this
gesture is not, as Shaw characterizes it, a "putting aside of effeminacy";
rather, it marks a more subtle effort to appropriate femininity, to attach
it to the achievement of a poet who will also, and in culminating fashion, be considered manly. In opposition to the cynicism that points up
the cultural marginality of "modern rhyme," and (much in the vein
of Pope) mocks the ephemerality of poetry as a material object—an
object that "May serve to curl a maiden's locks"—the speaker responds, "To breathe my loss is more than fame." He thus once again
embraces an emphatically feminized devotion, which ostensibly repudiates worldly fame. But he thereby does something more than, as Shaw
describes it, grant "female utterance" "a temporary superiority over
the values of public life" (81). More boldly, he lays claim to incorporate
within public, masculine life, the claim to that authoritative subjectivity
which is usually associated with the feminine. Whereas the grieving
widow is relegated to a static, unreflective abasement, the poet's grief
is subsumed in a dynamic self-discipline. The speaker's apparent renunciation thus veils a gesture of empowerment, which—again, following not only Mill but Carlyle—submits to a larger audience an
insistence on the heroic *sincerity* of the poet's utterance as the true voice
of feeling, anchored in an unwavering devotion rather than in any concern for "fame." And the reception of Tennyson's poem secured for
that expression of devotion the fame for which it professes not to care.

The exorbitance of Tennysonian suffering thus proved to be a successful analogue to the uncouthness of Carlylean prophecy: both mark
a resistance to gendered decorum that works to secure recognition of
a new form of masculine authority. Tennyson's imaginative identification with feminine personifications and subject-positions not only "liberates the voice of feeling," as Marion Shaw puts it (77), but attempts
to break down, in order to enlarge and reconfigure, the structure of
masculine identity. In one regard, this conclusion simply reiterates the
familiar post-Enlightenment allowance for greater "sensibility" in mod-

els of manhood.[14] But again, Tennyson is characteristic of early Victorian culture—and helps to define that culture—by likening this project to a model of androgynous identity. Critics often find this ideal of "man-woman" in Tennyson's tributes to Hallam as an emblem of "manhood fused with female grace." To be sure, such an ideal does not fundamentally reconfigure gender relations; by vesting masculine empowerment with a less brutal or rigid outward bearing, it obscures its operation, thereby strengthening its hegemonic force. That understanding of the ideal, however, fails to acknowledge the force of self-abasement at work in portions of *In Memoriam* and *Maud*, which point to a more extreme questioning of gender. This reconfigured norm of masculinity is better phrased as manhood fused with female *suffering*. The oblique expression of pride in the capacity for such suffering—those solicitations of "the praise that comes of constancy"—may occasionally let us hear in *In Memoriam* the inflections of Uriah Heep, which are more obvious in Saint Simeon's disclaimers of influence and pride: "It may be I have wrought some miracles" (134). Masculine self-abasement, Heep's "'umbleness," that is, may function as an avenue for the socially marginal to gain access to established norms of masculine power—an avenue all the more effective because it masks more familiar deployments of such power. But an insistence on suffering injects a subtle instability into regimens of manhood. The requisite capacity for suffering may be indulged to the point that it overwhelms the "manly" work of regulation; indeed, as we shall see in the writings of Charles Kingsley, discipline itself may become eroticized as a form of masochism, which breaks down economies of manhood beyond repair.

Tennyson's preoccupation with spectacles of male suffering points the way to this possibility as it heralds the increasingly equivocal position of lyric poetry in relation to norms of masculinity. In this larger context, Saint Simeon Stylites turns out to be a surprisingly resonant figure not only in Tennyson's career but in the gendering of Victorian poetry. Matthew Arnold in "Stanzas from the Grande Chartreuse" also looks to spectacles of ascetic discipline as models for his own vocation, in both its emotional integrity and its social marginality: "Their faith, my tears, the world deride— / I come to shed them at their side" (89–

---

14. "If a single cultural reflex could establish what was Victorian about Victorianism," Armstrong urges, "it was the insistence that a form of authority whose wellsprings were the passions of the human heart ultimately authorized writing" (14).

90), he writes of "the Brotherhood austere" he visits (65). Tennyson's
example, though unmentioned, evidently figures prominently among
those predecessors of whom Arnold declares, "we learnt your lore too
well!" "What helps it now," he asks, that Byron bore across Europe
"the pageant of his bleeding heart?" (133–36). Whatever its social utility, Byron's pageantry "helps" as a model of identity for the male poet,
which Arnold finds himself following even as he strives to distance himself from it. Arnold, after all, is constructing an emotional pageant of
his own—and with it, his own "Brotherhood austere," the elusive "we"
distinguished by a shared, elect, vanishing capacity for suffering: "last
of the race of them who grieve," fellow outcasts with the "last of the
people who believe" (110, 112). Arnold frames this designation in implicit response to the question he poses on his arrival: "What am I,
that I am here?" (66). But his response takes its special point from the
fact that both "the race" and "the people" with which he affiliates
himself are exclusively male. "What am I, that I am here?" A man
aspiring to be a poet, is one answer. I think we should read a similar
specificity in the bewilderment of Saint Simeon Stylites's question,
"What am I?" That question, Tucker contends, "represents the questioning of the self's status with which the modern dramatic monologue
came into being" (128). But Simeon's "prolonged crisis of identity"
has a special urgency in figuring the predicament of a man who in
1831 is beginning a career writing lyric poetry of agonizing, inchoate,
seemingly endless suffering. And it was the capacity for suffering to
which Arnold again paid tribute in "The Scholar Gypsy" (1853):
"Amongst us one, / Who most has suffered, takes dejectedly / His
seat upon the intellectual throne; / And all his sad experience he / Lays
bare of wretched days" (182–86). We cannot be certain whether it was
Goethe or Tennyson whom Arnold had in mind, but in either case
"the intellectual throne" is an elevation much like Simeon's pillar.[15]

THE DANDY ON THE SCAFFOLD

The understanding of masculinity as a rhetorical fabric of self-
presentation, exemplified in both "St. Simeon Stylites" and *Sartor Re-*

15. David DeLaura points to a further model in arguing that "Carlyle's system, in Arnold's eyes, virtually came down to this: I suffer, therefore I am" ('Carlyle and Arnold" 144). At this stage in his career, Arnold seems not to have moved much beyond
Carlyle.

sartus, shapes claims to new forms of power and authority in a wide range of Victorian discourse. By representing masculinity as a public spectacle, Carlyle and Tennyson reproduce in a visual register the struggle analyzed in Hegel's account of the master-slave dialectic. Like Hegel's master, the Carlylean hero requires recognition of his stature, in the form of hero-worship, in order to confirm his mastery, yet he thereby becomes locked into the worldly rivalry that he had ostensibly transcended in his very identity as a Master. "The Dandiacal Body" renders this predicament in a satire of the dandy's quest for recognition. But Tennyson in "St. Simeon Stylites" reminds us that some version of Hegel's paradox is endemic to postromantic conceptions of authorship, which are riven by a conflict between an ideal of transcendent genius and the demands of the marketplace—a conflict rehearsed in Tennyson's representation of the poet as spectacle.

These struggles for masculine authority have a still more mundane and pervasive analogue in the incessant Victorian preoccupation with defining a true gentleman.[16] As the ideal of the gentleman broadened—at least in theory—it also gave new moral urgency to the seemingly banal task of distinguishing between sincerity and performance. If the status of gentleman is not secured by inherited distinctions of family and rank, but is realized instead through behavior, how does one distinguish the "true" gentleman from the aspirant who is merely "acting" the part? This was less of a challenge for the Augustan age, not only because of more circumscribed social mobility, but also because the gentleman's role accommodated a degree of theatricality. But the rise of an ideal subjectivity defined in opposition to theatricality energized the anxieties informing Carlyle's obsessive preoccupation with the dandy. It was not merely that the gentleman might become a purely social role or status-marker disjoined from any moral substance. Equally—in some ways more—disturbing, that same threat incarnated the remarkable power of social mediation to shape human identity, and thus seemed to rob the individual subject of a fundamental autonomy.

---

16. The Victorian gentleman is such an elusive concept that anyone trying to pin down its attributes may be tempted to defer to Trollope's Duke of Omnium: "The word is too vague to carry with it any meaning that ought to be serviceable to you in thinking of such a matter" (*The Duke's Children* 67). But that indeterminacy reflects the extraordinary energies of competing efforts to appropriate the term. My account of the tensions informing the ideal owes most to Curtin, *Propriety and Position*; Gilmour, *The Idea of the Gentleman in the Victorian Novel*; Girouard, *The Return to Camelot*; Haley, *The Healthy Body and Victorian Culture*; Honey, *Tom Brown's Universe*; Newsome, *Godliness and Good Learning*; and Vance, *The Sinews of the Spirit*.

The force of this threat to autonomy figures centrally in Victorian fiction, which, as John Kucich points out in *Repression in Victorian Fiction*, stresses the often labyrinthine struggles of characters to break free of concern for "external regard," which is typically represented as a mode of entrapment. Amanda Anderson has located a similar preoccupation with what she calls "attenuated autonomy" in the Victorian preoccupation with fallen women, who embody forms of character in various ways determined by circumstance. The dandy's persistence in mid-Victorian debates over the nature of the gentleman—and hence over access to the authority of the norm—captures a differently gendered version of the same complex of anxieties. The Carlylean dandy, one might say, is a fallen man, whose compromised autonomy arises from a paradoxically willful abrogation of masculine self-sufficiency, rather than (as is typical in representations of fallen women) a failure in regulating a habitual and prescribed exposure to an imagined gaze. More precisely, the dandy functions as a sort of Derridean supplement to the gentleman. Both figures are defined in resistance to degrading involvement in economic competition, or (more broadly) to economic schemes of value (Gilmour 52); both ideals at least in principle repudiate self-interest, claiming instead devotion to a rigorous and impersonal code of duty (hence the ascetic pretensions of dandyism that Baudelaire celebrates and Carlyle mocks). But whereas the Victorian gentleman typically refers his duty ultimately to a religious sphere, the dandy's imperatives are overtly and fundamentally social. In stressing this dimension of the dandy, Carlyle turns the figure into an embodiment of a theatricality purged from the true hero, or gentleman, whose authenticity is manifested (ideally) in an absence of self-consciousness. As Charles Kingsley put it, the "secret" of the gentleman "was very simple, if one could attain it; but he attained it by not trying to attain it, for it was merely never thinking about himself" (*Life and Works* 2:189). Kingsley here enlists Carlyle's "anti-self-consciousness theory" (in Mill's phrase) to enforce a familiar Victorian mystification of social authority. Like many middle-class men, Kingsley ostensibly repudiates aristocratic notions of the "gentleman born," yet he implicitly appeals to a new version of that concept when he disowns the anxious self-consciousness of any man who *aspires* to become a gentleman. The mystification of an authority that resides in "never thinking about himself" depends on the ability to separate the true gentleman from an inauthentic (because theatrical) simulacrum, the dandy.

From the retrospective view of the fin de siècle, the difficulty of distinguishing the gentleman from the dandy becomes an energizing paradox—reminding us that the dandy always comes into focus as a textual mark, one might say, of masculine identity under stress or revision. For Wilde, in a precise reversal of earlier valuations, the gentleman exemplifies what has since been called the performing self; the gentleman is a fundamentally theatrical being, whose "nature" is emphatically a pose. In mid-Victorian literature, however, the potential confusion of the two figures typically represents a source of profound social and moral disorder. Although the preoccupation is perhaps most obvious in Thackeray, it likewise informs the obsessive representation of disaffected, deracinated men of privilege throughout Dickens's later fiction, most often in a structure of rivalry with another, contrasting male figure, typically of lower social caste yet upwardly aspiring, and thus earnestly engaged in economic and social struggle. *A Tale of Two Cities* (1859) situates this concern in especially suggestive relation to Carlyle. The novel is famously indebted to Carlyle's *French Revolution*; in all the attention devoted to the two works as historical narratives, however, it is less often noted that Dickens's hero, Sydney Carton, enacts a broadly Carlylean quest for a vocation, which is figured in the very image that typically distinguishes the Carlylean hero, that of the wanderer in the wilderness: "Waste forces within him, and a desert all around, this man stood still on his way across a silent terrace, and saw for a moment, lying in the wilderness before him, a mirage of honourable ambition, self-denial, and perseverance" (97). The "mirage" is a social incarnation (appropriately hazy) of the virtues that distinguish Carlylean earnestness: "honourable ambition, self-denial, and perseverance." Carton glimpses from afar an image of vocation, that Carlylean mirror in which he will finally discover the lineaments of his spirit. Carton's progress toward his glorious end thus seems to reenact the historical displacement of an aristocratic (or dandiacal) idleness by a distinctively bourgeois heroism.

Yet Dickens's portrait of Carton reproduces the blurring of dandy and hero suggested in *Sartor Resartus*. In this novel of mirrors and mirrored faces, Carton makes his entrance as Darnay's "double of coarse deportment," whose "especially reckless" and "careless" manner bespeaks a radical lack of self-discipline redundantly emblazoned in his "careless," "slovenly," "torn" attire (81–83). Although Beau Brummel would have protested such regalia, Carton is clearly a Carlylean dandy-dilettante, inasmuch as he is a standing affront to the "earnestness" so vividly engraved in Darnay's countenance. At the same time, however, Carton's disregard for decorum intimates his affinities with the Carlylean hero, in whom such disregard likewise affirms a tenacious integrity and self-sufficiency, which will of course support Carton in his crowning self-sacrifice. For Carton as for Carlyle, one's approach to redemption depends importantly on one's powers of contempt—including self-loathing. Carton's apparently casual *contemptus mundi* extends to a repudiation of economic responsibility: "Business! Bless you, I have no business!" he tells Lorry at their first meeting (88). But this avowal points to a reconfiguration of "business" as a higher vocation—a more lofty and exacting "care," as in "my father's business"—of which a mundane version is realized in Lorry's tenacious fidelity to his clients (clearly distinguished from the more self-interested dedication of Carton's aptly named partner, "Stryver"). Carlylean heroism, after all, shares with the creed of gentleman and dandy alike the repudiation of "business" as a narrowly economic struggle. And of course Carton's triumph will further underscore the profound affinities of dandy and prophet, as Carton becomes a literally self-made—which is to say, re-made—man. His reconfiguration begins from a fundamental deracination—"I care for no man on earth, and no man cares for me" (91)—and culminates as the affirmation of a new identity in a triumphant spectacle, in which Carton strikingly realizes the power of pure appearance. His triumph, like that of both dandy and "John the Baptist in Cockney-land," is an eminently theatrical achievement, which is realized through Carton's capacity to capture the gaze of an eager, public "curiosity" (363) that is riveted by his features yet incapable of fathoming them. In this light, Carton's death confirms the reign of Carlylean dandyism in the novel, underscoring the efficacy of a wholly mediated selfhood, which betrays no hint of a discordant identity that resides in some imagined, essential depth of being. Yet Dickens would have us regard this performance as the culminating act of a process of self-discovery, which builds on a truly heroic capacity of self-restraint, crowned by self-annihilation. Indeed, the young seamstress seems introduced largely to encourage an emblematic view of Carton's death, in which the particular triumph of the "stranger" is submerged in the divinity of heroism. The spectacle on the scaffold is neither Carton nor Evremonde, but a paradigm of triumphant manhood, obviously modeled on Christ: "I think you were sent to me by Heaven" (365).

Carton's death represents one imagined escape from the compromised autonomy that haunts ascetic self-fashioning. Only martyrdom can finally guarantee a perfect autonomy in self-discipline; in *A Tale of Two Cities*, as Kucich points out, "any desire for extremity that stops short of self-annihilation becomes impure by being implicated in the temporal arena of rivalry" ("Purity" 134). Dickens's novel thus discovers a narrative logic implicit in Carlyle's rhetoric of heroism. But Carton's visibility—and that of Dickensian manhood generally—differs importantly from that of Carlyle's heroes in its motivation, which in turn reflects the very different imaginative contexts in which Dickens represents the spectacle of masculinity. When Carlyle contemplates his permanent move to the alien world of London, he imagines himself concertedly making a spectacle of himself, proclaiming his alienation in the guise of a latter-day John the Baptist. In revolutionary Paris, Sydney Carton does not have to incite such attention; he cannot help becoming the object of a gaze, since the French Revolution, as Catherine Gallagher points out, functions throughout the novel as an omnipresent stare ("Duplicity" 134). There is no need, in other words, to launch an affront to social decorum, since that decorum is the implicit antagonist of every individual. Under such surveillance, Carton's only path to heroism lies in trying to become, as it were, merely a sight rather than a spectacle; he must avoid arresting that omnipresent stare until he has the opportunity to remake himself as the simulacrum of another man. So pervasive and bewildering is the specular logic in this world of mirrored pseudonyms and disguises—Jacques upon Jacques upon Jacques—that a form of intimacy can be established simply as a momentary arrest of the play of impersonation, even—paradoxically— by addressing someone as "stranger." This is the word uttered by the young seamstress to signal her awareness, as they are about to leave the prison, that Carton is not who he purports to be—or rather, that he possesses an identity apart from that of "Evremonde."

Carlyle, too, frequently insists on "the mystery of a Person," but as an ontological attribute, an index of divine origin that can never be fully fathomed by any human being (*Sartor Resartus* 99). In Dickens's novels such mystery operates principally as a social structure, secrecy, which is generated by, and in turn sustains, a pervasive dynamic of surveillance. That surveillance is of course what makes Dickens's novels so responsive to Foucauldian readings. As Gallagher points out, *A Tale of Two Cities* shares with the revolution it describes the sustaining premise that plots and hidden identities lurk everywhere, and hence every human being is a spectacle that requires investigation. This shared preoccupation shapes the famous opening of the third chapter, where the narrator announces the "wonderful fact" that "every human being is constituted to be that profound secret and mystery to every other," and that death marks "the inexorable consolidation and perpetuation of the secret that was always in that individuality," the secret that is Everyman's (as well as Evremonde's) "natural and not to be alienated inheritance" (21). In thus linking secrecy with mystery and death, Dickens energizes the vigilant reflexivity of surveillance throughout the novel (Hutter 10). To contemplate the mystery of another person is always to be reminded of one's own secrets, and thus of the disjunction between outward appearance and some "inner" identity, a disjunction that creates the possibility of exposure as well as the necessity of performance. In this passage, then, Dickens follows Carlyle in suggesting that secrecy is not merely a social strategy but an ontological condition. In doing so, however, the novelist augments his own professional resources, since he lays claim to a limitless supply of secrets to be fathomed. In thus naturalizing secrecy, moreover, Dickens implicitly aligns himself with the paranoid revolutionary imagination, for whom appearances are always hiding *something*: from such a perspective, there are no innocent spectacles.

A world devoid of innocence cannot accommodate the idyllic spaces of Victorian domesticity. Indeed, *A Tale of Two Cities* exemplifies Dickens's tendency to present those spaces as an increasingly overt realm of wish-fulfillment. To be sure, Carton's ostensible motivation for his heroic self-sacrifice, his love for Lucie, sharply differentiates him from Carlylean heroes, who reflect Carlyle's contempt for the consolations of romance. Carlyle's ascetic heroes are never motivated by desire for women; they work either in open antagonism to such desire, as in *Sartor Resartus*, or in entire isolation from it, as in *Past and Present*. But Carton's desire is profoundly equivocal in its relation to the domesticity that marks its ostensible fulfillment. Lucie is of course the apotheosis of domestic femininity, and as such she presides over Carton's final meditation:

> I see the lives for which I lay down my life, peaceful, useful, prosperous and happy, in that England which I shall see no more. I see *her* with a child upon her bosom, who bears my name. . . . I see that I hold a sanctuary in their hearts, and in the hearts of their descendants, generations hence. I see her, an old woman, weeping for me on the anniversary of this day. I see her and her husband, their course done, living side by side in their last earthly bed, and I know that each was not more honoured and held more sacred in the other's soul, than I was in the souls of both.
>
> I see that child who lay upon her bosom and who bore my name, a man winning his way up in that path of life which once was mine. I see him winning it so well, that my name is made illustrious there by the light of his. I see the blots I threw upon it faded away. I see him, foremost of the just judges and honoured men, bringing a boy of my name, with a forehead that I know and golden hair, to this place—then fair to look

upon, without a trace of this day's disfigurement—and I hear him tell
the child my story, with a tender and faltering voice. (367)

Although Carton celebrates domesticity, he does so in confirming his
own exclusion from it, save in the pleasures of imagination. His vision,
however, offers as much exemption as exclusion—particularly in light
of Dickens's own embattled domestic situation while he was composing
A Tale of Two Cities. Carton's meditation offers a vicarious experience
of domesticity as a cult of hero-worship, in which he is a divinity freed
from further responsibility in human affairs. The vision is a proleptic
variation on Tennyson's fantasy in the Choric Song of "The Lotos-
Eaters," where the mariners pay tribute to a domesticity that satisfies
only from a safe distance, and through the haze of retrospection. "Dear
is the memory of our wedded lives," the mariners sing, yet they recoil
from the possibility of returning to those lives; it is the *memory* that
charms.

   In thus displacing domestic life into a world of vision or daydream,
Carton's self-sacrifice cuts short the trajectory subsequently completed
by Eugene Wrayburn in *Our Mutual Friend*, another of Dickens's aristocratic idlers who ultimately embraces, in Eve Sedgwick's characterization, "the enforcing position of the paterfamilias" (*Between Men* 177).
Carton's meditation, however, appropriates the authority of the paterfamilias in an imagined history, in which his authority persists beyond
(and through) his death in the organization of something like a religious cult devoted to his memory. (Fittingly, Carton's vision of the Darnay family does not include Darnay himself—save in imagining his
death: "I see her and her husband, their course done, living side by
side in their last earthly bed . . .") Thus reenacted, tributes to Carton's
self-sacrifice become a further mode of resurrection in a novel obses-
sively concerned with being "restored to life." More generally, however, Carton thus imagines his sacrifice inaugurating a new form of
patriarchal authority, akin to Comte's "subjective immortality," in
which the influence of his heroism will be confirmed and extended by
the reinscription of his name with each new generation. Carton's invention of tradition thereby reclaims masculine authority for a male
figure outwardly deprived of the appurtenances of manhood.

   The concluding fantasy of *A Tale of Two Cities* thus captures a structure of compensation echoed throughout Victorian representations of
marginal masculinities of intellectual labor, or (more generally) constructions of masculinity outside the marketplace and domestic relations. Carton's final solace, after all, is a muted, more intimate echo of

the fiercer satisfaction that Carlyle derives from imagining the man of letters "ruling (for this is what he does), from his grave, after death, whole nations and generations who would, or would not, give him bread while living" (*Heroes* 383). And Carlyle's thinly veiled revenge fantasy in turn recalls Shelley's self-consoling tribute to poets as "the unacknowledged legislators of the world." All of these apologies summon up varieties of the sense of estrangement and dispossession so arrestingly embodied in Carlyle's figure of John the Baptist in Cockneyland. And widely disparate Victorian rhetorics of masculinity share in an appeal to imagined masculine traditions—replete with elaborate structures of ritual observance—in order to legitimate marginal forms of masculine identity. Thus Pater's fascination with the idea of "renaissance," for example, closely recalls Dickens's imagination of "rebirth" in *A Tale of Two Cities*, not only in the shared meaning of the terms, but in the extension of both concepts into structures of ritual commemoration. Participation in tradition compensates for present marginality with an imagined community articulated through history. The appeal to homosocial tradition thus both incorporates and reinforces an increasingly anxious and complicated semiotics of masculine identity, which would discover membership in an elite group by means of outward signs of shared wisdom or companionable selfhood.

The Oxford Movement, I will argue in the next chapter, represents an early and profoundly influential example of the authorization of a dissident masculinity through a conjoint appeal to tradition and to a solidarity manifested through an ostentatious regimen of ascetic discipline. Thus summarized, the community that formed around the example of John Henry Newman at Oxford seems uncannily like the Abbey of St. Edmundsbury that Carlyle conjures up in *Past and Present.* But Newman's influence underscores the importance to Victorian culture of the logic of heroism that Carlyle found so unsettling: the dandy and the prophet in the wilderness shadow each other with remarkable persistence as spectacles of a masculine self-fashioning estranged from, yet inevitably staged before, "the world." And the kinship of prophet and dandy may suggest in turn a new vantage on Carlyle's influence, as it was summed up in A. H. Clough's famous lament. "Carlyle has led us out into the desert," Clough complained to Emerson in 1848, "and has left us there." For Clough the desert was a place of confusion and betrayal; the writings of Carlyle, Tennyson, and Dickens, however, all envision the desert as a realm of anxious, incessant masculine self-fashioning. It is an especially fitting arena for spectacles of masculinity.

CHAPTER TWO

"A Sort of Masonry": Secrecy and "Manliness" in Early Victorian Brotherhoods

I have strange glimpses of the power of spiritual union, of Association among men of like object.

Thomas Carlyle, *Two Notebooks* (1896)

"What I feel daily more and more to need," Thomas Arnold confided to a friend in 1836,

> is to have intercourse with those who take life in earnest. It is very painful to me to be always on the surface of things. . . . It is not that I want much of what is called religious conversation . . . but I want a sign, which one catches as by a sort of masonry, that a man knows what he is about in life,—whither tending, and in what cause he is engaged. (Stanley, *Life* 275)

Arnold's longing for solidarity sheds unexpected light on the psychic and social economies informing that familiar Victorian virtue, earnestness. As it dwells in a deep subjectivity, defined in antagonism to the "surfaces" of life, earnestness tends to be a very lonely discipline. For those under its sway, most forms of social affiliation seem superficial. If earnestness is to find collective embodiment, it can only be as a community hidden or withdrawn from the larger society. And this logic is borne out when Arnold imagines fellowship in earnestness as a form of secret society, "a sort of masonry" ratified in the shared recognition of an arcane "sign."

In light of this longing for fellowship, it is all the more remarkable that Thomas Arnold was a vehement, public critic of secret societies, particularly, as he put it, "Trades Unions, a fearful engine of mischief, ready to riot or to assassinate, with all the wickedness, that has in all ages and countries characterized associations not recognized by the law" (Stanley, *Life* 237). "Associations not recognized by the law" invariably subvert the law; secret societies, Arnold complains, "regard the law as their worst enemy" (Stanley, *Life* 304). From this perspective, Arnold's imagined fellowship in earnestness models itself on a social structure that he himself declares to be anathema; his desire for solidarity stands condemned in its very utterance. Such ambivalence captures a widespread double bind governing associations between men in early and mid-Victorian England. It is a structure closely akin to homophobic inflections of what Eve Kosofsky Sedgwick calls the homosocial continuum. In Arnold's writings, a homosocial desire to affiliate with other men is checked by his own recoil from the idea of men in groups outside legal surveillance. But the recoil is not homophobic; instead, it marks an overtly political fear of "combination," to use the early-nineteenth-century term for illegal association. Over the course of the Victorian era, however, this fear becomes sexualized: secrecy among men becomes the sign less of potential insurrection than of sexual deviance. And that transition is vividly encapsulated in the widespread Victorian preoccupation with secret societies and brotherhoods, real and imagined.

There is an obvious, immediate context for Arnold's unease: growing working-class political unrest and agitation in the 1830s. In 1838, Parliamentary investigations into Trades Unions purported to uncover elaborate machinery of ritual and initiation that made them sound very much like masonic lodges; Disraeli cribbed a great deal from these reports in his lurid representation of a Chartist meeting in *Sybil* (1845) (Brantlinger *Spirit of Reform* 96–98). But the preoccupation with secret societies reflect an ongoing fascination as well as fear—a fear of insurrection answered by a desire for collective intimacy among men. In this regard, Arnold's ambivalence responds not only to explicitly political anxieties, but to a more encompassing, more diffuse, but quite pronounced unease aroused by the proliferation of strangers. The pressure here is less one of Foucauldian surveillance than of the sheer novelty of a daily routine increasingly given over to encounters with unfamiliar

faces—one important product of the increasing social mobility bound
up with the rise of industrialism. Such unease found paranoid embodiment in fantasies of secret societies that threatened to subvert a civic
order that seemed ever more tenuous. But the adoption of an increasingly guarded stance toward the world at large also made intimate
friendship between men seem increasingly difficult to enjoy outside the
domestic realm.

In many respects, this ambivalence mirrors the paradox embodied
in Carlylean hero-worship. Carlyle echoes Arnold's longing for solidarity in his early tribute to the power of "spiritual union" among men,
which he most famously envisioned in the form of hero-worship, "the
soul of all social business among men," as he calls it in *Past and Present*
(39). As it joins two or more together in reciprocal bonds of recognition and devotion, hero-worship is the foundation of all Carlylean
schemes of society. Yet Carlyle's rhetoric of heroic integrity, as we saw
in the previous chapter, fuses the model of the solitary prophet with a
romantic discourse that reserves moral authority for social marginality.
If the hero affirms his integrity as a "wild," "savage" disruption of all
social economies, how is hero-worship to form the basis of a new order?
The dilemma follows from Carlyle's charismatic conception of authority; to envision heroism as a mechanism of social renewal requires what
Weber called the routinization of charisma. In the terms of Carlyle's
construction of his own vocation, the solitary eremite must be brought
in from the wilderness in order that a society might form around his
example. For this project, Carlyle in *Past and Present* turned to the
model of the medieval monastery. In the process, however, Carlyle formulated a model of society that erased the very existence of women,
and in effect, as Herbert Sussman has argued, identified the condition
of England question with the condition of English manliness. Carlyle
in *Past and Present* sets forth, in Sussman's phrase, "a foundation myth
of manliness for an industrial society" that would redirect and regulate
masculine desire; virility is separated from sexuality, and "manhood"
is understood as an incessant self-regulation, a psychic economy ad-
justed to the demands of early Victorian political economy. In this
scheme, the monk represents the "heroic or virtuoso case of the regulation of desire that defines manhood," manhood realized in an all-
male community ordered around a charismatic leader (38).

The regimen of masculinity set forth in *Past and Present* radically
challenges Victorian domestic ideology, in that it is realized entirely
outside relations with women; under its authority, in Sussman's phrase,
the marriage plot gives way to the masculine plot, a narrative of initi-

ation into manhood. Yet variations on this pattern are surprisingly pervasive in Victorian constructions of privileged manhood. Most obvious, the rapidly expanding public-school system increasingly undermined the sway of domesticity by challenging the family as the boy's primary source of identity. Indeed, Carlyle's St. Edmundsbury strikingly resembles Arnold's vision of Rugby School as a proving ground for the Christian gentleman—or at least the idealized Rugby presented in A. P. Stanley's almost exactly contemporary *Life and Correspondence of Thomas Arnold* (1844). But Carlyle's monastery represents a more radical revision of manhood, inasmuch as it did not propose the ascetic community as a transitional stage. Carlyle had a more immediate and exact contemporary model, however, in the Oxford Movement, which had been denounced almost from its inception in 1833 as a "priesthood," and whose leaders recently had inflamed controversy with a tentative revival of religious orders, most notably John Henry Newman's "retreat" at Littlemore. The Tractarians were very much on Carlyle's mind when he announced the completion of *Past and Present* to Emerson in 1843: "It is a somewhat fiery and questionable 'Tract for the Times,' *not* by a Puseyite, which the horrible aspect of things here has forced from me" (*Collected Letters* 16:76). Although Carlyle on several occasions expressed contempt for Newman, their organizations of discipline had much in common. Carlyle, after all, proposed a model of manhood that, whatever its economic utility, fervently rejects economic rationality: "Thou wilt never sell thy Life. . . . Give it, like a royal heart; let the price be Nothing . . ." (*Past and Present*, 204). Like Arnold at Rugby and Newman at Oxford, Carlyle sought to remove inner-wordly asceticism, in Weber's phrase, from a world where it had been corrupted by the god of getting-on, to purify it by returning to a monastic realm from which it had emerged. The Carlylean hero, Arnold's Christian gentleman, and the Tractarian priest are all defined through an ascetic discipline within the confines of an all-male society. Each figure, moreover, offers to his followers a sense of identity largely derived from membership in a sect ordered around his charismatic influence.

The many parallels among these three communities confirm the authority of virtuoso discipline in early Victorian rhetorics of masculinity. But these congruences have been largely obscured not only by familiar theological disputes, but by the development of a sexualized discourse of "manliness" that has anachronistically exaggerated the disjunctions between the three projects. That discourse, as I argue in this chapter, was largely organized around anxieties over male secrecy. An increasing number of twentieth-century accounts of the Oxford Movement have suggested that the widespread hostility it aroused was from the very outset an attack on a perceived sexual deviance. In fact, however, the earliest attacks on the Movement denounced it as a priesthood, appealing to a *civic* ideal of manhood defined above all as an ideal of honest, straightforward conduct—the same ideal to which Arnold appealed in attacking secret societies.[1] As the shifting forms of this hostility helped to codify a newly rigid norm of "manliness" defined against subtlety and obliquity of any kind, they also help to explain the widespread appeal of the Oxford Movement to various cultural dissidents: the Movement offered the model of an elite, heterodox social formation that defined itself through the shared possession of arcane wisdom or values. The ostentatious mystery of Tractarian "reserve" in this context came to function for many of Newman's followers as the masonic "sign" for which Arnold yearned. Only gradually did the aura of secrecy associated with the movement come to be emphatically sexualized—most notably in Kingsley's famous attacks on Newman. In this regard, the changing reception of the Oxford Movement encapsulated a momentous, many-faceted transformation in Victorian culture and its norms of masculinity: the broad shift from models of identity founded in kinship and rank to forms of "deep," putatively classless subjectivity came into arresting focus in the genealogy of the closet.

"THE TONE OF EARNESTNESS": STANLEY'S *LIFE OF ARNOLD*

It is not easy today to appreciate the immense and sustained popularity enjoyed throughout the Victorian era by A. P. Stanley's *Life and Correspondence of Thomas Arnold, D.D.* (1844). Filial and other forms of piety of course generated a staggering number of memoirs of Victorian clergymen. None, however, approached the impact of Stanley's *Life*, which by 1890 had sold hundreds of thousands of copies in at least fifty editions (McCrum 153n) and made Arnold so eminent a figure of Victorian hagiography that he called out the best ironic weapons of the devil's chief advocate, Lytton Strachey. Largely through Stanley's influence, "Dr. Arnold" has been enshrined as the man who rescued Rugby School—and thence English public schools generally, and thereby (still further) the moral life of the privileged classes—from the swamp of

---

1. Dowling, *Hellenism and Homosexuality,* traces this ideal of civic manhood back to the tradition of classical republicanism analyzed by J.G.A. Pocock.

brutality and barbarism that was the legacy of Georgian lassitude. It was a triumph of staggering moral energy and unflagging devotion to duty—the keynote of a character captured in a letter Arnold wrote to Stanley in 1835: "My love for any place or person, or institution, is exactly the measure of my desire to reform them" (Stanley, *Life* 238).

Yet this familiar account of Arnold as, in Basil Willey's words, "the great Headmaster who changed the face of education all through the public schools of England" (52), is largely a myth. As T. W. Bamford and others have pointed out, the changes Arnold effected were not dramatic, they were confined largely to his well-known delegation of formal authority to the senior pupils, they did not have a profound impact on other schools, and they became famous less through the subsequent achievements of his pupils—distinguished as some of those were—than through Stanley's *Life*. Stanley's work, in turn, was a concerted effort to rescue Arnold from the main source of his fame in his own lifetime, as a fierce controversialist who allegedly had turned Rugby into a breeding ground for Radicalism (Bamford 78–79). Stanley successfully transformed this image by in effect abstracting from Arnold's varied public activities and writings the model of a heroic *character* that transcended sect or party.[2] In this regard, he was faithful to Arnold's own approach to religious controversy, which typically resolved theological conflict by appeal to underlying moral norms. In Stanley's treatment, the Radical reformer was lost in the Christian gentleman, a being distinguished above all by what one pupil called "the tone of earnestness." Arnold's significance thus came to be identified with an ideal type of manhood, the Christian manliness he so famously and strenuously attempted to inculcate in his pupils. And the reception of Stanley's *Life* confirms that the middle-class public was eager for just such an ideal. James Martineau, for example, argued in the *Prospective Review* in February 1845 that

> however great the loss of Arnold's Roman History, it is as nothing to the wealth he leaves us in this Biography. From what a good man *does* there is no higher lesson to be learned than what he *is*; his workmanship interests and profits us as an expression of himself, and would become dead and indifferent if it were the product of some mechanical necessity. That Arnold has lived, and shown how much nobleness and strength may

2. Even Thomas Hughes, who is often credited with shaping the cult of Arnold through his *Tom Brown's Schooldays* (1857), claimed that it was Stanley's *Life* which first made him aware of Arnold's greatness (Mack and Armytage 43).

maintain itself in an age of falsehood, negligence, and pretence,—with this let us rest and be satisfied. (1:44)

Even W. R. Greg, whose review of Stanley's *Life* passed over Arnold's career at Rugby to focus on his liberal theology, nonetheless concluded by paying tribute to Arnold's earnestness as "the capacity for which above all others we honour him," and lamenting, "In times like ours, a man so *real* could ill be spared" (380–81).

The rhetoric of authenticity in such tributes—the satisfaction of finding "a man so *real*"—is a tellingly Carlylean emphasis. (Indeed, Greg invokes the epigraph of *Past and Present*—Schiller's *ernst ist das Leben*— as the epitome of earnestness [380].) But that emphasis is faithful to Stanley's portrait, in which Arnold's innovations in the educational structure of Rugby are far less prominent than his mesmerizing personal influence over his pupils. Those achievements for which Arnold is best known today—particularly his delegation of formal disciplinary authority to the "praepostors" of the sixth form—Stanley emphatically subordinates to the portrait of a charismatic leader. Even more than in Carlyle's account of St. Edmundsbury, the institution is submerged in the individual. "Throughout," Stanley writes, "the one image that we have before us is not Rugby, but Arnold" (*Life* 62); "the system is lost in the man" (79). This design seems at odds with Arnold's own tributes to the formative influence of the institution and its traditions, that "something very ennobling in being connected with an establishment at once ancient and magnificent" (Stanley, *Life* 62), which would become so prominent in *Tom Brown's Schooldays* and later Victorian celebrations of the public-school system. But Stanley transfers to Arnold himself the reverence and solemnity typically invoked by such appeals to tradition. In a strategy likewise central to contemporary representations of Newman's and Carlyle's authority, the leader's personal attributes not only carry the authority of, but seem to incarnate, the awe-inspiring force of tradition.

Carlylean heroism was an especially important model for Stanley inasmuch as he, too, wished to ennoble an often-belittled male career. In the eighteenth century, learning was found primarily in books, and the schoolmaster's popular image was that of a rather mean, beleaguered, perhaps ludicrous functionary. In Stanley's account the figure is transformed into a source of profound moral guidance, whose influence might indelibly shape not only his pupils' social opportunities, but their very salvation. The traditional figure persists in the young Arnold's jocular references to his "trade" (24), as well as in his awareness of the still-equivocal "place of a schoolmaster in society," which, as Arnold put it, cannot yet "stand by itself in public opinion as a liberal profession; it owes the rank which it holds to its connexion with the profession of clergyman, for that is acknowledged universally in England to be the profession of a gentleman" (350). Stanley's Arnold, however, reanimates that "connexion" through a newly attentive ministry to the spiritual welfare of his charges; a renewed pastoral relationship thus supplants the schoolmaster's traditional identification with the drudgery of rote learning. This transformation would have profound importance in Victorian social history, since it provided the expanding middle classes with a moral rationale for public-school education to supplement the less disinterested appeal of social utility. The public school was no longer an anarchic, often brutal aristocratic rite of passage, nor simply a path to more assured social ascent; instead, it offered the experience of a comprehensive discipline, which turned out not only young men of privilege but Christian gentlemen. In the course of this transformation, the charismatic influence of the male teacher or headmaster came to replace the more general ideal of culture informing Georgian education (Rothblatt 133–35). To be sure, the very ambitious Arnold often seemed less sanguine about the nobility and authority of his calling: "I should like to be *aut Caesar aut nullus,*" he wrote in 1823, "and as it is pretty well settled for me that I shall not be Caesar, I am quite content to live in peace as *nullus*" (Stanley, *Life* 18). Stanley in turn acknowledges a similar attitude when he imagines his reader lamenting that "a man fit to be a statesman should be employed in teaching school-boys" (*Life* 57). Yet Stanley's *Life* aspires to counter any sense of waste or frustration at Arnold's career by minimizing the discrepancy between statesman and schoolmaster. Arnold, he remarks, governed the school "precisely on the same principles as he would have governed a great empire," and thereby, "in the simplest relations of the boys towards each other, or towards him" was able to put into practice "the highest truths of theology and philosophy" (58). In a sense, Stanley's biography succeeded by suggesting that the schoolmaster's calling may not only elicit a heroic force of character, but may rival the gravity of the statesman's calling in its power to influence human conduct.

Stanley's success in his project is reflected in the extent to which mid-Victorian accounts of manly character and self-discipline invoke Arnold as a model. For both William Acton and Samuel Smiles, Arnold's education formed young men into superb examples of *homo economicus,* distinguished by their power of self-control (Cominos 40; Smiles

84–85, 91, 93). And yet the very gravity of Arnold's achievement reflects a fundamental insecurity in the headmaster's reign. As many commentators have noted, Arnold's whole enterprise is founded on a
profound suspicion of the beings with whose welfare he was charged.
On assuming the headmastership of Rugby in 1828, Arnold announced, "My object will be, if possible, to form Christian men, for
Christian boys I can scarcely hope to make" (Stanley, *Life* 50). Boyhood
figures as a state of apparently irremediable evil, which is the subject
of his repeated laments. "In the nakedness of boy-nature, one is quite
able to understand how there could not be found so many as even ten
righteous in a whole city" (99); "it is quite awful to watch the strength
of evil in such young minds" (154). Evil could be conquered only by
hastening the onset of moral manhood. And that goal prompted objections from the very outset of Arnold's career that what Stanley calls
"preparation for Christian manhood" (64) was in fact a premature
forcing of it.[3] Yet the rigor of Arnold's discipline was not idiosyncratic;
it bears the impress of his Evangelical upbringing, which taught him to
regard life as an arena of stark and perpetual moral trial. In this regard
Arnold and Stanley's *Life* figure centrally in the social milieu that Samuel Butler would recreate in *The Way of All Flesh*, whose central character, Ernest Pontifex, bears a name reflecting his birthdate in 1835,
the period at which "earnestness" began to pass into wide currency.
And there is ample evidence in the *Life* of the bleak, often fanatically
single-minded rigor that Butler captures. Thus, for example, Arnold
complains in 1839 of "childishness in boys" as a "growing fault" to
be ascribed to "the great number of exciting books of amusement, like
Pickwick and Nickleby . . ." (Stanley, *Life* 355). A death in the school,
Arnold remarks, "is as nothing when compared with the existence of
any unusual moral evil in the school" (423); an additional daily prayer
for the sixth form is initiated when Arnold experiences too great a
"contrast" in the change from "attendance on the death-bed of one
of the boys in his house to his school-work" (74). Even Arnold's defense of his exacting discipline is adamantine. Although he professed
himself "pained" to find that the tone of his sermons was "generally
felt to be hard and severe," he also rejected complaints that "they carry
the standard so high as to unchristianize half the community": "I do
not see how the standard can be carried higher than Christ or his

3. For example, Fitzjames Stephen's review of *Tom Brown's School Days* in the *Edinburgh
   Review* in 1858, which prompted Matthew Arnold to compose his elegy, "Rugby
   Chapel."

Apostles carry it, and I do not think that we ought to put it lower"
(29).[4]

It is remarkable that such discipline did not, in Stanley's account,
call out more resistance.[5] But Stanley's Arnold commands obedience
through sheer force of character, something akin to pure charisma. His
wordless influence is bodied forth in his very being, his mere presence
in a room, which incarnates the animating force of his own self-
discipline. Early on, Stanley cites a tribute from Bonamy Price, a Rugby
master whom Arnold tutored before taking over at Rugby: "His hold
over all his pupils I know astonished me. It was not so much an enthu-
siastic admiration for his genius, or learning, or eloquence which
stirred within them; it was a sympathetic thrill, caught from a spirit that
was earnestly at work in the world—whose work was healthy, sustained,
and constantly carried forward in the fear of God . . ." (22–23). The
romantic note in the "sympathetic thrill" may remind us that Arnold
was an exact contemporary of Keats (and may also help to explain why
Price was able to recount so vividly an influence that he experienced
for only two months at the age of eight). But Arnold's "spirit" is firmly
located in a different milieu by the invocation of "earnestly at work":
the ineffable appeal that Keats found in exquisite song, or female
beauty, is discovered here in the spectacle of disciplined labor dedicated to a "mission" in the world. Arnold's authority, like that of the
Carlylean hero, is conveyed through his own self-discipline, through an
exacting earnestness that is communicated without words—"the startling earnestness with which he would check in a moment the slightest
approach to levity and impatience" (79). That expressive character is
most forcefully registered when Arnold appears in Chapel—the sight,
and site, which would figure so powerfully in tributes from other Rugbeians, especially Thomas Hughes in *Tom Brown's Schooldays*. "More
than either matter or manner of his preaching, was the impression of
himself" (94); for his hearers (as distinct from "the mere readers of
his sermons") "it was the man himself, there more than in any other

4. Such rigor recalls that of Newman, who when Samuel Wilberforce protested the harsh-
   ness of his sermons, responded, "We *require* the 'Law's stern fires.' We need a continual
   Ash Wednesday" (Newsome, "Evangelical Sources" 25).
5. Most accounts suggest that Stanley "simply didn't grasp the violence around him"
   owing to his quick advancement to the Fifth Form and the unusual deference of other
   pupils toward him (Bamford 78–79). But there is also a moral logic in his apparent
   oversight; the persistence of violence in the school might call into question the efficacy
   of Arnoldian heroism.

place, concentrating all his various faculties and feelings on one sole object, combating face to face the evil, with which directly or indirectly he was elsewhere perpetually struggling" (94).

Arnold's forbiddingly grave and stern discipline is thus rendered charismatic as the direct and uncalculating expression of his entire being. This impression is reinforced by a tribute likening the young Arnold to the Apostle Paul: the discipline of both men is attributed to an immediate apprehension of realities that others knew only at second hand, only "believed" or "talked about," "so that like St. Paul he seemed to be battling with the wicked one, and yet with the feeling of God's help on his side" (16–17). Although in some of his pupils, Stanley concedes, "the sternness of his character" aroused "mere dread," that reaction was also "mingled with an involuntary and, perhaps, an unconscious respect inspired by the sense of manliness and straightforwardness of his dealings, and still more by the sense of the general force of his moral character." Listeners were struck by (here Stanley quotes tributes from other pupils) "a truthfulness . . . a sort of moral transparency," "by a consciousness, almost amounting to solemnity, that 'when his eye was upon you, he looked into your inmost heart'; that there was something in his very tone and outward aspect, before which anything low, or false, or cruel, instinctively quailed and cowered" (100).

Such tributes shape Arnold's influence into a social structure, inasmuch as they rest on a distinction between initiates and outsiders: only those who had heard or witnessed Arnold in person could fully experience his authority. It is in the school chapel, a headmaster of Harrow wrote, that the school "learns that it has a corporate life; there it stands face to face with its chief, and there the lessons of brotherhood can be enforced" (Wilkinson, *Gentlemanly Power* 55). Such "lessons"—amply celebrated by Stanley—implicitly discount any criticism of the school or its leader that comes from outside, as proceeding from those who have no "face-to-face" experience of the "chief." In this regard, the pupils of Rugby—and those of the Sixth Form in particular, who enjoyed an especially close contact with Arnold—approximated the structure of the secret society for which Arnold himself longed. But what held them together was less a common cause or "mission" than Arnold's charismatic discipline. And that discipline, in turn, was clearly modeled on the divine paragon of the Christian gentleman. Stanley's Arnold incarnates a perfectly disinterested authority, whose punishment is loving in its very severity, motivated solely by concern for the welfare of the punished; his discipline is inexorable, his gaze omniscient, like that of Milton's "great Taskmaster's eye." Under such a discipline, submission is freedom.

Stanley thus constructs around Arnold a society closely akin to a religious sect. And this aspect of his influence disturbed some observers almost from the beginning of Arnold's tenure at Rugby. Many historians of the English public school have pointed out that Arnold's discipline exemplified an increasingly exacting regulation of public school life that deprived boys of what had been considered a fundamental aspect of boyhood—their freedom (Chandos 167–95). One might recast this objection in Foucauldian terms, to suggest that Stanley's Arnold mystifies the work of a rather different form of discipline: Arnold's apparently omnipresent "eye," whose reach was extended by the discipline of the praepostors, represents an impressive system of surveillance, whose monitory power is almost wholly internalized in Stanley's devotion to Arnold. To be sure, Arnold's authority hardly displays the reach and efficiency of Foucauldian "power," yet Foucault's emphases are helpful here in pointing up the extent to which Arnold's discipline not only depends on adversaries, but may indeed create them. Even as Stanley describes a willing and entire submission to Arnold's authority, Arnold's own letters repeatedly single out pockets of resistance, which invariably take the form of boys in groups. For Arnold, "the great curse of the public schools" (in Stanley's words) was "the spirit which was there encouraged of combination, of companionship, of excessive deference to the public opinion prevalent in the school" (*Life* 67). "At the very sight of a knot of vicious or careless boys gathered together . . . , 'It makes me think,' he would say, 'that I see the Devil in the midst of them'" (67). "Vicious" seems redundant here, inasmuch as "knot" carries the pejorative overtones of conspiracy, which almost always shadows contemporary use of the term "combination," associated as it is with trade unions. "Companionship" among boys thus energizes the very suspicion informing Arnold's attacks on secret societies: it represents a "servile submission to unlawful authority," which is "fatal . . . to all approach to sympathy between himself and his scholars—to all free and manly feeling in individual boys—to all real and permanent improvement in the school itself" (67).

As "companionship" becomes the nucleus of potential insurrection, a pronounced double bind in Arnold's authority emerges. No boy can be adequately disciplined unless he is absolutely individuated, "free and manly," in his relation to Arnold. At the same time, however, the boy can only be disciplined through participation in an elaborately structured social hierarchy that inculcates uniform submission to "lawful authority." The necessity for such submission—and with it a constraint on "all free and manly feeling"—informs Arnold's public response to those who complained of flogging at Rugby. Such criticism, he objected, "originates in that proud notion of personal independence which is neither reasonable nor Christian—but essentially barbarian. . . . At an age when it is almost impossible to find a true manly sense of the degradation of guilt or faults, where is the wisdom of encouraging a fantastic sense of the degradation of personal correction? What can be more false, or more adverse to the simplicity, sobriety, and humbleness of mind, which are the best ornament of youth, and the best promise of a noble manhood?" (67). A "proud notion of personal independence" is here "essentially barbarian," yet it is just what Arnold demands in opposition to the evil of "combination"; in the one instance he insists on group loyalty, in the other he calls it the source of all evils. Arnold's discipline can never escape its fundamental suspicion of boys in groups; it can only intensify it. Even Stanley seems to acknowledge this when he remarks that Arnold's earnestness "prevented him from fully appreciating" many aspects of "the peculiar humour of boys." But Stanley immediately praises the "quick and far-sighted eye" with which Arnold "became familiar with the face and manner of every boy in the school": " 'Do you see,' he said to an assistant master who had recently come, 'those two boys walking together? I never saw them together before; you should make an especial point of observing the company they keep;—nothing so tells the changes in a boy's character' " (*Life* 95).

The psychic pressures entailed by this regimen of suspicion are reflected in Arnold's notorious flogging of an innocent boy named Marsh, which aroused a controversy that prompted Arnold's public defense of flogging. When the boy told Arnold that a particular lesson he had not prepared had not been assigned, the Headmaster accused him of lying, despite Marsh's vehement protestations and unblemished record, and gave him eighteen strokes with a cane—although Arnold later apologized to the assembled school when the boy's innocence was established (Bamford 49–53). More than one commentator has referred this incident to Arnold's "pathological hatred of lying" (McCrum 76) but the pathology reflects a larger, cultural conradiction: more than a few middle-class Victorian men were led to the verge of breakdown by violent alternation between unwavering suspicion of conspiracy, on the one hand, and the wish to participate in, or to direct, a "combination" of their own. In effect, the regimen of earnestness undermines the very camaraderie, that "sort of masonry," for which Arnold longed. The tension is powerfully akin to those embodied in Carlyle's distinctive rhetoric: as he celebrates the communality of hero-worship, Carlyle nonetheless can only represent heroic integrity as a proud solitude, defined in strenuous antagonism to social norms. Indeed, this same double bind shaped the hostility of outside observers toward Arnold's rule—whether they assumed that Arnold's school was itself a subversive "combination" devoted to Radicalism, or, like William Johnson (Cory), an influential master at Eton, criticized the very intensity of the pupil-master bond Arnold created. "We are content to have pupils, and do not aim at disciples," was Johnson's disdainful comment (Chandos 270). Ironically, Johnson's career was destroyed by suspicions of his own intense relationships with pupils.

That readers of Stanley's *Life* largely overlooked such internal tensions reflects the eagerness with which a middle-class readership welcomed not only a moral rationale for the public school, but a model of virtuoso discipline in an age fearful of social upheaval. Arnold's discipline, moreover, was explicitly modeled on the Christian paradigm that ostensibly grounded all Victorian schemes of value. Yet even in Stanley's *Life* one can glimpse a subtle tension between Christian piety and an emerging idea of the "manly." When Arnold himself urges that the Society for the Diffusion of Useful Knowledge should aim at a union "between goodness and wisdom;—between everything that is manly, sensible, and free, and everything that is pure and self-denying, and humble, and heavenly" (*Life* 157), he tellingly separates the "pure and self-denying" attributes of his discipline from those which are "manly." Stanley echoes this usage in describing the Headmaster's presence in Chapel as "the complete image of his union of dignity and simplicity, of manliness and devotion" (89). Of course it was Arnold's distinctive achievement, in Stanley's account, to reconcile manliness and devotion; that is the very essence of the Christian gentleman. Yet the persistent resolution of that achievement into gendered components suggests the precariousness of the ideal. In particular, it underscores the susceptibility of Arnold's regimen to a renewed association of "manliness" with forthright self-assertion, with a concomitant suspicion of all forms of manhood that celebrate an inwardness cultivated by self-restraint, and hence are not transparent to the world's scrutiny. Although this association will gain wide currency with the rise of so-called muscular Christianity, a version of it is already subtly inscribed throughout Stanley's *Life* in Arnold's suspicion of boys—and men—in groups. And a similar suspicion assumed even greater force, and reverberated far more widely, in the exactly contemporary reception of another elite male society—the Oxford Movement.

"CREDO IN NEWMANUM": TRACTARIAN HERO-WORSHIP

If the popularity of Stanley's *Life of Arnold* takes some effort to explain, the extraordinary hold of John Henry Newman on the mind of Oxford in the 1830s is still more elusive. Clearly one cannot explain in exclusively theological terms the heady appeal that is captured in a letter of 1837 by J. F. Russell, a Cambridge undergraduate who visited Oxford and recounted his conversations there:

> The talk naturally fell upon Pusey, &c. It was allowed that the Doctor [Pusey] and Newman *governed the university*, and that nothing could withstand the influence of themselves and their friends. Every man of talent who during the past six years has come to Oxford has joined Newman, and when he preaches at St. Mary's (on every Sunday afternoon) all the men of talent in the University come to hear him, although at the loss of their dinner. His triumph over the *mental* empire of Oxford was said to be complete! (Liddon 1:406; Russell's emphasis)

An imperial hold on the thought of Oxford—the doctrinal center of the Church of England—was obviously an influence to be reckoned with; such tributes help to explain why Newman would come to strike many as a national power, and perhaps a national danger. Russell's youthful exhilaration at the imagined overthrow of the intellectual establishment is familiar enough in postromantic cultural avant-gardes. But the implicit structure of this "mental empire" is closer to that of a religious sect, for it is organized to an extraordinary extent around the charismatic authority of a single man. This is the recurrent burden of tributes like that of R. W. Church: "None but those who can remember them can adequately estimate the effect of Mr. Newman's four o'clock sermons at St. Mary's. . . . While men were reading and talking about the Tracts, they were hearing the Sermons; and in the sermons they heard the living meaning, and reason, and bearing of the Tracts, their ethical affinities, their moral standard" (93). In such influence, the doctrinal teachings of the priest are of less moment than the charismatic aura of Weber's ethical prophet, whose personal example demonstrates the way to salvation (*Sociology of Religion* 55).

Virtually all commentators agree that young adherents of Tractarianism were drawn less by theological worries than by the ethical and spiritual regimen epitomized by Newman. In the words of Henry Liddon, "The Movement appealed to a desire to lead a holy life rather than to any craving to fill up gaps which the 'reason of faith' could not but detect in an imperfect creed" (Allchin 37). And this appeal formed an important bond between Newman and Arnold that is often obscured in accounts of their theological differences (Houghton, *Victorian Fame* 231). "No sermons," Church wrote, "except those which his great opposite, Dr. Arnold, was preaching at Rugby, had appealed to conscience with such directness and force"; they urged above all, Church continued, "a passionate and sustained earnestness after a high moral rule, seriously realised in conduct" (22)—the very impulse that distinguished Arnold's Christian gentleman. Even Stanley himself paid tribute to the shared earnestness of the two men: what drew students to Newman, he explained, was "chiefly the grasp of ethical precepts, the appeals to conscience, the sincere conviction of the value of purity and generosity, in which many of his hearers recognized the reverberations, in a more subtle, though not in a more commanding form, of those stirring discourses which had thrilled them from the pulpit of Rugby" ("The Oxford School" 310). Stanley had reason to know: when he arrived at Oxford from Rugby in 1835, Newman powerfully reminded him of Arnold, and he underwent a "short but severe bout of Newmanism" (Woodward 34–36).

For all their theological antagonism, then, both Newman and Arnold were identified with a newly energetic regimen of spiritual and ethical discipline. And as their example was manifested above all in their sermons, so in turn the firsthand experience of those sermons helped to define a masculine community that divided the world into outsiders and initiates. Numerous Victorian memoirs pay tribute to what E. T. Vaughan called a "mysterious bond of union" derived from the experience of Newman's preaching at St. Mary's (DeLaura, "O Unforgotten Voice" 85). Indeed, such tributes came to constitute a Victorian tradition so powerful that, as David J. DeLaura has pointed out, what Matthew Arnold called Newman's "unforgotten voice" was often recalled by writers who had never heard Newman preach—including Arnold himself (81).[6] Such tributes, DeLaura shrewdly infers, provided

6. Matthew Arnold's account, probably the most famous "recollection," appears in the opening passage of "Emerson": "Forty years ago he was in the very prime of life; he was close at hand to us at Oxford; he was preaching at St. Mary's pulpit every Sunday;

elegiac solace to those who recounted them, by sustaining "an enduring myth of a lost generation, permanently caught between an irrecov-
erable past and the unspeakable future" (97). Yet the striking parallels
between memories of Newman and memories of Arnold suggest that
"the bond of union" among both men's admirers had a larger and
more complex cultural appeal. That bond was also enjoyed as an emphatically contemporary sense of brotherhood formed around a shared
encounter with charismatic male authority, a community that was
deeply satisfying to young men looking for new forms of authority in
a world of religious, political, and social upheaval—a community, in
short, remarkably akin to Carlyle's St. Edmundsbury.[7]

"With us," Matthew Arnold wrote in 1864, "the universities are, at
best, but the continuation of the sixth form of Eton, Harrow or Rugby"
(4:331). Arnold was referring to the character of university instruction,
but his remark captures important continuities in emotional and social
life as well. As R. W. Church pointed out, the passions aroused by the
Oxford movement were fueled by the insular character of the University, in which "feelings were apt to be more keen and intense and
personal than in the larger scenes of life . . . the man who attracted
confidence and kindled enthusiasm, whose voice was continually in
men's ears, and whose private conversation and life was something ever

---

he seemed about to transform and renew what for us was the most national and natural institution in the world, the Church of England. Who could resist the charm of
that spiritual apparition, gliding in the dim afternoon light through the aisles of St.
Mary's, rising into the pulpit, and then, in the most entrancing of voices, breaking
the silence with words and thoughts which were a religious music,—subtle, sweet,
mournful? I seem to hear him still, saying: 'After the fever of life, after weariness and
sicknesses, fightings and despondings, languor and fretfulness, struggling and failing,
struggling and succeeding; after all the changes and chances of this troubled, unhealthy state,—at length comes death, at length the white throne of God, at length
the beatific vision' " (10:165).

7. Tellingly, tributes to Newman's preaching figure its effect as that of a melody. In part,
this motif furthers the insistent identification of heroic influence with charismatic
sympathy rather than doctrine; tributes to the "music" of Newman's voice obscure
what Matthew Arnold calls his "impossible" solution to "the doubts and difficulties
which beset men's minds today" (10:165), as the wearying experience of intellectual
combat is lost in the pure, engrossing affect of Newman's being. In this light, one
might expand the Carlylean ascetic continuum noted at the outset of the previous
chapter, to claim that charismatic manhood constantly aspires to the condition of
music, where music is understood on the model of that familiar romantic emblem of
undivided selfhood, the bird's song. Certainly that ideal informs Arnold's evocation
of Newman in St. Mary's as an ethereal being, a seemingly weightless "spiritual apparition, gliding in the dim afternoon light."

new in its sympathy and charm, created in those about him not mere
admiration, but passionate friendship, or unreserved discipleship"
(114).[8] In this regard, Oxford preserved something of the highly
charged emotional atmosphere of public school life—an atmosphere
captured less in Stanley's *Life* than in Disraeli's exactly contemporary
hymn to Etonian friendships in *Coningsby* (1844): "The influence of
the individual is nowhere so sensible as at school. There the personal
qualities strike without any intervening and counteracting causes. . . .
At school, friendship is a passion. It entrances the being; it tears the
soul. All loves of after-life can never bring its rapture, or its wretchedness . . ." (72).

Newman's educational and ecclesiastic positions in many respects
attempted to systematize the "intense and personal" feelings of Oxford
life by insisting on "the personal element" in all forms of human understanding. Several years before the beginning of the *Tracts for the
Times*, Newman attempted to place that element at the heart of undergraduate instruction, by arguing that the existing lecture system at Oriel
be supplemented by a highly individualized, pastoral relation between
each tutor and a few pupils personally selected by him. "The tuition
revolutionized," as Thomas Mozley called it, proposed "an exacter regard to the character and special gifts of each undergraduate, and a
closer relation between him and his tutor," in which the tutor ideally
would stand (as Mozley claimed Newman did) "in the place of a father,
or an elder and affectionate brother" (1:230, 1:181). "It was a large
and novel proposition in those days," Mozley continues (1:230)—but
of course it is strikingly akin to the influence that Arnold was proposing
to exert at Rugby at precisely the same time.

Newman's proposal for a more personal and pastoral mode of instruction evidently had a special appeal for undergraduates such as
Mark Pattison, the future rector of Lincoln College (and militant skep-
tic), for whom arrival at the University brought an excruciating sense
of self-consciousness and isolation, which frustrated "that communion
of mind with mind, and soul with soul, for which I was all the while
inwardly pining; pining unconsciously, for I did not know exactly what
it was that was wanting" (52). Such inchoate longing for intimacy may

8. Newman's comments in the *Apologia* on William Palmer, one of the initial Tractarians,
suggest the exclusionary logics inherent in this tightly knit sense of community: "Coming from a distance, he never had really grown into an Oxford man, nor was he
generally received as such; nor had he any insight into the force of personal influence
and congeniality of thought in carrying out a religious theory" (44–45). Palmer was
a Fellow of Worcester College, but he was Irish.

be an inescapable fact of late adolescence, but it seems to have been especially pronounced at Oxford in the 1830s and 1840s. With the beginning of a gradual but decisive shift of the University from ties based on sponsorship and "interest" to the more impersonal criteria of proficiency measured by examinations, and with an increasing social mobility not yet answered by the mid-Victorian expansion in public school enrollment, an unusually large segment of undergraduates were entering the University lacking the social networks provided by family connections or school affiliations. Such students, moreover, were more likely than their more privileged and better-connected peers to be responsive to an ideal of earnestness, and to appreciate a tutor acting as surrogate father or elder brother. Newman himself had been such a student, and both his pedagogy and his theology clearly formalize his exhilarating discovery of intellectual and emotional fellowship. In this regard, Newman himself worked to define the terms in which his own influence would later be celebrated. Like accounts of Arnold in Rugby Chapel, accounts of Newman preaching in St. Mary's record a sense of uncannily sympathetic insight into the hearer's inmost being (Brilioth 214). "He laid his finger how gently, yet how powerfully, on some inner place in the hearer's heart," J. W. Shairp recalled, "and told him things about himself he had never known till then" (Church 101). J. A. Froude, in his autobiographical novel, *Nemesis of Faith* (1848), similarly described Newman's power as a startling grasp of the listener's inmost self:

> While so much of our talk is so unreal, our own selves, our own risings, fallings, aspirings, resolutions, misgivings, these are real enough to us; these are our hidden life, our sanctuary of our own mysteries. . . . It was into these that Newman's power of insight was so remarkable. I believe no young man had ever heard him preach without fancying that some one had been betraying his own history, and the sermon was aimed specially at him. It was likely that, while he had possession so complete of what we did know about ourselves, we should take his word for what we did not. (144)

"When his eye was upon you, he looked into your inmost heart": this recollection of Arnold might equally be applied to Newman (Stanley, *Life* 100).

Tellingly, when Froude recalled Newman's influence in 1881, his tribute echoed a passage in the *Apologia* that describes "the special power of scripture" to communicate with the reader as with an intimate friend. In the *Apologia*, scripture possesses "this Eye, like that of a portrait, uniformly fixed upon us, turn where we will" (29); Newman's sermons, Froude recalls, "seemed to be addressing the most secret consciousness of each of us—as the eyes of a portrait appear to look at every person in a room" ("Oxford Counter-Reformation" 186).[9] Although this trope pays tribute to Newman's moral insight, its Gothic genealogy has a subtle but powerful resonance in Newman's career. On the one hand, Froude hints at a profound ambivalence captured in many tributes to Newman's "fascination"—a word that likens his influence to the irresistible force of a magic spell, which exhilarates through an apparent suspension or evasion of rational agency.[10] Such associations were eagerly seized on by adversaries such as Kingsley, who would depict Newman's influence as a poisonous dart hidden within his "calm eloquence," "one little barbed arrow which . . . he delivered, as with his finger-tip, to the very heart of an initiated hearer, never to be drawn again" ("What, Then?" 362). But Froude's trope is Newman's own, and as such it reflects the central importance of British romanticism— above all the writings of Scott—in Newman's own intellectual heritage.[11]

Froude's experience of private self-understanding as "real" in a way that social forms and exchange are not reflects an ideal of romantic selfhood central to Newman's thought—perhaps nowhere more evocatively than in his famous sermon, "The Individuality of the Soul," in which he imagines an observer in the midst of a crowded city:

> Every being in that great concourse is his own centre, and all things about him are but shades. . . . He has his own hopes and fears, desires, judgments and aims; he is everything to himself, and no one else is really any thing. No one outside of him can really touch him, can touch his soul, his immortality; he must live with himself for ever. He has a depth within him unfathomable, an infinite abyss of existence; and the scene in which

9. The authority of personal communication is subtly underscored by the framing of the passage in the *Apologia*: Newman is in fact quoting Keble, who in his Bamford lectures attributed this remark to a "Mr. Miller."

10. The word is echoed widely in tributes of the period. Conservatives feared Thomas Arnold's "fascination" over his pupils (Bamford 76); a motto affixed to a memoir of Frederick Faber, a Tractarian who preceded Newman in going over to Rome, points up the etymology of the praise with a passage from *Cymbeline*, "such a holy witch / That he enchants societies unto him" (Faber 230). Over the course of the century, such tributes were to become increasingly equivocal.

11. The best overviews of Newman's important debt to British romanticism are those of Bright and G. B. Tennyson.

he bears part for the moment is but like a gleam of sunshine upon its surface. (*Parochial and Plain Sermons* 4:82–83)

As in the poetry of Wordsworth, it is the evocation of solitary, even solipsistic, depths in the individual soul that most powerfully reached Newman's young audience. Indeed, the recollections of his listeners suggest that they experienced his sermons in a manner akin to Newman's famous concentration of his own thoughts on "two and two only absolutely and luminously self-evident beings, myself and my Creator" (*Apologia* 16). In Newman's thought, such apprehension is connected to a Coleridgean distinction between Imagination and Reason to form the basis of all his speculation on the nature of faith and belief, in an array of associations Newman called "the principle of personality." Although that principle would be most fully developed in *A Grammar of Assent* (1871), it is vividly sketched in *The Tamworth Reading Room* (1840): "The heart is commonly reached, not through the reason, but through the imagination, by means of direct impressions, by the testimony of facts and events, by history, by description. Persons influence us, voices melt us, looks subdue us, deeds inflame us. Many a man will live and die upon a dogma; no man will be a martyr for a conclusion" (*Selected Writings* 101). This understanding of influence prepares the way for tributes to Newman's own impact on his audience as a "mesmeric influence" (Church 101) or "a magnetic stream" (Froude, *Nemesis* 221), and Tractarianism itself, in Mark Pattison's more cynical recollection, as a "whirlpool" (171, 182). A. P. Stanley, noting an "enthusiasm" for Newman even among students who did not share his "ecclesiastical sympathies," referred it to "the wonderful charm of his mysterious and almost unknown personality . . . [T]here was no contact with the hidden springs of action which controlled the movements of this inscrutable personage." This same charm, Stanley continues, drew undergraduates to seek out Newman's retreat at Littlemore; their "curiosity bordering on impertinence," of which Newman complained in the *Apologia*, was inspired by "a sentiment of irresistible awe, to ascertain the real nature of his place of retirement and devotion" ("The Oxford School" 312).

Here is a hero-worship that Carlyle might have commended; indeed, Abbot Samson exerts a similar sway of "irresistible awe" over his abbey, and himself displays the noble curiosity of hero-worship in his desire to exhume the body of Saint Edmund, which palpably incarnates the sanctity that is more elusively attached to Newman. The parallel is still more exact, inasmuch as Newman, like the Carlyean hero, commands loyalty less through action than through an essential *being*—which in Carlyle's account of Abbot Samson is something profoundly akin to Christian holiness. One particularly vivid testament to this congruence is Froude's 1848 novel, *The Nemesis of Faith*, which is largely organized around an explicit comparison of Newman and Carlyle (and which achieved instant notoriety when it was publicly burnt by the Senior Tutor of Exeter College, where Froude was a Fellow). For his generation, Froude explains, these were the two examples of "genius," which "alone is the Redeemer," and which he defines in stark, Carlylean antagonism to the smooth blandishments of "respectability": "Say not, say not, it is a choice. . . . They do not ask for it. They are what they are from the Divine power which is in them. . . . They alone never remember themselves; they know no end but to do the will which beats in their hearts' deep pulses. Ay, but for these, these few martyred heroes, it might be after all that the earth was but a huge loss-and-profit ledger book" (*Nemesis* 142). Here is precisely the sensation of necessity that animates Carlylean heroism. And it is in this context that Froude introduces Newman, in markedly Carlylean prose, as a prophet come to scourge "a foolish Church, chattering, parrot-like, old notes, of which it had forgotten the meaning . . . selfishness alike recognized practically as the rule of conduct, and faith in God, in man, in virtue, exchanged for faith in the belly, in fortunes, carriages, lazy sofas, and cushioned pews" (152).

As he likens Tractarian discipline to Carlylean heroism, Froude lays special emphasis on their common antagonism to domesticity: the "respectability" they renounce is not Carlylean gigmanity, but a world of "sweet smiling home, and loving friends, and happy family" (140). Many contemporaries noted the wrenching disruptions of families caused by early Victorian discoveries of vocation—whether Evangelical, Tractarian, Catholic, or Carlylean. But Froude, whose family history was especially tumultuous, suggests that the sanctification of domestic life is closely bound up with the construction of a heroism that ruptures domesticity. "Home is the one perfectly pure earthly instinct which we have," and "scenes of home" sometimes seem "religion itself" (102–4), yet that purity cannot satisfy "the gifted man." Froude's heroes thus reenact the biblical injunction that the true believer must leave family behind. What most powerfully connects the Carlylean hero and the Tractarian priest, however, is their shared embodiment of the charismatic subjectivity that Froude calls "genius," which is intimated as an unfathomable depth of being, "a spring in which there is always more behind than flows from it. The painting or the poem is but a part of him inadequately realized, and his nature expresses itself, with equal or fuller completeness, in his life, his conversation, and personal presence. . . . Greatly as [Newman's] poetry had struck me, he was himself all that the poetry was, and something far beyond. I had then never seen so impressive a person" ("Oxford Counter-Reformation" 182–83). Froude thus echoes the ideal of heroic selfhood informing Martineau's tribute to Arnold: "From what a good man *does* there is no higher lesson to be learned than what he *is*; his workmanship interests and profits us as an expression of himself" (Martineau 1:44). And as the power of Newman's "fascination" confirmed his genius, it enabled Froude to liken him not only to Carlyle, but to Caesar:

> In both there was an original force of character which refused to be moulded by circumstances, which was to make its own way, and become a power in the world. . . . Both were formed by nature to command others; both had the faculty of attracting to themselves the passionate devotion of their friends and followers; and in both cases, too, perhaps the devotion was rather due to the personal ascendancy of the leader than to the cause which he represented. . . . *Credo in Newmannum* was a common phrase at Oxford, and is still unconsciously the faith of nine-tenths of the English converts to Rome. ("Oxford Counter-Reformation" 179)

Once again, the tribute chimes with an insistent emphasis in Newman's own writings, which are nearly as steeped in martial heroism as those of Carlyle: even the collection of Tractarian poetry, *Lyra Apostolica*, bears as its motto Achilles's words on returning to battle: "You shall know the difference, now that I am back again" (*Apologia* 40).

THE FASCINATION OF RESERVE

That the Tractarian priest could be represented in the 1840s as a Carlylean hero may seem surprising today. But the two patterns of masculinity share a common derivation from the ethos of earnestness— and from the paradigm of that discipline, Christ's self-denying faith and moral fervor. The hero as Tractarian priest becomes an increasingly incongruous figure, however, over the course of a momentous shift in norms of masculinity, under which the Carlylean hero and Tractarian priest were associated with virtually antithetical types of manhood. To be sure, one finds intimations of this shift in early criticism of the movement: James Stephen's review of Hurrell Froude's *Remains* (1838), for example, denounced the Tractarians' "unmasculine horror of everything vulgar in belief and sentiment"—singling out Froude's "contrite reminiscences of a desire for roasted goose" (528, 532)— and an 1843 attack by Henry Rogers in the *Edinburgh Review* similarly complained of insufficient vigor in Tractarian criticism of "Popery": "There is as great a difference between *their* tone and that of the Reformers, as between the playful tap of a coquette's fan and the vigorous stroke of a boatswain's lash" (291). But such attacks are still framed within a traditional rhetoric of civic manhood that celebrates courage and moral vigor, and judges Tractarian discipline lacking in energy. Over the next two decades, however, such gendered language increasingly become associated with a specifically sexual deviance. This new rhetoric is most famously associated with Kingsley, whose notorious 1864 attack on Newman clearly conjoins to an accusation of lying a further insinuation of sexual treachery: "Truth, for its own sake, had never been a virtue with the Roman clergy. Father Newman informs us that it is not, and on the whole ought not to be; that cunning is the weapon which Heaven has given to the saints wherewith to withstand the brute male force of the world which marries and is given in marriage" (*A Correspondence* 298). The priest's transgression is recast as a failing of "brute male force," which embraces not only martial valor but the sexual energies summoned up by "the world which marries and is given in marriage"—a nice distillation of all that Kingsley held most dear.

Such vehement reaction to male celibacy may seem a form of hysteria peculiar to Kingsley's "muscular Christianity" and its energizing anxieties about the male body and its drives. Indeed, scholars have recently argued that Kingsley's long-standing antipathy to Newman was animated less by mendacity than by sexuality—or rather, by Newman's ideal of priestly celibacy, which was a standing affront to Kingsley's celebrations of marital bliss, celebrations that sublimated Kingsley's hard-won accommodation with his own disturbing sexual desire. But the terms of Kingsley's characterization have had a strangely persistent afterlife. Thus, for example, Geoffrey Faber's influential "group portrait" of 1933, *The Oxford Apostles*, suggested that there was something "forced and morbid" in all the Tractarians, and speculated at some length (albeit obliquely) on the homoerotic component of "this unusual capacity for emotional friendships," even invoking sexuality to explain Newman's conversion (215–234, 204). On the other hand, Pusey, Faber urged, "was, in fact, what Newman never was—a man. Let Newman, with his escort of hermaphrodites, succumb to those alien, imperious fascinations. He would not believe it" (346). In a similar vein, Bamford compares Thomas Arnold and his contemporary "Noetics" at Oriel with the Tractarians: "Outside their studies the men of Oriel were a virile set. There was nothing about them to suggest the celibate introversion of their successors, John Henry Newman and Hurrell Froude. Arnold himself had an eye for the opposite sex" (10). This last comment represents an especially suggestive collapse of logically disjunct categories, under which "introversion" is set against a "virile" "eye for the opposite sex" that is also (somehow) a form of extroversion. Under such logic, Arnold confirmed his sociability by siring ten children.

Ironically, these homophobic accounts have been cited in more recent and more sympathetic studies as evidence that *contemporary* reception of the Movement was homophobic—that it was a pronounced homoerotic aura attached to the Tractarians that incited such fervent attacks. Tellingly, however, such accounts typically draw their evidence only from the late 1840s onward, concentrating above all on Kingsley's quarrel with Newman, which is where one sees early suspicions of the movement becoming emphatically sexualized. Of course this is not to argue that Newman's desires were *not* powerfully homoerotic. My point is rather to urge a respect for the complex historicity of gender ideology. When commentators call on indictments of the "unmanly" in belief and demeanor as evidence of homosexuality, they collapse the distinction between sexuality and gender, and in the process lose sight of a social hermeneutic that Newman cannily grasped, and whose force as a mode of social control he keenly experienced.

There is no question that Newman from the outset understood his Christian discipline to be an affront to prevalent, broadly aristocratic norms of masculinity. His early essay on poetry, which dates from 1826, well before any vestige of a "movement" appeared, declares that "the virtues peculiarly Christian are especially poetical—meekness, gentleness, compassion, contentment, modesty, not to mention the devotional virtues; whereas, the ruder and more ordinary feelings are the instruments of rhetoric more justly than of poetry—anger, indignation, emulation, martial spirit, and love of independence" (G. B. Tennyson 41). An adherence to "the virtues peculiarly Christian" represents a direct and profound challenge to the ascendancy of those "ruder and more ordinary feelings" traditionally associated with a masculine realm of rhetoric and public life. Recognizing this logic, J. A. Froude boldly summed up the Tractarian ideal (with a telling change in the affiliations of "poetry") as a radical challenge to the dominant English conception of manhood: "To make England cease to produce great men—as we count greatness—and for poetry, courage, daring, enterprise, resolution, and broad honest understanding, substitute devotion, endurance, humility, self-denial, sanctity, and faith. This was the question at issue" (*Nemesis* 150). But this contest is closely akin to earlier, Evangelical challenges to aristocratic manhood, which similarly inform Arnold's ideal of the Christian gentleman. Both of these programs likewise promoted an ideal of masculine discipline traditionally reserved for a priestly caste. Why, then, did they not incite such fierce, and fiercely gendered, attack as Tractarianism? The Oxford Movement was far more vulnerable to attack than Arnold's Rugby, not only because it could not enjoy the license accorded to youth, but because it was widely associated with the sinister designs of a secret society.[12]

Initial attacks on the Tractarians in the 1830s almost invariably centered on a long-standing Protestant demonization of "Priesthood." The fear of such bodies was epitomized in conservative notions of "Romanism" as a conspiracy aimed at the very heart of English religious life and political sovereignty. Such suspicion had long been directed at English Catholics, but it had a special force against the professedly Protestant Tractarians, who seemed guilty of a double duplicity. They were not only promulgating suspect doctrine from Oxford, the citadel of Anglicanism, but they were suspected of withholding or reserving their true principles in the very process of doing so. Such suspicion was inflamed by Tractarian insistence on the importance of "reserve" in religious knowledge, which entailed that the communication of religious belief might be adapted to the character of an audience; certain beliefs might be "economized," portions of them held in reserve. Not surprisingly, this doctrine confirmed the suspicions of many observers that the Tractarians were merely Roman priests in disguise. With characteristic relish, Arnold distinguished the Roman Catholic from the

12. Stanley's *Life* also accommodated, if only marginally, the domestic world that is so glaringly absent in early Tractarian discourse. But even Arnold's domesticity can only be described in negative terms, as a release from pressure, a "softening" of that which is rigid but nonetheless defining of one's manliness. As such, Arnold's domestic life occupies a space that remains largely out of view in the *Life*, obscured not only by physical barriers but by the "sanctity" that was beginning to envelop the middle-class home. It emerges only in glimpses, in the liminal state of Arnold's study, which marks the delicate equilibrium of public and private realms, and their attendant virtues: here "severity and playfulness" are united, "expressing each in their turn the earnestness with which he entered into the business of life, and the enjoyment with which he entered into its rest" (Stanley, *Life* 128).

"Newmanite" as a declared enemy from a spy: "The one is the French-man in his own uniform . . . the other is the Frenchman disguised in a red coat. . . . I should honour the first, and hang the second" (Stanley, *Life* 434).[13] Arnold's attacks on the Tractarians in this regard share the animus and animation of his attacks on trades unions as threats to the rule of law. And popular suspicion of the Oxford Movement was further intensified when it came to nationwide notice in the pages of the *Times* in 1839, in exact conjunction with nationwide panic over the prospect of Chartist insurrection, following the 1838 publication of Hurrell Froude's *Remains* and Isaac Williams's Tract 73, "Reserve in Commu-nicating Religious Knowledge." Both phenomena incited fears of vast foreign conspiracies, both linked to Ireland, whose ultimate aim was nothing less than the overthrow of English sovereignty—the one by force, the other by guile. Thus a *Times* leader of 21 November 1839 linked "Chartist power" to "the power of the Irish priesthood," both dedicated to "the surrender of the British monarchy, and the breaking up of political society" (3a). Such fears frequently blossomed into par-anoid narratives worthy of a Gothic novel. In 1868, Disraeli announced in Parliament that "High Church Ritualists and Irish followers of the Pope had long been in secret combination and are now in open con-federacy" (Sage 44); as late as 1897, in *The Secret History of the Oxford Movement*, Walter Walsh claimed that the Movement had been from its outset a mission from Rome sent to conquer England on behalf of the pope.

Laughable as such narratives may seem, an aura of conspiracy seems to have been part of the appeal of the Movement to many of its younger followers. As one of them recalled, during the early, "golden age" of the movement, "some readily accepted the charge of conspiracy, and were far from prompt to disavow that there was more in the back-ground" (Mozley 1:342); Hurrell Froude in particular seems to have cultivated "the air of a chivalrous conspiracy, at once exclusive and dangerous" (Brendon 137). The deliberate solicitation of public hos-tility points to a crucial feature of the Movement as a masculine social formation, which was cannily grasped by Thomas DeQuincey in an 1847 essay, "Secret Societies." As a child, DeQuincey claims, the fear of secret societies prompted him to wonder, "When wickedness was so easy, *why* did people take all this trouble to be wicked?" (7:174). As he points to the paranoia that informs many accounts of secret societies, DeQuincey also suggests an important sociological appeal in the Tractarians' inculcation of reserve. Everyone, DeQuincey urges, must

> regard with a feeling higher than vulgar curiosity small fraternities of men forming themselves as separate and inner vortices within the great vortex of society . . . connected by the link either of purposes not safe to be avowed, or by the grander link of awful truths which, merely to shelter themselves from the hostility of an age unprepared for their reception, are forced to retire, possibly for generations, behind thick curtains of secrecy. To be hidden amidst crowds is sublime; to come down hidden amongst crowds from distant generations is doubly sublime. (7:173)

There was something "sublime" in the aura of secrecy emanating from Tractarian reserve—a form of charisma akin to what Arnold imagines in his quest for "a sort of masonry." In recognizing this attraction, DeQuincey suggests that Tractarian reserve came to function as a version of the masonic "sign" that Arnold sought; reserve, that is, might be deployed in part to solicit the hostility of the world at large, and thereby to underscore the corporate integrity of the Oxford Movement as a male order akin to a secret society.

The importance of reserve in Tractarian theology reinforces, and to a degree grows out of, Newman's insistence on the force of personality in all forms of human understanding. The ideal of learning as a highly personalized transmission of wisdom, which informed Newman's attempted "revolution" of teaching at Oriel, was evidently what also first drew Newman to accounts of Church tradition as a structure founded on oral communication (Matthew 208). As this notion was codified in the doctrine of the apostolic succession, it informed the central ecclesiastical tenet of the early Movement: the clergy's authority could not be abridged by the state, since it was a spiritual possession, transmitted in direct succession from Christ's original apostles through the process of ordination effected by the laying on of hands. It is thus fundamental to religious authority, in Newman's view, that "tradition in its fulness is necessarily unwritten . . . and it cannot be circumscribed any more than a man's countenance can be conveyed to strangers in any set of propositions" (Ker 142). On this model, the truths borne by tradition can only be conveyed through the ineffable influence of personal contact—and in this respect truth itself is always distinguished by reserve. All such knowledge, in other words, is sacramental in character, and is perhaps best exemplified in any encounter with another human being,

where the outward, visible reality palpably suggests the indwelling presence of something more than meets the eye, an ineffable mystery that
can only be intimated, never fully stated. Thus Newman's insistence on
the primacy of "the personal element" is bound up with his sacramental understanding of the world, and both stances in turn are inseparable from the doctrine of reserve in the communication of knowledge.

Reserve has a number of closely connected functions in Tractarian
thought and influence. For Newman himself, reserve was first and foremost part of a sacramental phenomenology, under which the visible
world is always the symbol or "shadow" of some indwelling spiritual
truth. As such, reserve also has a hermeneutic significance, since it
informs a model of scriptural interpretation that stresses typological
representation. Reserve also defines a model of personal and ecclesiastical discipline: as Newman describes it in *The Arians of the Fourth Century* (1834), reserve is a "self-restraint and abstinence ... in the
publication of the most sacred doctrines of our religion" (49–50). Such
discipline in turn informs an understanding of reserve as a rhetorical
strategy (sometimes called "economy"), under which certain aspects
of truth may be withheld in deference to the knowledge and character
of an audience. Finally—and most important for my argument—the
concept of reserve closely links hermeneutic understanding with social
forms. As reserve enforces a distinction between sacred and profane
significance, it also separates the world into initiates and outsiders. If,
as W. David Shaw notes, literary strategies of reserve functioned "to
keep the uninitiated at bay," they did so within both a textual and a
social hermeneutic (67). Reserve, in other words, could readily be
translated into a fact of behavior that structured social relations (G. B.
Tennyson 47–48). It thereby differentiated Tractarians from Evangelicals, who were notoriously fervent in their emotional displays, but
whose exacting sense of religious discipline in other regards closely
resembled that of the Tractarians. Reserve in this respect confirmed
what Selby calls Newman's horror of "excitement," under which he
regarded "all formal and intentional expression of religious emotion"
as a form of dissipation, "a drain and waste of our religious and moral
strength" (Newman, *Parochial and Plain Sermons* 2:397; Selby 90). More
generally, however, reserve set Tractarians apart from all who did not
participate in their discipline—and thus it might function as the masonic "sign" for which Arnold longed as the mark of a comrade in
earnestness. Reserve might become, that is, the social embodiment of
some form of inward, spiritual elevation; much like Carlylean "rudeness," it could be the outward index of an inner depth that distin-

guishes the man possessed of a calling. In both instances, the refusal of, or obliviousness to, certain forms of decorum is presented as the index of heroic powers.

Reserve could thus be manifested in a paradoxical dynamic of social presentation, whereby its ostensible emphasis on "retiredness and absence of self," as Pusey put it, could be turned into a mode of self-assertion. This was a possibility grasped by many of Newman's young admirers, who attempted to reinforce the social integrity of the movement—to underscore its structure as a form of brotherhood—by adapting distinctive modes of behavior and dress, which operated as "badges" of party loyalty.[14] Soon after coming up to Oxford in 1839, Frederick Temple (later archbishop of Canterbury) mocked the distinctive behavior of young Tractarians: it was "very absurd to see them all hold their heads slightly on one side, all speak in very soft voices, all speak quick and make very long pauses between their sentences, and all on reaching their seats fall on their knees exactly as if their legs were knocked out from under them" (Ward 312). Newman's long-tailed coat, Mozley recalled, "almost became the badge of his followers"; "it was so long kept up by the Oxford school as to be likely to become as permanent as the distinctive garb of the Quaker" (1:206). In the 1840s, waistcoats "buttoned all the way up to the cravat" became favored by so many High Churchmen that they were deemed "distinctly Popish," and became known among London tailors as the "M.B."—for "Mark of the Beast"—waistcoat, a fact gleefully seized upon in *Punch* caricatures of Tractarian clergy (Bowen 117).

Not surprisingly, sympathetic commentators on the Movement tend to find in such phenomena only trivial affectation, religion as fancy-dress. Adopting a Carlylean stance of their own, they follow earlier commentators in dismissing such allegiance as a kind of dandyism, from which they emphatically exclude Newman and the other leaders of the Movement. "Nothing could be more alien to them than to want to parade their self-discipline" (Brilioth 248). Whereas the Evangelicals "wore their hearts on their sleeves," David Newsome writes, "Keble and his friends concealed their emotions, lest by advertising them they should seem to cheapen their love" ("Evangelical Sources" 23–24). Here is precisely the repudiation of the histrionic that informs Carlyle's analysis of dandyism. Yet Carlyle's inability entirely to extricate his own activity from forms of "advertising" should make us pause. Might Trac-

<hr/>

14. Mary Coleridge, for example, disapproved of "party badges," and urged "a more Protestant fashion as to externals" (Allchin 67).

tarian self-discipline, like that of the Carlylean hero, be inescapably entangled in the theatrical "parade" that reflects the persistent complicity of social exclusion and social exclusivity? Certainly Newman captures this logic when he describes reserve in an 1830 sermon, arguing that God's "marvellous providence" "works beneath a veil, which speaks but an untrue language; and to see Him who is the Truth and the Life, we must stoop underneath it, and so in our turn hide ourselves from the world. They who present themselves at kings' courts, pass on to the inner chambers, where the gaze of the rude multitude cannot pierce" (Selby 56–57). As the act of hiding from the world turns out to elevate one above "the rude multitude," so reserve may be a means of resisting the gaze of that multitude while nonetheless soliciting its attention. In effect, that is, reserve may turn a manifold "hiddenness" into a sign of social and moral exclusivity—precisely on the analogy of the masonic sign that Arnold sought. And the special appeal of such distinction to young Tractarians is suggested by the contrast with the broadly parallel discipline of Rugby. Whereas Rugby's Sixth Form was an elite demarcated by clear and formal marks of membership, the nascent Tractarians lacked such distinct outlines. The sense that the Oxford movement defined a community possessed of a social as well as an intellectual integrity and mystique could be powerfully reinforced by turning its members' sense of a shared world of hidden or arcane meaning into a mark of public distinction.

Evangelicalism of course offered a precedent for such self-definition, and Newman—as many commentators have stressed—was profoundly influenced by Evangelical discipline (Brilioth 211; Ker 95; Hill 124). As David Newsome points out, the great Evangelical leader William Wilberforce wished to discover an emphatically *visible* elect, who were "marked off from all others by the possession of the quality of 'seriousness.' It was this quality—a peculiar earnestness which showed in one's bearing and demeanor—which gave to Evangelicalism its spirit of fire and zeal, and also established a kind of mint-mark whereby the faithful could be immediately discerned" ("Evangelical Sources" 17). As it inculcated such theatricality, Evangelicalism struck unsympathetic observers as something akin to Carlylean dandyism. In the Oxford of the 1830s, such self-display on behalf of the spirit had become a byword of vulgarity, as A. H. Clough made plain in a letter of 1838 commending "the Newmanists": "These people however have done a great deal of good at Oxford, where anything so 'ungentlemanly' and 'coarse' and 'in such bad taste' as 'Evangelicalism' would never be able to make very much way" (1:67). Yet Newman himself (as Newsome concedes) wished to experience a very similar sense of spiritual zeal and elevation without making any outward claim on its behalf. Thus he explicitly cautioned against the dandyistic mannerisms of some of his followers, what in the *Apologia* he calls their "extravagances" (86). In a frequently quoted letter of 1837, for example, he warns against "a danger of getting peculiar in interests, i.e. formal, manneristic" (Ward 312)—the term "peculiar" recalling the Tractarian slang term for Evangelicals, "Peculiars," and hinting at the snobbery that informed Tractarian decorum. Newman's caution also echoes Pusey's insistent warnings against self-display: "Do not act or think as though you were the Apostle of some new doctrine, but inculcate duty simply, plainly, and earnestly" (Liddon 2:145).

But such self-effacement was not easily reconciled with the powerful proselytizing impulse of the Movement, which Newman himself helped to inaugurate in the very first of the *Tracts for the Times* (published on 9 September 1833).[15] While writing as an anonymous "fellow Presbyter, like yourselves," Newman urged that the clergy insist on the apostolic succession as a "gift" which distinguished their authority: "Let it not be said that you have neglected a gift; for if you have the Spirit of the Apostles on you, surely this is a great gift . . . make much of it. Show your value of it. Keep it before your minds as an honourable badge, far higher than that secular respectability, or cultivation, or polish, or learning, or rank, which gives you a hearing with the many. Tell them of your gift" (Church 84). Such a project demanded first and foremost sheer visibility. "To be recognized as a fact is everything," Newman wrote to Frederick Rogers in 1837; "If you form a knot in London and set about puzzling the Peculiars, etc., I shall not regret one bit being left alone" (Ward 311). The vaguely conspiratorial "knot" of Tractarians—Newman's use of the term recalls Arnold's accounts of potential insurrection at Rugby—represented an emphatic self-assertion on the part of the clergy, who thereby claimed both religious and social prerogatives. Indeed, this claim to authority, along with the remoteness enforced by reserve, ultimately would be reinforced even in the spatial configurations of Tractarian ecclesiology and church architecture, which made the new importance of the priest "literally visible" by sep-

15. This irony also helps to explain the inconsistency noted by Piers Brendon in his biography of Hurrell Froude: that the same Tractarians who counseled reserve in the expression of religious belief were fierce interrogators of the religious beliefs of others.

arating the clergy from the laity and elevating the priest above the congregation (Bright 397–98).

Critics of Tractarianism quickly seized on such configurations of authority as a revival of "priesthood." But priesthood was suspect above all as a political configuration, and was attacked in rhetorics of class conflict. The class bias informing the Tractarian recoil from "vulgarity" made them easy targets of a well-established middle-class rhetoric that denounced aristocratic pretension as effete and "unmasculine." A more damning and widely echoed criticism, however, attacked Tractarian conceptions of authority as "Popish," because they regarded the Church, in Thomas Arnold's words, as "a sort of chartered corporation," by membership in which "any given individual acquires such and such privileges":

> This is a priestcraft, because it lays the stress, not on the relations of a man's heart towards God and Christ, as the Gospel does, but on something wholly artificial and formal,—his belonging to a certain so-called society. . . . There is something so monstrously profane in making our heavenly inheritance like an earthly estate, to which our pedigree is our title. And really, what is called succession, is exactly a pedigree, and nothing better; like natural descent, it conveys no moral nobleness. (Stanley, *Life* 296)

In this criticism, "priestcraft" is an aristocratic structure, starkly opposed to the broad, more fervent, and more democratic faith that Arnold envisioned—ultimately in the form of a Church that would be coextensive with the state. The society of the apostolic succession figures in this attack as a rotten borough, or an unreformed Rugby School, in which any claims to "moral nobleness" were submerged in the prerogatives of status and the privileges of formal membership, which derived from the pedigrees of both the corporation and its members. But in thus attacking Tractarianism Arnold points to a central source of its appeal: this very sense of elevation and exclusivity was immensely seductive not only to young men pondering a clerical career, but to the many obscure clerics throughout Britain who were glad to be reminded, as Desmond Bowen points out, that they shared in the same succession as their bishop (52–53). However arcane theological debate may have seemed to observers outside Oxford, Froude observed, to Oxford students, "particularly to such of them as form the opinion of Oxford, theology is itself the profession" (*Nemesis* 138). In this regard, as Arnold's phrasing presciently suggests, the social formation of the Oxford Movement anticipated the motivations and organizational structures of the professional associations that would proliferate in the Victorian period, as "disinterested" expertise and authority were invoked to rationalize economic and social rewards. As Froude pointed out, sacerdotalism gave the clergy "professional consequence" ("Oxford Counter-Reformation" 220)—a point taken up by Harold Perkin's description of the Movement as an effort to professionalize the clergy (362).

One may redescribe this nascent professionalism in terms of an intractable intellectual conflict within the Movement. As Ingve Brilioth points out, the idea of the Church as an elect community distinguished by the holiness of its members, an essentially static body, is at odds with a historical conception of the Church, in which the ministry is the most essential component (260). This is the tension one sees in Newman's vacillation between the positions of priest and prophet: while professing a priestly obeisance to church authority, Newman also gave ample support to followers who wished to cast him in the iconoclastic role of the prophet. And as that conflict is bodied forth in the social dynamics of reserve, it reproduces the tensions that beset the Carlylean hero's claims to charismatic authority. As different as Tractarian reserve may seem from Carlylean "rudeness," both are forms of decorum defined in resistance to an eager solicitation of public regard. This was Newman's persistent complaint of Evangelical preaching: "What I shrink from," he wrote in 1835, "is their rudeness, irreverence, and almost profaneness . . . the poorest and humblest ought to shrink from the irreverence necessarily involved in pulpit addresses, which speak of the adorable works and sufferings of Christ, with the familiarity and absence of awe with which we speak about our friends" (Newsome, "Evangelical Sources" 24). The caesura enforced by the comma after "pulpit addresses" underscores a significant ambiguity, which we have already encountered in Carlyle: might reserve enforce a discipline so severe that it is inconsistent with "pulpit addresses" of any kind? Those who recall hearing Newman's sermons uniformly stress that he always read them, and rather stiffly, in a quiet, subdued voice with relatively little dynamic range or emotional heightening (DeLaura, "O Unforgotten Voice" 93–94). In contrast to the "familiarity" of Evangelical preaching, Newman's delivery seems to refuse any hint of ease. It might thus seem an ecclesiastical counterpart of the physical clumsiness of Dobbin in Thackeray's *Vanity Fair*. In both instances, the lack of ease serves (again, on the model of Carlylean uncouthness) as a warrant of spiritual depth and moral probity in a world of polished but barren surfaces.

Yet Newman's refusal of demonstrative conduct retains an element of self-conscious, superbly disciplined grace that sets him apart from Dobbin. The "gliding" form and the "musical" voice hint at this element, which seems essential to that exacting self-regulation evoked in the word "subdued"—Newman's favorite word to denote Christian eloquence and conduct of life (Griffiths 67).[16] Observers thus point to a complex, even paradoxical logic in the operation of reserve, which Newman himself would acknowledge: reserve is frequently difficult to distinguish from theatricality, precisely because it enforces a vigilant self-consciousness. As Selby points out, for Newman reserve enforced a sense not only of social exclusion but also, in Newman's words, "what is sometimes called consciousness, the painful perception of the presence of self, quite distinct from self-importance and self-conceit though looking like them to undiscriminating eyes" (Selby 93–94). This is the "spiritual fastidiousness" emphasized by many commentators, which is so resonantly captured in the passage from "The Individuality of the Soul" quoted above. And though Newman disavows in such individuality any calculated appeal to onlookers, Tractarian disciplines of humiliation and self-denial, like all ascetic regimens, are structured by an implicit audience. Even Newman's account of "consciousness" tellingly enforces a distinction between "undiscriminating eyes" and more perceptive ones. Contemporary accounts confirm that such inward remoteness could indeed be an entrancing spectacle, as it was to Stanley and his friends, and as it would be, if only in the imagination, to many later Victorians.

When scholars of the Oxford Movement relegate its dandyistic elements to what Brilioth calls the "epigoni," then, they reproduce a Carlylean rhetoric of essential selfhood. They are disavowing, by projecting onto the margins of the Movement, a potential theatricality inherent in the largest intellectual ambitions of the Tractarians—as in emergent forms of masculine discipline throughout the Victorian period. Like Victorian celebrations of the gentleman, sympathetic accounts of Tractarianism attempt to mystify the potential social utility of the Movement as a program of masculine self-fashioning. But the dandyism of ostentatious reserve and its solicitation of political suspicion were extremely effective means of solidifying the corporate integrity, autonomy, and

16. I thank David DeLaura for this helpful complication.

exclusivity of the Movement. Even R. H. Hutton, in his sympathetic study of Newman's career, characterized the Tractarians as men living "more like a colony of immigrants among a people of different language and customs, than like a band of patriots who were reviving the old glories of their native country" (55). A movement attacked as fundamentally alien to British habits of life and thought quickly became identified with an entire ethos hostile to middle-class respectability—which, most commentators agree, was the central appeal for most young adherents. But it is therefore misleading to claim, as Mozley does, that the Tractarians had "no earthly inducement whatever" for their activities (2:1). They in fact sacrificed more conventional forms of advancement in order to enjoy the empowering sense of membership in an intellectual elite through which, in Mozley's words, "Oxford resumed its historic place as the centre of religious activity" (1:342).

DeQuincey's wry question, "*Why* did people take all this trouble to be wicked?" can thus be answered in sociological terms: an ostentatious secrecy offers those who participate in it a sense of corporate solidarity. In this regard, DeQuincey's analysis of the "sublime" appeal of secrecy anticipates the late-century sociology of Georg Simmel, who stresses the extent to which secrecy functions, irrespective of its content, to define structures of group membership and its attendant prerogatives. The shared possession of secrets—or even the belief by others that secrets are being shared—divides the world into initiates and outsiders. In this regard, Simmel suggests, secrecy as a social form operates much like adornment, such as those "badges" which are so prominent in accounts of the Oxford Movement. Moreover, as it confirms membership in an elite group, secrecy also allows each member to embody the charismatic aura of the group—that quality DeQuincey calls "sublime." Simmel, again, explains this appeal: "If the utmost attractiveness of another person is to be preserved for us, it must be in the form of vagueness or impenetrability. This is the only substitute which the great majority of people can offer for that attractive value which the small minority possess through the inexhaustibility of their inner life and growth" ("Secrecy" 461–62). The power of Tractarian reserve to intimate such deep subjectivity, such "inner life and growth," is amply borne out by contemporary accounts of Newman's "fascination."

In Simmel's analysis, secrecy is something more complex than a mere defense against surveillance. Responses to Tractarian reserve energized a social paradox, whereby reticence turned into a canny mode of self-assertion, which laid claim to special privileges. And contemporary hostility to the Tractarians seized on this political dimension. Arnold, for instance, quickly grasped in Tractarianism a reactionary social formation, "that sort of religious aristocratical chivalry so catching to young men"—a "chivalry" that Arnold regarded as "Antichrist" because it subordinated duty and character to the purely social attribute of "Honor" (Stanley, *Life* 327,140).[17] And this distinction was especially crucial to Arnold, for he knew that his own "disciples" were susceptible to similar appeals and could be denigrated in similar fashion. They, too, enjoyed a social mystique derived from membership in an elite fraternity; indeed, some commentators suggest that "Rugby men" elicited as much attention from Oxford undergraduates in the late 1830s and early 1840s as did their rival Tractarians (Bowen 71). Their distinction likewise derived its contemporary force largely from the charismatic transformation of an ancient institution, yet like the elitism of the Tractarians, the intellectual or moral stature attached to Rugbeians could be readily denigrated as mere status, an attribute derived solely from pedigree. Still further, their elitism also incited suspicions from conservative outsiders that Rugby was a secret society devoted to inculcating Radical principles.[18] Indeed, in reviewing *Tom Brown's Schooldays*, Fitzjames Stephen could even call Rugby "a semi-sacerdotal fraternity of premature men" (Mack 331). A precisely analogous characterization sums up much criticism of the Oxford Movement, whose men were arraigned not as "premature" but "unmanly."

The disciplines of Newman and Arnold, then, were both susceptible to a broadly middle-class suspicion of male elites as effete and subversive.[19] Tractarian reserve, however, became a lighting rod for attacks

17. The shrewdness of Arnold's comment would be confirmed by the brief efflorescence of "Young England" in the early 1840s, whose cult of "aristocratical chivalry" was most memorably celebrated by Disraeli after Arnold's death.

18. The local conservative paper inveighed against his influence by warning away parents of prospective applicants, posing such questions as, "Am I performing the part of a father in exposing my son to the fascination of such talent as Dr. Arnold possesses, when I know he will be taught the language of heresy, and be nurtured up in the cradle of Radical Reform?" (Bamford 76). And in a pleasant historical irony, when Thomas Hughes presided over an effort to set up a town of Rugby, Tennessee, as a settlement for English emigrants, the project foundered in part owing to local suspicions that "the Rugby colony was a 'society' or a 'Brotherhood,' entry to which could be obtained only by pronouncing some shibboleth" (Mack and Armytage 240).

19. Carlyle's portrait of St. Edmondsbury seems to have escaped such innuendo, partly because Carlyle's monastic community was safely distanced from the present, and partly because Carlyle's rhetoric was so distinctive, and so antagonistic to elite social

on all the various strands in the indictment of "Priesthood"—that the movement was reactionary, authoritarian, elitist, formalistic, devious. Ironically, this power to provoke suggests an additional reason why the Oxford movement would come to have a widespread appeal to a variety of Victorian writers and artists, such as the Pre-Raphaelite Brotherhood, Morris and Burne-Jones, Pater, and Wilde. The Tractarians offered the model of an elite brotherhood that defined itself through the possession of arcane (and presumably unorthodox) wisdom or values. That same structure helps to explain the popularity of later Tractarianism, or "ritualism," among gay men, which has been documented by David Hilliard. It was not just theology that led Wilde to repeatedly request the works of Newman for his reading material in prison: the structure of Tractarian reserve parallels in remarkable detail Wilde's preoccupation with the double life, another extremely exacting mode of masculine discipline.

But the potential affiliation of reserve with dangerous sexuality does not seem to have informed early responses to Newman—or if it did, the connection was not very troubling to observers. In early attacks on that reserve as something "unmanly," the gendered norm prosecutes class antagonism or a failure of courage rather than sexuality. Even Kingsley's earliest attacks on the movement focus on its elitism—as in his letter of 1851 expressing the wounded sense of social exclusion that dogs his entire career: "In all that school, there is an element of foppery, even in dress and manners; a fastidious, maundering, die-away effeminacy, which is mistaken for purity and refinement; and I confess myself unable to cope with it, so alluring is it to the minds of an effeminate and luxurious aristocracy" (*Life and Works* 1:260). This is a passage of some moment in studies of Victorian masculinity, which have widely cited Hilliard's claim that Kingsley's use of "effeminacy" in this letter represents "the usual nineteenth-century caricature of male homosexuality" (Hilliard 188). Tellingly, however, Hilliard offers no evidence for this conclusion. In fact, Kingsley clearly uses the term here (as throughout his writings) in its older, traditional sense, to refer to a male person or institution weakened by luxury or inactivity; thus Hazlitt, for example, in "On Effeminacy of Character" (1824), applies the term to Keats. When Kingsley characterizes the entire British aristocracy as "effeminate," he is not insinuating that they are animated by same-

decorums, that it could always be dismissed as merely idiosyncratic: he was "a whole sect in himself," as a writer in the September 1844 *Fraser's* put it (*"Historic Fancies"* 318).

sex desire.[20] Instead, Kingsley develops the same associations we have seen in other critics of the Movement: the discipline of reserve that underwrites the elitism of the Tractarians is denigrated as the "fastidious maundering" of the dandy, which Kingsley in good Carlylean fashion decries as a feeble echo of an already-enervated aristocracy, and thus a standing affront to middle-class manhood.

Newman himself acknowledged widespread suspicion of his discipline as something "unmanly." But he attributed the label to a gender surveillance concerned above all with secrecy. In his 1843 sermon, "Wisdom and Innocence"—the very sermon, ironically, that Kingsley would invoke twenty years later in his attack on Newman—Newman wrote that "the world" mistrusts innocence as "craft" because "sobriety, self-restraint, control of word and feeling have about them an air of being artificial, because they are not natural; and of being artful, because artificial." Thus self-restraint, he continues, "is the first thing which makes holy persons seem wanting in openness and manliness" (*Sermons* 299–300). Under such a hermeneutic, even Thomas Arnold's Christian gentleman would fall short. And that is precisely what would happen under the reign of "muscular Christianity," as David Newsome has observed. In "Wisdom and Innocence," Newman cannily anticipates the dynamics of Kingsleyan manliness well before its public manifestation. Under the suspicion Newman evokes, "manliness" is implicitly identified with straightforward, frank, unhesitating action and utterance; it is a norm of bluff, direct communication shorn of subtlety and any hint of equivocation. As a contributor to *Fraser's* put it in an 1838 exchange, "Frankness, openness, and manliness seem altogether strangers to this class of writers!" ("Treason within the Church" 757). This is of course a long-standing association in British culture, one that Newman himself was willing to exploit in his Anglican polemic against the Roman Church. "We Englishmen like manliness, openness, consistency, truth," he wrote in January 1840; "Rome will never gain on us till she learns these virtues" (Ker 188). The norm seems to have been invigorated, however, by the social dislocations attendant on the rise of industrial capitalism, along with its concomitant culture of information, and the recurrent fear of mass insurrection, under which the challenge

20. Kingsley is remarkably consistent in his many uses of the term: as late as 1868 he denounces "the effeminacy of the middle class, which having never in its life felt bodily pain, looks on such pain as the worst of all evils" (*Life and Works*, 4: 13). Tellingly, Kingsley directs his comments against those who preach the power of "circumstances," most notably "Mill and his followers"—against, that is, the logic of the Carlylean dandy.

of knowing the characters of other persons began to seem both newly urgent and newly difficult. Thomas Arnold's agitation over secret societies certainly exemplifies this development, commingling as it does a powerful desire to know the character of strangers with a deep-seated fear that whenever strangers band together they threaten the rule of law. The Tractarian project manifests a similar complexity: Newman's desire to secure more direct and personal forms of association sets itself against the individuating structures of industrial society, yet at the same time Tractarian reserve exploits those structures by invoking secrecy to enforce a barrier between initiates and outsiders. Those suspicious of that enterprise proscribe the possession of secret and arcane meanings as a violation of "manliness."

The connection between hermeneutic complexity and gender deviance is already implicit in the reaction to Newman's famous *Tract 90*, which was widely regarded as a virtuoso close reading of the Thirty-Nine Articles of the Anglican Church undertaken to destroy their authority. "The Art of Perjury Made Easy" would be an apt title, Henry Rogers complained in the April 1843 *Edinburgh Review*. His *Edinburgh Review* article of January 1843, "The Right of Private Judgment," had asked to what extent the Tractarians "have their esoteric doctrine to which the public is not yet to be admitted" (198). Rogers takes up that widely echoed insinuation by attacking the mystifications of "that obscure, imposing, and truly Delphic style" (275), in which "seldom is anything said plainly and absolutely, but with a perpetually tortured and guarded expression," leaving the reviewer to conclude that Tractarianism is "a hieroglyphical religion" (288) and "the 'Church' is just Mr. Newman or Dr. Pusey—not unbecomingly disguised in the habiliments of a somewhat antiquated lady, and uttering their 'private judgments' as veritable oracles" (278). In this intriguing foreshadowing of *Jane Eyre*, the wily and oversubtle theologian is transformed into a female fortune-teller. Even Kingsley's earliest attacks on the Movement—more than twenty years before the fiasco that led to the *Apologia*—concentrated on an elitist hermeneutics rather than sexuality. In an 1842 letter, he counsels his future wife to avoid the "mystifying subtlety and morbid fear" of the Tractarians: "Do not be too solicitous to find deep meanings in men's words. Most men do, and all men ought to mean only what is evident at first sight on their books..." (*Life and Works* 1:93). In such advice, the Puritan strain in a widespread religious perplexity has been isolated and intensified by the "lawless allegorizing" of the Tractarians, which, in Kingsley's words, "prevents men from accepting God's promises in their literal sense, with simple childish faith, but drives them to spiritualize them away—i.e., to make them mere metaphors, which are after all next door to lies!" (1:138) Kingsley's social resentments thus converge with his religious anxiety to anathematize Tractarian subtleties, those elitist "allegories" which Kingsley would later denounce at wearying length in his novel *Hypatia.* And this reaction helps in turn to explain widespread mid-Victorian suspicion of hidden or oblique meaning in art. In Kingsley's logic, the search for "deep meanings" marks a failure of the manliness that speaks "plainly and absolutely." From this perspective, the poetry of Browning, as well as the work of Pre-Raphaelite painters and poets— particularly the "fleshly" poetry of Rossetti and Swinburne in the 1860s—was scandalous not only in its sensuality but in its obscurity.

In early attacks on the Oxford Movement, then, we see the codification of a gendered hermeneutic of suspicion under which male secrecy is proscribed, but not overtly sexualized. The subsequent sexualizing of attacks on the Movement parallels the pronounced mid-century shift that J. R. Honey has noted in the discourses of public-school morality. In schoolmasters' references to "immorality," "vice," and "sin" in the 1830s, these transgressions are associated with drunkenness and indiscipline, rather than "sexual impurity"—an emphasis in keeping with Arnold's vigilant guard against insurrection. By the 1860s, however, the terms had assumed an "increasingly explicit sexual connotation," which by the 1880s had in many schools narrowed down to an obsessive preoccupation with sexuality—whether masturbation or homosexuality (Honey 167–78).[21] This development is strikingly mirrored in Kingsley's changing responses to Tractarianism. His early hostility, to be sure, is informed by tacit but powerful sexual anxieties. Newman's ideal of celibacy was a powerful affront to Kingsley's hard-won reconciliation with his own sexual drives. (Moreover, when Kingsley first met his future wife, she was about to enter a Tractarian sisterhood—a coincidence that further inflamed Kingsley's resentment of Newman's influence.) But Kingsley found a therapeutic outlet for these struggles in his most famous contribution to Victorian culture: the peculiar amalgam of athletic and devotional rhetoric that would become known as "muscular Christianity," within which the body became a central locus of value. In the early 1840s, the young Kingsley, still profoundly envious of Newman's prominence, phrases his attack

21. Honey links the shifting preoccupation to an increase over the course of the century in the proportion of sexually mature boys in any school, owing to earlier puberty and a consolidation of age range in school enrollment (168).

in the language of class. By 1864, however, Kingsley no longer had any incentive to attack Newman in those terms; Newman had become a social outcast following his conversion to Rome in 1845, and Kingsley himself had in the intervening years become much more conservative, pleased to be affiliated with the aristocracy he had once called effeminate. But he now had a different rhetoric ready to hand, the sexualized rhetoric of muscular Christianity. Thus in his famous review of 1864, the charge that Newman condoned lying and deception—an extension of the long-standing vilification of the Tractarians—is conjoined with the claim that celibate priests lack "brute male force."

Arising from the turbulent political milieu of the 1830s, attacks on the Tractarians solidified a gendered structure in which male secrecy eventually came to be identified narrowly and specifically with sexual transgression. That momentous historical development is unwittingly rehearsed in the 1881 *Reminiscences* of the Oxford Movement by Thomas Mozley, Newman's brother-in-law and (in the 1830s) close sympathizer. Of all contemporary memoirs, Mozley's most suggestively connects Tractarian reserve to forms of everyday social interaction. Many commentators, he points out, professed amazement at the outcry prompted by Isaac Williams's 1838 Tract "On Reserve in Communicating Religious Knowledge," which, wrote R. W. Church, "to the astonishment of everyone, was like the explosion of a mine" (180). Mozley, recognizing the naïveté of this reaction, mocks both the tract and its reception. Williams "in truth only made a pretty theory of what all the world does in one way or another," yet "the world fell or affected to fall into a paroxysm of terror at the infernal machinations preparing against it. . . . It was the awful indefinite . . . reserve that made ten thousand pulpits tremble to the very foot of the steps" (1:436). For Mozley, the very omnipresence of reserve makes a mockery of both the public outcry and of the solemnity with which the concept was enunciated by the Tractarians:

> All the world practices all kinds of reserve, but never mentions the word. The world does not write in large letters over this spot "secret"; over that "strictly private"; over another, "a deep mystery"; over another, "a dark corner"; and over the darkest corner of all, "this is what you come to at last." If, as it is said, there is a skeleton in every closet, it is kept in a closet, and the closet door is not labelled "a skeleton here." (1:433)

This mockery, however, turns out to capture a surprisingly complex ambivalence toward "reserve." On the one hand, Mozley infers that

Williams actually had no secrets to hide, or he would not have claimed his possession of them; in this light, Tractarian reserve is something of a charade. Yet Mozley's inference rests on the assumption that calculated reserve has a pervasive and momentous role in everyday life. One would not broadcast one's possession of a secret because secrecy is at once seemingly omnipresent and highly dangerous. The merest hint that one has a secret is sufficient to incite an observer to attempt to penetrate it, thereby magnifying its potentially compromising significance through a dynamic of intensification neatly reproduced in Mozley's own prose. The inquirer passes from "secret" to "strictly private" to "a deep mystery" to "a dark corner" to "the darkest corner of all" to the closet hiding a skeleton. Over the course of the sentence, reserve becomes increasingly less playful and more provokingly redundant: why insist that one has a secret, when "all the world" possesses dark closets, and every closet hides a skeleton? The more somber implications of Mozley's gibe have of course been elicited by the subsequent history of his culminating trope, which has become pointedly associated with a hermeneutic of suspicion directed principally against men. Secrecy among men, we have been taught to assume, is always ultimately *sexual* knowledge, and "the closet" is the space that contains the secret of male homosexuality.

Mozley's mockery of Williams's motives in extolling reserve thus rehearses the social logic within which male secrecy came to be interpreted as an index of homoerotic desire. From the suggestions that Tractarian piety was "unmanly," twentieth-century commentators have inferred that contemporaries associated the movement with a transgressive sexuality. But there is little or no evidence of such association in early responses to the Movement. Even Tractarian devotion to celibacy aroused little antagonism—not surprisingly, given that all Fellows of Oxford colleges in the 1830s still were required to be unmarried, celibate males. To be sure, Newman wished to restore what had become a largely formulaic social constraint to its central place in religious discipline, to make chastity a focal point of an ascetic regimen. But that ideal seems to have been attacked only insofar as it reinforced the larger, encompassing objection that Tractarianism celebrated priesthood. After all, Newman's vow of celibacy is but a logical extension of other greatly influential contemporary varieties of masculine discipline—most importantly, Carlyle's. And in this light, celibacy could readily be described, as it had been in early Christian monasticism, as an eminently masculine and martial discipline. In R. W. Church's account, "to shrink from it was a mark of want of strength or intelligence, of an unmanly preference for English home life" (248). Such appeals turn "manliness" against its ostensible proponents; if celibacy, in the words of Newman's novel, *Loss and Gain*, is not "unnatural" but "supernatural" (195)—or, in Weber's terms, is "a symptom of charismatic abilities" (*Sociology of Religion* 238)—then the Tractarian priest, like Carlyle's Abbot Samson, is a standing rebuke to the manhood of Kingsley's world that marries and is given in mariage. The provocative power of celibacy in the 1830s—as in most eras—is not its affiliation with transgressive sexuality, but its disturbingly powerful challenge to gender norms, to structures of masculine identity and authority, in which it was at one with "the virtues peculiarly Christian," as Newman well understood.

But as Stanley's *Life* suggests, the effort to redefine manhood as a fusion of traditionally masculine and feminine attributes leaves the ideal susceptible to redescription as a profound confusion of gender— a susceptibility that is writ large in Tennyson's *In Memoriam*. Under such rigorous gendering of experience, those who mistrusted Newman's authority could readily isolate an "effeminate" strain in his influence. In such characterizations, however, gendered designations are powerfully overdetermined, embracing a wealth of antagonisms to patriarchal stability. The newly rigorous gendering of life in early Victorian England made it possible for the "unmanly" to assume protean attributes, and to serve as a ready vehicle for the expression of novel, often inchoate anxieties. Hence arises the remarkable fact that suspicions of Tractarian secrecy, like the secrecy of Popish plots, could be cast as antithetical forms of deviance, which are connected only by their common denomination as threats to patriarchy. Not long after Kingsley proclaimed Newman's lack of "brute male force," the House of Lords was in an uproar over the perceived threat that priests posed to the women of England. And once again, the focal point of agitation was secrecy—not the secrecy of "reserve," but the secrecy associated with auricular confession.

Debates over the place of confession in the Anglican Church became central in what has been called the "second phase" of the Movement, after the secession of Newman in 1845 and the diffusion of Tractarian influence had made the Movement less narrowly associated with Oxford.[22] Although confession incorporates numerous strands of Tractarian doctrine—a stress on rigorous discipline, an elevated role for the clergy as spiritual guides, an emphasis on personal communication—

22. Pusey, however, certainly had begun to encourage auricular confession by 1839.

the practice incited denunciations of secrecy even more fervent than those aroused by Tractarian "reserve," primarily because in confession the effects of a treacherous secrecy seemed carried into the heart of domesticity itself. Auricular confession exposed "the sacredness of the hearth to a prying and morbid curiosity," as Archbishop Thomson declared (Bowen 30–35). It also represented a devious attack on the "purity" of Victorian womanhood, since, as one Evangelical journal put it, "the very reduction of sins of impurity to language . . . must result in making them the fuel of fresh sin, and in fanning the flame of a more dangerous temptation" (Reed 220). This tendency exacerbated yet a further danger, that of "bachelor priests prying into all the inmost feelings and most secret thoughts and acts of maidens and wives" (Reed 220). Here, as with reserve, the crime is emphatically the subversion of patriarchal order: as Samuel Wilberforce, the bishop of Oxford, explained it, confession "supersedes God's appointment of intimacy between husband and wife, father and children . . . producing reserve and estrangement where there ought to be perfect openness," and thereby disrupting the prerogatives of the patriarch (Reed 224). But now the priest's transgression of gender norms is cast as an emphatically heterosexual treachery, as the discordant, dangerous presence of an unmarried man intruding on the most private realm of women in their own households. The priest's transgression is the apprehension of other people's secrets, a violation that is characteristically figured as something akin to rape. Hence the otherwise bizarre paradox that contemporary attacks on celibate priests—Jesuits in particular—tend to figure them as at once emasculate and sexually predatory, intent on destroying the "purity" of the family.[23]

The outcry against confession captures in especially stark antagonism an ambiguity increasingly associated with bachelors—as the phrase "bachelor priest" might suggest.[24] The complexity is produced less by the construction of a new form of masculine identity, than by the shifting relation of unmarried males to an increasingly pervasive and anxious surveillance of both public and domestic life. Mr. Slope in

---

23. These shifting associations are vividly captured in the many *Punch* caricatures of Tractarian priests from the 1840s through the 1870s.
24. This emphasis is somewhat different from the ambiguity in the figure of the bachelor noted by Sedgwick (*Epistemology* 188–212). Studying the figure as a character type in Victorian fiction leads to the conclusion that the bachelor is "housebroken by the severing of his connections with a discourse of genital sexuality" (190), whereas pamphlet warfare over confession suggests that the bachelor could figure as a far more overt, if indeterminate, sexual threat.

Trollope's *Barchester Towers*, for example, who is associated with inscrutable design, also seems to occupy constantly shifting, sometime contradictory gender spaces—but so, too, does Dr. Arabin, his ostensible adversary in theology. When domestic space admits a single man identified with the acquisition of knowledge—whether a father-confessor, a doctor, or a detective—his entrance perplexes the boundaries of public and private and creates a corresponding gender dissonance that is then attributed to his agency. By exposing the domestic realm to a public gaze, the confessor turns private space into a repository of secrets. That collapse of privacy into secrecy in turn undermines the aura of security and ease that virtually defines the home in Victorian domestic ideology. Still more disturbing, the confessor not only exposes the family's shared privacy to a prurient gaze, he thereby brings to light secrets that potentially divide wife from husband, parent from child. The confessor not only creates secrets; his presence brings to light secrets that have always already existed within that ostensibly idyllic space of perfect confidence and repose. (Mozley's remarks on the reaction to Tractarian reserve suggestively capture this dynamic.) And this discovery of a pervasive secrecy within domesticity energizes a profound sexualizing of discourse and social space, not only in attacks on confession but in the rise of the sensation novel in the 1860s. The entrance of a figure specifically concerned with knowledge "gothicizes" domesticity, so to speak, hinting that dangerous secrets lurk everywhere. And the figure who sets in motion this profound destabilizing of domesticity will inevitably confound norms of gender: he will be labeled "unmanly."

The association of the priest with conflicting modes of sexuality underscores the remarkable fluidity in early and mid-Victorian suspicions of male secrecy. Those suspicions in turn reflect the extraordinary looseness, and thus versatility, with which the epithet "unmanly" could be employed as a mechanism of social exclusion and control. Ultimately this complex historicity in categories of gendered identity should prompt reflection on our own current critical and historical practice. Interpretations that assume that a male realm of the hidden or withheld always defines the closet of homoerotic desire are trying to stabilize an exasperating, because ultimately undecidable, ambiguity. If early Victorian secrecy corresponds to a closet, it is the closet of the father-confessor, who outrages Victorian patriarchy not through the content of his secrets, but through the mere fact that he possesses them. By assuming that these secrets were always already sexual, we may be reproducing the suspicions of the anxious Victorian paterfamilias, whose own desire for mastery is likewise confronted by a disturbing opacity in a world he desires to render transparent.

CHAPTER THREE

Imagining the Science of Renunciation: Manhood and Abasement in Kingsley and Tennyson

Political economy, the science of wealth, is therefore, at the same time, the science of renunciation. . . . The science of a marvelous industry is the science of *asceticism* . . .
   Karl Marx, "Economic and Philosophical Manuscripts" (1844)

It is all right. All under rule.
   Charles Kingsley on his deathbed (1875)

In the *Saturday Review* in 1858, a glowing review of Charles Kingsley's *Andromeda and Other Poems* opened with a tribute to "the great Apostle of the Flesh" and went on to praise the poem as "the production of one who enters as heartily into what is rather priggishly called the 'sensuousness' of the Homeric life as Walter Scott does into chivalry." The poem needed only to be compared with "Simeon Stylites on his pillar," the reviewer urged, to see the "distinctive philosophy of Mr. Kingsley and his school": "The spirit of the young gentleman described in the lines we have quoted could hardly be very anxious to be released from its carnal prison-house . . ." ("Kingsley's *Andromeda*" 594). Flippant as it might seem, the reviewer's exuberance calls attention to the important personal and cultural history sketched in the previous chapter:

Kingsley's apostolic mission was indeed incited by, and defined against, a phenomenon for which Simeon Stylites was an apt emblem, the ascetic discipline of the Oxford Movement. Moreover, Kingsley's very personal response to Newman's example quickly came to define a "school" less of theology than of masculinity; it became emblematic of a new model of manhood in Victorian Britain. The remarkably rapid diffusion of "muscular Christianity," as Kingsley's "distinctive philosophy" was soon christened, marks a crucial shift in Victorian norms of masculine identity. To be sure, as David Newsome points out, there had been muscular Christians before Victoria came to the throne (*Godliness* 203). Yet Kingsley, Newsome notes, became the most popular exemplar of a "manliness" very different from that of Coleridge and Thomas Arnold: the ideal of *arete*, "the fulfilment of one's potentialities in the living of a higher, better and more useful life," gave way to *thumos*, "robust energy, spirited courage, and physical vitality." What had seemed a set of qualities essentially *adult* was displaced by a cult of aggressively physical masculinity (*Godliness* 197). In the phrases of James Fitzjames Stephen's 1858 *Edinburgh Review* article that the *OED* quotes in defining "muscular Christianity": "The principal character of the writer whose works earned this burlesque though expressive description, are his deep sense of the sacredness of all ordinary relations and the common duties of life, and the vigour with which he contends . . . for the great importance and value of animal spirits, physical strength, and hearty enjoyment of all the pursuits and accomplishements which are connected with them." In many respects, this regimen marks a revival of aristocratic norms of manhood, and as such seems to have appealed to middle-class men (and boys) anxious to align themselves with more traditional sources of masculine identity. Indeed, Kingsley's celebration of the "animal spirits" informing both martial vigor and sexual potency in many respects recalled the stereotype of rakish Georgian masculinity that had been demonized by Evangelical and Tractarian alike. From the perspective of those newly austere disciplines, Kingsley's program might well seem akin to a return of the repressed—or at the very least, in Newsome's widely-echoed view, the "complete antithesis" of Tractarianism (*Godliness* 198).

But "Muscular Christianity" as it is represented in Kingsley's writings is itself a far more strenuous discipline than one might think. Indeed, the rapid diffusion of Kingsley's "school" reflects the readiness with which it was adapted to, and helped in turn to sustain, two demanding ascetic regimens: the Victorian cult of athleticism, and British imperial rule. "If asked what our muscular Christianity has done," one late-Victorian headmaster famously pronounced, "we point to the British Empire" (Mangan, *Games Ethic* 148). Kingsley's rise to national prominence in the 1850s coincided with a series of crises involving Britain's status as a world power: fears of French invasion in the early 1850s (commemorated in such Tennyson lyrics as "Form, Riflemen, Form") soon were succeeded by the disasters of the Crimean War, and then the Indian Mutiny of 1857. Each of these events raised the specter of an enfeebled Britain unable to enforce its far-flung dominion, and prompted anxieties about both the leadership and the fortitude of Britons charged with upholding the empire. These requisite values were especially central to the discipline of a public school education, which (far more than university life) stressed physical hardiness, corporate identity, and submission to authority—qualities epitomized in success on the playing fields. The social authority of the public schools was already attaining greater ascendancy at Oxford in the wake of Tractarianism, which had eroded Oxford's traditional status as a form of national seminary by undermining the theological ascendancy of the Anglican Church (Matthew 215–17); at the same time, the spiritual austerity of both Arnoldian and Tractarian masculinity was challenged by a norm of "muscular" manhood more readily adapted to the growing public-school population. The association of "manliness" with physical norms was further strengthened by expanding concern with public health and sanitation reform, and (more generally) by the extension of scientific and medical authority as what Foucault calls "medico-juridical" discourses, discourses that ultimately would claim to legislate standards of masculine identity grounded in the imperatives of science.

Kingsley's important affiliations with both imperial and medical discourses, along with the widespread popularity of schoolboy novels—especially Hughes's *Tom Brown's Schooldays*—help to explain his central place in any study of Victorian masculinity. Yet his works are most representative of larger cultural formations as they struggle to reconcile physical virility with the imperatives of self-discipline—which is to say, as they participate in earlier rhetorics of manliness that might seem a "complete antithesis" to Kingsley's own. Even the *Saturday Review* account of *Andromeda* hints at a conflict widely noted by contemporaries: if Kingsley's "school" inculcated little more than energetic sensuality, it was an affront not only to Simeon Stylites but to the demands of Victorian domesticity. Many critics objected that Kingsley's celebrations of unreflecting impulse seemed to sanction male profligacy; others, more hostile, suggested that his gospel contained more pantheism than Christianity.[1] But although Kingsley celebrated bodily impulse, he also wrestled constantly with the Pauline imperative to keep the body in submission. This was not a merely formal deference to authority; Kingsley was in fact powerfully, even erotically, drawn to the asceticism he attacked. That attraction is registered explicitly in his poetry—such as his early narrative of the martyrdom of St. Elizabeth of Hungary—as well as in his correspondence with his future wife, which is filled with descriptions of flagellation, as well as drawings of naked men and women in various forms of bondage (drawings first printed in Susan Chitty's 1975 biography of Kingsley). Even without such graphic evidence, however, one can discover a powerfully masochistic impulse in Kingsley's novels, where his heroes typically experience an unusually violent oscillation of desire and restraint. But Kingsley thus depicts more than a personal pathology; the very idiosyncrasies of his sensibility made him an acutely sensitive register of the stresses inherent within an ascetic regimen of manhood. Self-discipline offers a powerful sense of the autonomy that is fundamental to manhood, yet it can only be realized through a perpetual and painful process of renunciation. The pangs of temptation, on the other hand, must be distinguished in turn from the feminizing anguish of frustration imposed from without— from that emasculating capitulation to "circumstances" that is the bane of nearly all Victorian proponents of heroic masculinity, whether Samuel Smiles or John Stuart Mill. "All true manhood consists in the defiance of circumstances," as Kingsley put it (*Historical Lectures and Essays* 203). But how can a man defy circumstances and at the same time remain, as Kingsley also demands, "bold against himself"? In the "true manhood" of ascetic discipline, one punishes oneself.

This logic is familiar enough in Christian understandings of the conscience. But a secular version assumed new authority in the nineteenth century, as Evangelical discipline converged with the discourse of political economy through the Malthusian logics common to both. Political economy offered future satisfaction based on the deferral of present desire; in Nassau Senior's influential formulation of 1836, approvingly quoted in Mill's *Political Economy* (2:400), profit was a reward for the *abstinence* of the capitalist. Even the capitalist came under the sway of what Marx called "the science of renunciation," in which future profit was justified in proportion to present pain. At the same time,

---

1. Thomas Hughes, in *Tom Brown at Oxford*, was especially concerned to rescue "muscular Christianity" from its association with profligacy.

however, desire had to be stimulated in order to encourage individuals to participate in the salutary discipline of economic life. And insofar as the market fanned new desires, it also intensified the need for self-discipline. Political economy thereby reinforced the struggle entailed by Evangelical insistence on innate human depravity, which posited a stern dichotomy between "strict renunciation" and "illimitable desires," in Christopher Herbert's account (33). Out of this cycle of intensified desire met by intensified regulation emerged a norm of middle-class masculinity exemplified in Archibald Alison's 1839 tribute to "professional men": their existence is "an incessant scene of toilsome exertion and of virtuous self-denial . . . their whole life is a sacrifice of the present to the future" (296), whereas the working classes, Alison contended, cannot master their "insatiable thirst for immediate enjoyment from the senses," and hence "their habits are, generally speaking, reckless and improvident in the extreme" (297).[2] Like many apologists for the middle class, Alison here transferred the burden of Marx's "science of renunciation" to the bourgeoisie and implicitly turned political economy into a distinctly male province. As it enforced an ascetic practice of virtuoso self-regulation, Victorian political economy defined a middle-class manhood distinguished by a forward-looking perspective and a capacity for deferred gratification.

The ideal of middle-class manhood authorized by political economy is articulated with special clarity and force in Victorian tropical fantasies. Because both political economy and economic manhood demand an incessant mastery of temptation, their ascetic regimen may be represented most suggestively in imagined realms apparently remote from its influence. The periphery of Victorian empire is an especially appropriate space in which to imagine the strength of Victorian discipline, precisely because it is so attractive as an imagined realm of self-indulgence. Hence the remarkable persistence with which Victorian celebrations of progress incorporate fantasies of escape to a tropical paradise; Tennyson's "Locksley Hall" is paradigmatic. But such fantasies also reveal the extent to which dreams of unreflecting abandon lie at the very heart of masculine discipline—not merely as a logical component of its definition, but as an active antagonist in its ongoing practice. After all, self-mastery is worth applauding only if one has wayward passions to master. Kingsley's evocations of self-mastery thus underscore the dependence of cultural and personal identities on the "otherness" they overtly expel or forbid. In the words of Peter Stallybrass and Allon

2. I thank Steve Pulsford for calling this article to my attention.

White, such constructions inevitably generate "unconscious heterogeneity, with its variety of hybrid figures, competing sovereignties and exorbitant demands" (194). In Kingsley's writings, tropical fantasies offer an imagined space in which the apparently unified regimen of muscular Christianity is dispersed across a variety of "hybrid figures"—offspring of miscegenation, hysterical men, "half-savage" women, men of uncertain class affiliation—all of which incarnate instabilities within the regimen of middle-class manhood. Such fantasies help to explain why the poetry of Tennyson had such a powerful hold on Kingsley's imagination, despite the apparent gulf between the bluff, slashing rhetorics of muscular Christianity and the introversions of Tennysonian anguish. Like Tennyson, Kingsley incessantly imagines manhood as a parade of pain, the staging of an excruciating ambivalence, in which the lure of unreflective abandon is checked by the imperatives of manly discipline.

Kingsley's writings in this regard reproduce the burdens of Carlylean heroism: the Apostle of the Flesh has far more in common with John the Baptist in Cockney-land, and Tennyson's ascetic Saint Simeon Stylites, than one might guess. But whereas Tennyson typically sublimates male suffering into a familiar scheme of rational progress, which reaffirms the traditional prerogatives of male authority, Kingsley frequently explodes those economies altogether, by suggesting that renunciation might afford an erotic satisfaction in its own right. Throughout Kingsley's influential celebrations of the healthy male body bodily vigor turns out to be most important not as an end in itself, but as it enables a man to endure correspondingly intense chastisements of emotional and physical suffering. If the true man punishes himself, then the science of renunciation operates constantly on the verge of its own dissolution: political economy and the manhood it underwrites might fail, not so much through a *lapse* of self-discipline, as through the *intensification* of self-discipline to the point that it becomes eroticized as mascochism, and thus becomes itself a form of "savage" abandon. As they explore this possibility, Kingsley's novels subject "true manhood" to a scrutiny even more corrosive than Tennyson's far better known parades of pain. For the Apostle of the Flesh, ironically, the authority of manly discipline is most keenly displayed at the point of its collapse in a self-destructive intensity.

TROPICAL FANTASIES, VICTORIAN MANHOOD

In his little-known travel narrative, *At Last*, which recounts an 1869 voyage to the West Indies, Kingsley evokes the burdens of Victorian discipline by describing their apparent lapse in the tropics. His description of Trinidadian laborers bears quoting at length:

> I lounged awhile in the rocking-chair, watching two Negroes astride on the roof of a shed, on which they were nailing shingles. Their heads were bare; the sun was intense; the roof on which they were working must have been of the temperature of an average frying-pan on an English fire: but the good fellows worked on, steadily and carefully, though not fast, chattering and singing, evidently enjoying the very act of living, and fattening in the genial heat. Lucky dogs: who had probably never known hunger, certainly never known cold; never known, possibly, a single animal want which they could not satisfy. I could not but compare their lot with that of an average English artisan. Ah, well: there is no use in fruitless comparisons; and it is no reason that one should grudge the Negro what he has, because others, who deserve it certainly as much as he, have it not. After all, the ancestors of the Negroes have been, for centuries past, so hard-worked, ill-fed, ill-used too—sometimes worse than ill-used—that it is hard if the descendants may not have a holiday, and take the world easy for a generation or two. (17: 308)

There is much to be said about this remarkable passage, and the abundant ideological "fruit" in its central comparisons. But I want to emphasize its central, breathtaking metamorphosis: while Kingsley lounges in a well-shaded rocking-chair, two men nailing shingles in blazing sun on a roof the temperature of an English frying-pan somehow come to embody "holiday"—or as the subsequent paragraph has it, "perpetual Saturnalia." We witness here, among other things, the remarkable power of Victorian racial ideology, under which not even the most arduous labor can defuse racist conceptions of the freed slave as a pampered, indolent, unreflective animal—the "Quashee" of Carlyle's notorious invective in "Occasional Discourse on the Nigger Question" (1850). Racial ideology, however, in this instance serves a further, more inclusive system of self-legitimation, which emerges more explicitly in the paragraph immediately following:

> The perpetual Saturnalia in which the Negro, in Trinidad at least, lives, will surely give physical strength and health to the body, and something of cheerfulness, self-help, independence to the spirit. If the Saturnalia be prolonged too far, and run, as they seem inclined to run, into brutality and license, those stern laws of Nature which men call political economy will pull the Negro up short, and awaken him out of his

dream, soon enough and sharply enough. (Kingsley, *Life and Works*
17:308)

Kingsley's invocation of "holiday" underwrites a scheme of discipline,
both individual and cultural, that he identifies with the laws of political economy. The warning casts a cold light on the ideological contexts of Victorian travel literature, in which flirtations with "perpetual
Saturnalia" are virtually a defining characteristic. In reading of travels
in the tropics, one may savor a temporary release from the disciplinary
burdens of "political economy," while at the same time experiencing
the extraordinary power of that economy, which not only makes possible Victorian travel, but also registers its "stern laws" in the starkly
contrasting social conditions of those less disciplined (albeit pictur-
esque) peoples whom the travelers encounter at their exotic destina-
tions.

More generally, however, the very blindness of Kingsley's appeal suggests that his disciplinary scheme—like all Victorian representations of
political economy—*required* a site of "perpetual Saturnalia" for its articulation. Typically, of course, we think of the two realms as dichotomous: the dream of "holiday" denotes the logical complement of
political economy, the *lapse* of its discipline. In fact, however, that discipline necessarily incorporates some version of that dream at its very
core, since desire is the motive force of disciplined work: "To civilize
a savage, he must first be inspired with new wants and desires," Mill
famously remarks in his *Political Economy* (1848; *Collected Works* 2:104).
And the necessity of such desire is reaffirmed whenever political economy is invoked to underwrite a norm of manly self-discipline. Alison's
tribute to "professional men," for example, is founded on the same
"insatiable thirst for immediate enjoyment" that it attributes to the
working classes: the professional *masters* the desire that is blazoned in
the working classes' "reckless and improvident behavior," but the longing for such perpetual saturnalia is at the heart of that mastery. Otherwise, the regimen merits no praise.

Victorian writers most frequently locate Kingsley's perpetual saturnalia, that realm beyond the pale of discipline, in "the lower orders"
and "the savage"—a conjunction that reflects the close association of
class and racial hierarchies in Victorian thought.[3] And it is in this con-

---

3. A tacit association of Blacks with the British working classes crucially informs, for example, the controversy over Governor Eyre's brutal suppression of Jamaican unrest in
1865; see Semmel (132–40) and Lorimer (172–94).

text that fantasies of tropical paradise have an emphatically political dimension and articulate with special clarity the burdens of Victorian discipline.[4] In Tennyson's "Locksley Hall," for example, the famous paean to progress, "Forward, forward let us range, / Let the great world spin forever down the ringing grooves of change," is both motivated by, and defined against, a fantasy of escape to "savage" abandon in the tropics. Tennyson's speaker imagines himself escaping to "summer isles of Eden"—

> There the passions cramped no longer shall have scope and breathing space;
> I will take some savage woman, she shall rear my dusky race . . .
>   (167–68)

—only to abruptly repudiate the dream:

> I, to herd with narrow foreheads, vacant of our glorious gains,
> Like a beast with lower pleasures, like a beast with lower pains!
>   (175–76)

This overt racism at the heart of one of the most famous credos of the Victorian period is not idiosyncratic, nor is it peripheral to the vision of progress Tennyson's speaker sets forth. On the contrary, the interlocked structures of progress and middle-class manhood are defined together—as they are throughout *In Memoriam*—through their joint triumph over an unreflective, undisciplined existence outside history. Kingsley's relieved deathbed utterance, "It is all right. All under rule," sums up widespread preoccupation with a comprehensive discipline that linked the rule of empire to an exacting regimen of self-control. And Kingsley recognized this dynamic in "Locksley Hall," to which he paid tribute in 1850 as "the poem which, as we think deservedly, has had most influence on the minds of the young men of our day" (*Literary and General Lectures* 114). "Locksley Hall," he continues, shows a

---

4. Alan Sinfield's salutary insistence on the politics of Tennyson's "exotic margins" unfortunately leads him to fold the poet into a virtually seamless, omnipresent, irresistible imperialism: "Ulysses *is* the hegemonic"; "The ultimate threat to remote spaces comes from Tennyson himself" (53, 50). On this reading, Tennyson is the unwitting agent of something like a demonic parody of the Christian deity, which is likewise defined by its power to inhabit both center and circumference simultaneously. I stress a resistance to Victorian discipline—including schemes of imperial rule—that the tropical fantasies of both Tennyson and Kingsley represent as crises of masculine identity, which expose abiding tensions within Victorian ideologies of progress and manhood.

young man that "the path of deliverance is . . . not backwards towards
a fancied paradise of childhood . . . but forward on the road on which
God has been leading him" (115). Kingsley's own writings, however,
like Tennyson's, complicate the trope: the path of deliverance always
leads *through*, rather than away from, the fancied paradise in the tropics.
The discipline that insists on the renunciation of paradise will also intensify the lure of regression, and thus is liable to leave Kingsley's young
man paralyzed with ambivalence.

This possibility is memorably explored in "The Lotos-Eaters," a
poem that reverberates throughout Kingsley's writings. Like Kingsley
in Trinidad, Tennyson's mariners encounter a perpetual Saturnalia, but
the experience prompts them to resist the burdens of Victorian political economy. In the timeless world of the lotos-eaters, "toil cooperant
to an end" has frayed into aimless, pointless struggle: "Why should we
only toil?" Although the "laws of Nature men call political economy"
make their presence felt in the implicit ironic frame of the poem—in
The Odyssey, Ulysses forced the mariners to return to their duty and to
Ithaca—Tennyson (unlike Kingsley) refuses to intervene overtly on behalf of those laws. Instead of awakening the mariners from their dream,
he creates a space of profound ambivalence poised between a self-
annihilating languor and the acutely individuating pangs of Victorian
self-discipline. Indeed, the addition of the sixth stanza of the "Choric
Song" in the 1842 edition of the poem, ostensibly an assertion of moral
rigor, only exacerbated the divided allegiance. As the imperatives of
duty and domestic life tellingly blur together into a single, somnolent
memory of their other "island home," the past and its imperatives are
set against nothing less than a longing for death—the logical culmination of the mariners' erotic and social abandon, at least from the
perspective of Victorian political economy. The poem is thus an especially rich embodiment of competing sovereignties, not least competing
ideals of manhood. Like the fantasy of miscegenation in "Locksley
Hall," the poem bodies forth a clash between an older ideal of manhood conceived as the enjoyment of seigneurial possession and a manhood affirmed precisely through the power of libidinal regulation,
which configures desire to the demands of political economy, in Kingsley's broad sense. This same conflict clearly animates Tennyson's recurrent depictions of a long-lost paterfamilias returning home to find
his place occupied by another man. Critics typically read this preoccupation—particularly in "Enoch Arden" (1864)—as a fear of patriarchal dispossession, but as Tennyson employs the motif in "The
Lotos-Eaters" (114–32) it expresses at least as much a sense of release

from the burdens of domesticity and civic duty: "Let what is broken so remain" (125).[5]

"The Lotos-Eaters" bears out the central conclusion of a wealth of recent criticism dealing with imperialism and travel narratives, that the work of cultural definition is especially energetic and anxious on the imperial frontier, where familiar norms are troubled by the discovery of, in the words of Mary Louise Pratt, "not only unfamiliar Others but unfamiliar Selves" (140). Such encounters reveal with special clarity the extent to which cultural norms, and the "selves" they help to shape, invariably depend on and animate the "otherness" they overtly expel or forbid. Just such an image of competing sovereignties is the fantasy of Europeans "going native," with its corollary but even more aggressively disavowed fantasy of cultural hybridity, miscegenation. These tropes of fear and longing are typically associated with narratives of high imperialism after 1870 or so, yet they are central to both "Locksley Hall" and "The Lotos-Eaters," where Tennyson's fantasies articulate an emergent cultural as well as personal identity. In "Locksley Hall," the speaker's fantasy of miscegenation—of taking a "savage wife" who will rear his "dusky race"—envisions empowerment through transgression of the most basic norms of middle-class life, including manly self-discipline. Ultimately, of course, the repudiation of that "dream" not only restores the regimen of disciplined progress it had seemed to disrupt; it reinforces that scheme, by affirming the power of self-discipline even in a man apparently relegated to the margins of society and its progress.

"The Lotos-Eaters," on the other hand, bears witness to the possibility that one might surrender to desire, and thereby unsettle the triumphant masculine conquest of self and circumstance. The erotic investment in Tennyson's tropical fantasies was suggested a half century ago by W. D. Paden, who first noted Tennyson's reliance in his early lyrics on narratives of European exploration and conquest. Tennyson's "Anacaona" (1830), which draws on Washington Irving's *Life of Columbus* (1828), is especially revealing in this context. In this lyric, never published in Tennyson's lifetime, the central figure is quite emphatically a projection of desire, but that desire is not disowned (as it is in "Locksley Hall") as something "savage" or bestial. Instead, Anacaona

5. Even Tennyson's Ulysses, recently interpreted as the very archetype of the imperialist, displays a strangely enervated and ambivalent will to power; like Tennyson's mariners, he seems poised between competing conceptions of "home," so much so that, as Matthew Rowlinson points out, "he seems not to know where he is" (267).

exerts throughout the lyric the erotic appeal established in the poem's
opening stanza: "A dark Indian maiden, / Warbling in the bloomed
liana . . . / Wandering in orange groves / Naked, and dark-limbed, and
gay, / Bathing in the slumbrous coves, / Of sunbright Xaraguay" (1–
9). Her significance as a sign of erotic freedom helps to explain, I
think, why Tennyson refused to publish this poem despite the entreat-
ies of friends. The ostensible reason was (of all things) the inaccuracy
of its scenic detail, but a jocularly nasty response to a request from
Monckton Milnes in January of 1837 suggests another concern. In that
letter, Tennyson asks "whether you had any occasion to threaten me
with that black b—— 'Anacaona' and her cocoa-shadowed *coves* of nig-
gers—I cannot have her strolling about the land in this way—It is neither good for her reputation nor mine" (*Letters* 1:149). The "threat"
of publication energizes a rather nervous parody of the rhetoric of
blackmail. Contemplated within the imagined, idyllic freedom of tropical Haiti, Anacaona is a figure of natural, fulfilled sensuality, "stepping
lightly flower-laden." Publication, however, would amount to transpor-
tation back to England, where, under the sway of a more vigilant discipline, such sensuality would become sexual license, and Anacaona,
"strolling about the land," a fallen woman, whose company would compromise Tennyson's reputation. "Anacaona" seems to have been un-
printable, then, at least in part because—in keeping with its lyric
structure—it refuses the burden of self-discipline that distinguishes
"Locksley Hall" (which was begun just about this time). But Tennyson's letter (which even Hallam Tennyson felt obliged to censor for
the *Memoir*) clearly rehearses the disciplinary work of the later poem,
by violently repudiating erotic tropical fantasy—fantasy that in "Locksley Hall" explicitly centers on miscegenation.

In effect, then, Tennyson in his letter to Monckton Milnes tries to
recontextualize the lyric as a dramatic monologue—something akin to
the "Choric Song" of "The Lotos-Eaters"—in which an expression of
desire is distanced, but not quite disowned, by more clearly framing it
with—and thus sharpening its antagonism to—the normative self-
discipline it resists. There is a further component, however, in Tennyson's uneasy relation to "Anacaona" (both the poem and its heroine).
Anacaona is admired for her songs as well as her beauty: in the poem,
Tennyson commends what Irving calls her "skill in composing the *ar-
ytos*, or legendary ballads of her nation" (Irving 2:420). She is thus a
poet, and as such she is for Tennyson a subject of identification as well
as an object of desire. Confirming the parallels between "Locksley
Hall" and *In Memoriam*, the poet and the "savage" woman are again

joined in their resistance to the demands of masculine self-discipline: the latter as a figure principally of erotic abandon, the former as one of extravagant emotion. Hence the suggestive ambiguity of "Locksley Hall," where the speaker imagines his "merry colleagues" mocking his passionate outcry in a manner that will be echoed in *In Memoriam.* "Weakness to be wroth with weakness! woman's pleasure, woman's pain—/ Nature made them blinder motions bounded in a shallower brain," he declares (149–50); yet the "weakness" of "woman's pleasure, woman's pain"—as well as the diminished mental capacity that the poem likewise attributes to the "savage"—in this instance refers to the poet's susceptibility, as well. The savage woman again becomes a surprisingly apt figure for representing not only masculine conquest but failures of "manliness," in which an estrangement from normative manhood is experienced as eroticized self-division.

Tennyson's edgily jocular concern with his own and Anacaona's reputations thus hints at an anxiety like that rehearsed in *In Memoriam:* as figures of imaginative and emotional abandon, both the poet and the princess incite the potentially violent discipline of a hostile culture. Indeed, in Tennyson's sources for "Anacaona" that hostility assumes harrowing form. As "The Lotos-Eaters" is shadowed by the reader's awareness of *The Odyssey,* the final stanza of "Anacaona" ("No more . . . no more . . .") only intimates the eventual fate of "happy Anacaona" known to readers of Irving: she was executed, and her people massacred by the Spaniards in "a savage and indiscriminate butchery" (2: 497). That parallel of implicit frames is underscored by the poems' common indebtedness to Irving's idyllic description of aboriginal life in Haiti (Paden 140): "When the Spanish mariners looked back upon their toilsome and painful life, and reflected on the cares and hardship that must still be their lot if they returned to Europe, it is no wonder that they regarded with a wistful eye the easy and ideal existence of these Indians," and asked Columbus to allow them to stay on Hispaniola (Irving 1:241). These parallels suggest a fundamental congruence between the violence of the Spanish and the unstated intervention of Ulysses that frames "The Lotos-Eaters"; in both instances Tennyson seems to align himself with the liminal position of the mariners who wish to remain in peace, yet cannot ignore the call of duty. This broadly European fantasy gains specificity in Tennyson's poetry as "duty"—the demands of both action and "wedded lives" (114)—is understood within schemes of secular progress and manhood, which are complexly interlocked by dynamics of self-discipline. And competing norms of masculinity are implicitly at issue in the long-standing critical debate about the poem's allegiances: are the lotos-eaters recovering an imaginative and sensuous freedom or descending into self-annihilating, bestial desire? The history of commentary on "The Lotos-Eaters" suggests how profoundly Tennyson's lyric represents the disciplinary burdens of Victorian culture through its evocation of a paralyzing ambivalence.

This ambivalence explains the extraordinary hold of "The Lotos-Eaters" on Charles Kingsley's imagination. He frequently quotes the poem in his writings, where it typically structures narratives of saturnalian temptation. For both Tennyson and Kingsley, the tropics beckon as a fantasy of social and erotic empowerment: the speaker of "Locksley Hall" is exemplary in looking to the tropics for a sense of manhood that in England has been frustrated by economic and social dispossession, which is frequently imagined as estrangement from a rightful inheritance. The dispossessed suitor of "Locksley Hall" and *Maud* has a counterpart in the young Kingsley's proposed *nom de plume*, "Earnest Lackland": "Lackland has meaning enough for the head of a ruined family," he wrote to his fiancée in the 1840s (Chitty 71). There was historical basis for both men's grievances, but—as in *Great Expectations*—inheritance also functions more generally in their works as a fantasy of resistance to political economy, a space of imaginative participation in an older, quasi-feudal economic and social order. The very title of *At Last*, which announces the satisfaction of a long-frustrated desire, suggests the imaginative recuperation of Kingsley's lost family possessions in the West Indies: "The Negro has had all I ever possessed," he once wrote, "for emancipation ruined me" (Martin, *Kingsley* 257–58). More generally, the title points to the centrality of "the tropics" throughout his writings as a space of manifold imagined empowerment—not merely economic, but social, imaginative, and physical as well.

The tropical fantasies recounted in Kingsley's best-known novel, *Alton Locke* (1851), are explicitly organized by "The Lotos-Eaters." The opening chapter recounts the thirteen-year-old Locke's "dream of Pacific Islands, and the free, open sea" as an escape from "the horror" of his oppressively confined urban life (*Life and Works* 7:116–17). His earliest attempts to write poetry envision "a pious sea-rover" on a South Sea island (7:198) and even his first trip into the countryside brings to mind a voyage to Raleigh's El Dorado (7:232). Finally, near the end of the novel, Locke's aristocratic patroness, Lady Ellerton, begins reading him the Choric Song from "The Lotos-Eaters" to speed his recovery from fever (8:230), and also (as it turns out) to prepare the "tailor-poet" to sail to the tropics, in order that he might realize her ideal of "a Tropic poet":

> One who should leave the routine imagery of European civilization, its meagre scenery, and physically decrepit races, for the grandeur, the luxuriance, the infinite and strongly-marked simplicity of tropic nature, the paradisiac beauty and simplicity of tropic humanity. I am tired of the old images. . . . See if you cannot help to infuse some new blood into the aged veins of English literature; see if you cannot, by observing man in his mere simple and primeval state, bring home fresh conceptions of beauty, fresh spiritual and physical laws of his existence. . . . Sin you will see there, and anarchy, and tyranny; but I do not send you to look for society, but for nature. I do not send you to become a barbarian settler, but to bring home to the realms of civilisation those ideas of physical perfection, which as yet, alas! barbarism, rather than civilisation, has preserved. (8:264–65)

Kingsley thus appropriates Tennyson's poem to anatomize the appeal of "perpetual saturnalia" as a stimulus to poetry. For all the moral dangers lurking in "barbarism," "civilization" can only be advanced by an encounter with its apparent antithesis; in the pursuit of a "physical perfection" central alike to biological, social, and imaginative regeneration, one must hazard an encounter with the primitive. The concerns are similarly conjoined near the end of Kingsley's career, in *At Last*: "What an untried world is here for the artist of every kind," Kingsley exclaims (17:288), not only in the tropical landscapes but in the inhabitants: "It was a comfort to one fresh from the cities of the Old World, and the short and stunted figures, the mesquin and scrofulous visages, which crowd our alleys and back wynds, to see everywhere health, strength, and goodly stature, especially among women. Nowhere in the West Indies are to be seen those haggard down-trodden mothers, grown old before their time, too common in England, and commoner still in France" (17:33).

The pursuit of a many-faceted "health" is central to Kingsley's "muscular Christianity," but here it perplexes the familiar binary of civilization and savagery. That binary is not a simple dichotomy; instead, in Kingsley's representations savagery is something akin to the Derridean supplement that Stallybrass and White discover in transgression. It is a vital energy at once essential to, yet always threatening to subvert, the comprehensive self-discipline that is the "health" of both the individual and civilization at large. This structure emerges strikingly in Kingsley's responses to what for many Victorians was the supreme icon of Western culture, the statuary of ancient Greece. Kingsley frequently invokes those forms in his lectures on sanitation as models of health, which should incite the beholder to personal emulation and social reform. But in this regard their function is that of "barbarism" in *Alton Locke*—and indeed, Kingsley's accounts of Greek art almost always incorporate their apparent contrary, the "savage." Greek sculptures are "a perpetual sermon to rich and poor," Kingsley urges, because they represent "men and women whose every limb and attitude betokened perfect health, and grace, and power, and a self-possession and self-restraint so habitual that it had become unconscious, and undistinguishable from the native freedom of the savage" (*Health and Education* 69). In a lecture delivered in the United States in 1873, Kingsley similarly calls Greek sculpture the product of "a people of rare physical beauty, of acutest eye for proportion and grace, with opportunities of studying the human figure such as exist nowhere now, save among tropic savages" (*Literary and General Lectures* 23). Ostensible antagonists, Greek art and "savagery" converge in Kingsley's mind as embodiments of a consummate physical vitality.

They are also, of course, decidedly erotic spectacles. Indeed, representations of Greeks and savages were perhaps the only realms of Victorian culture in which naked bodies could be made available to the gaze of the respectable classes.[6] But in Greek sculpture the artist's mediation was taken to sublimate physical and erotic vigor into a superbly disciplined sexuality. The unrestrained desire that was thereby disciplined (or disavowed) was in turn displaced onto the "savage," whose purported lack of self-restraint served to confirm by contrast the strength of Greek (and Victorian) discipline. In viewing Greek sculpture, that is, the middle-class spectator was authorized to contemplate the body as a consummately rational, and hence moral, achievement: "the native freedom of the savage" could be enjoyed vicariously under the aegis of supreme "self-possession and self-restraint." We glimpse here the remarkable diffusion of German Hellenism in Britain as a basis for authorizing vicarious satisfaction within a puritanical culture.

But the projection of unrestrained sexuality onto the "savage" also entails that the rejuvenating contact with physical vigor in the tropics

6. As of this writing, there is no comprehensive study of the significance of the nude, or even Greek sculpture, in Victorian culture, although Gay, *Education of the Senses* 379–402, and Jenkyns, *Dignity and Decadence*, offer helpful overviews.

is fraught with danger, since the "native freedom" that allows for such vigor also represents a lapse of self-discipline. Not surprisingly, Kingsley's celebrations of physical vitality among black West Indians, for example, are typically agitated at the same time by intense moral— which is to say sexual—disturbance. Every European, he urges, will experience "a shock—and that not a slight one—at the first sight of the average negro women of Port of Spain. . . . their masculine figures, their ungainly gestures, their loud and sudden laughter . . . and their general coarseness, shocks, and must shock" (*Life and Works* 17: 93). The spectacle of gender norms confounded embodies a complex instability in Kingsleyan discipline. On the one hand, what strikes Kingsley as a lack of restraint in the women has the effect of masculinizing them in a way that he insists is repugnant. At the same time, however, the shock is emphatically sexualized: the usual "license" of seaport towns is here, Kingsley urges, "aggravated by the superabundant animal vigour and the perfect independence of the younger women. It is a painful subject. I shall touch it in these pages as seldom and as lightly as I can" (17:93). Predictably, this refusal to "touch" figures of sexual license is a disavowal that initiates a sustained preoccupation with the provocative behavior of young black women. "When you have ceased looking— even staring—at the black women and their ways, you become aware of the strange variety of races which people the city" (17:94)—but it is evidently not easy for Kingsley to cease looking. There is another energy at play, however, in the mesmerizing fascination of black women: like Tennyson's Anacaona, they are both objects of desire and subjects of identification. For Kingsley, after all, even momentary lapses of self-discipline feminize the male traveler, thereby implicating him in the very confounding of gender norms by which he is fascinated. Moreover, the imagined escape from such discipline is a central impetus in all of his tropical fantasies; only through "native freedom" can one encounter "superabundant animal vigour."

The profound ambivalence energizing Kingsley's tropical fantasies explains the extraordinary hold of "The Lotos-Eaters" on his imagination. Tennyson's poem presides over not only the fantasy of emigration in *Alton Locke*, but a number of imagined voyages that likewise envision the tropics as at once an extension of, and a site of resistance to, the demands of Victorian discipline. The most striking example of this appears in Kingsley's most popular novel, *Westward Ho!* (1855). Written during the Crimean War and dedicated to the Rajah Brooke of Sarawak, an Englishman who had brutally suppressed insurrections of the Dyaks in Borneo, the novel is best known as a bellicose tribute to the conquests of Elizabethan mariners: "a most ruthless bloodthirsty book it is, (just what the times want, I think)," as Kingsley himself put it (*Life and Works* 2:179). But the narrative is faithful to "the times" of both mid-Victorian Britain and early modern Europe in its dream of an enchanted tropical civilization—in which, as it turns out, the "ruthless bloodthirsty" impulses of the novel are powerfully suspended, at least for a moment. In chapter 24, "How Amyas was tempted of the Devil," Kingsley quotes lines 93–98 of "The Lotos-Eaters" as an epigraph to a prolonged, emphatically sexual temptation of his hero, Amyas Leigh, which is precipitated when two of Amyas's men disappear into the Northern Amazon forest with Indian brides. Once again, miscegenation is the focal point of a "dream" of indolent, erotic satiation from which the mariners must be awakened. In foiling the temptation, the novelist in effect takes up the disciplinary burden of "those stern laws of Nature which men call political economy," which Kingsley invokes to curtail "perpetual Saturnalia" in *At Last.*

But Kingsley's intervention reproduces the profound ambivalence of Tennyson's poem, enacting an acute crisis of authority. Amyas's initial outrage is quickly and surprisingly restrained: when he comes upon his men in the idyllic landscape, "he had hardly heart to wake them from their delicious dream," and his deliberation is prolonged for more than six pages: "Amyas stood silent for a while, partly from noble shame at seeing Christian men thus fallen of their own self-will; partly because—and he could not but confess that—a solemn calm brooded above that glorious place, to break through which seemed sacrilege even while he felt it a duty. Such, he thought, was Paradise of old; such our first parents' bridal bower! Ah! if man had not fallen, he too might have dwelt for ever in such a home" (6:157). As he surveys the idyllic indolence, the authority of Christian discipline (whose force underwrites political economy as Kingsley understands it) is temporarily suspended. Moreover, when Amyas finally rehearses the objection of Tennyson's speaker in "Locksley Hall," that the men are "living thus the life of a beast" (6:159), he is answered by a sustained rebuke from one of the mariners, expressed with such disconcerting eloquence that Amyas takes it to be a sign of possession by "some evil spirit." "And yet he could not answer the Evil One. His English heart, full of the divine instinct of duty and public spirit, told him that it must be a lie: but how to prove it a lie?" (6:160). The ambivalence is paralyzing, and Amyas is never able to muster a countering argument. Indeed, he is on the verge of yielding—"Was not your dreamer right? Did they not all need rest? What if they each sat down among the flowers, beside an

Indian bride?" (6:161)—when the idyllic scene is abruptly shattered
by a jaguar crashing down from the rocks onto one of the Indian
women. "'O Lord Jesus,' said Amyas to himself, 'Thou hast answered
the devil for me!'" It is a measure of the seductive power of the tropical
fantasy that Kingsley cannot dispel its charm by invoking Christian belief, or even "duty and public spirit"; it can be defeated only through
an irruption of natural violence that, despite Kingsley's Christian gloss,
appeals to the most banal instinct of self-preservation.

Kingsley's narrative closely follows Tennyson's earlier rhetorical strategy, in effect recasting Spenser's Bower of Bliss. The psychic discipline
of mid-Victorian life is invoked in isolation from the ideology that underwrites its claim to be "natural"; as a result, that discipline undergoes
a crisis of authority of the sort that Homi Bhabha has identified with
"hybridity" in imperialist discourse (173). When disciplinary authority
is thus compromised, it can be reestablished only through violence, in
this instance by appeal to "nature" acting as the arm of a Protestant
Christ who upholds the authority of political economy. To embrace this
scene of idyllic bliss—which is carried out under the sign of miscegenation—would entail rejecting Victorian political economy and the domestic ideal that helps to sustain it.

But the spectacle of such bliss is tempting indeed—so much so that
Kingsley elsewhere in his writings more nearly embraces it. Throughout
At Last, Kingsley finds *himself* in an "Earthly Paradise" (17:410). In the
midst of one such rhapsody over his surroundings, he pauses to offer
fulsome tribute to "a gallant red-bearded Scotsman" living on a tiny
island with "a handsome Creole wife and lovely brownish children":
"I looked at the natural beauty and repose; at the human vigour and
happiness, and I said to myself, and said it often afterwards in the West
Indies: Why do not other people copy this wise Scot?" (17:132–33).
Once again, the apparently singular bliss takes on emblematic significance through the fantasy of the lotos-eaters. The Scot is "an old sailor,
and much-wandering Ulysses" who has found an island home far away
from his original island home; indeed, he is "practical viceroy of the
island, and an easy life of it he must have." This Ulysses, however, has
not abdicated his responsibility; nor is his miscegenation occasion for
Tennyson's savage invective in "Locksley Hall." On the contrary, the
Scot and his wife rearing their dusky race are offered as an emblem of
health at once physical and mental, which participates in the pervasive
"natural beauty and repose" of their physical surroundings.

Why, then, do people *not* copy this "wise Scot"? It might seem that
they do: the dream of becoming "practical viceroy" of an island en-

capsulates the ambitions of many a British imperialist. In Kingsley's
account, however, this island life is a pastoral fantasy that refuses the
imperial economy of expansion and accumulation: "He needs nothing,
owes nothing, fears nothing. News and politics are to him like the distant murmur of the surf at the back of the island; a noise which is
nought to him . . . He has all that man needs, more than man deserves,
and is far too wise to wish to better himself" (17:132). Kingsley's "wise
Scot" represents a refusal of modernity itself, a rejection of the capitalist mode of production in favor of a subsistence economy. And this
fact suggests an answer to Kingsley's question in the terms of his own
criticism of the tropics elsewhere. The "wise Scot" is not more often
copied because this idyllic tableau incarnates the "perpetual Saturnalia" of Trinidadian life, and thus is a standing affront to the moral
imperatives of Victorian manhood and its political economy. Not only
Kingsley's own criticism of that "holiday," but nearly all attacks on
black laborers by Victorian commentators (most famously Carlyle's ven-
omous "Occasional Discourse on the Nigger Question") focused precisely on their repudiation of wage labor in favor of a subsistence
economy (Semmel 33). Why, then, does Kingsley here refuse the opportunity for outrage or even warning? The reason, I think, is only
partly a matter of racial ideology—that is, of Kingsley commending in
a Scot what he might at best tolerate in a black Trinidadian. Instead,
miscegenation here presides over a profound ambivalence toward industrialism itself, which recalls us to the circumstances of Kingsley's
emergence as a public figure in Victorian England.

   Ironically, Kingsley established his reputation in England in the late
1840s through his *attacks* on "political economy." The great Chartist
rally planned for Kennington Common on 10 April 1848, which ter-
rified Londoners fearful of mass working-class insurrection, crystallized
Kingsley's belief that the Church of England could defuse calls for democracy only by accommodating working-class political sentiments. He
found an outlet for his views in a new periodical, *Politics for the People*,
which articulated the claims of what became known as Christian Socialism, and to which Kingsley contributed "Letters to the Chartists"
under the pseudonym of Parson Lot. In 1850, he printed over the same
name a pamphlet titled "Cheap Clothes and Nasty," in which he fu-
riously denounced the sweating system among London tailors, and argued for the formation of independent associations among working
men. "Why should we not work and live together in our own work-
shops, or our own homes, for our own profit?" he asked, adopting the
fictive identification with the urban artisan that developed into the

novel *Alton Locke* (7:76). The widespread denunciation provoked by the pamphlet was in many ways predictable, but it is unexpectedly illuminating in the context of Kingsley's tropical fantasies. When not being charged with inciting insurrection, Kingsley was arraigned for his ignorance of political economy; as W. R. Greg put it in the *Edinburgh Review*, Kingsley would cocoon men with "artificial environments which shall make subsistence certain, enterprise superfluous, and virtue easy, low-pitched, and monotonous" ("English Socialism" 17). In effect, Greg objects, Kingsley would have workers living in a perpetual saturnalia.

Kingsley would later renounce these early socialist sentiments, along with even a theoretical belief in human equality, as the radical Parson Lot gave way to Canon Kingsley, Chaplain to Queen Victoria.[7] Yet even his later writings remain centrally preoccupied with the debilitating effects of industrial labor on English masculinity. That preoccupation reflects the markedly paternalistic, even feudal, strain in Kingsley's ideal of working-class manhood. The truly masculine working man should follow the example of Kingsley's "wise Scot," who is "far too wise to wish to better himself." That imagined contentment reaffirms one of the central polemics of *Alton Locke*, which insists that the working man who wishes access to middle-class privilege is a traitor to his class. Kingsley thus appropriates the strange amalgam of capitalist and feudal labor patterns that distinguishes so much Victorian commentary on labor: the working man is held to middle-class norms of self-discipline, but is denied any compensation in the form of upward social mobility, the reward of deferred gratification typically proffered to "the middle ranks." At the same time, however, Kingsley persistently envisions spaces of release from such pressures—which are also spaces for the containment of frustrated political desire—in escapes from the pressures of modernity itself. With such release comes the recovery of a virility that is evoked in *At Last* under the image of Ulysses. There Kingsley praises a self-sufficient resourcefulness and "manhood" that is now disappearing "under the money-making and man-unmaking influences of the 'division of labour' ": "He is vanishing fast, the old bee-keeping, basket-making, copse-cutting, many-counselled Ulysses of our youth, as handy as a sailor: and we know too well what he leaves behind him;

---

7. In a letter of 1866, Kingsley wrote "I held that doctrine [that humans are "congenitally equal"] strongly myself in past years, and was only cured of it, in spite of its seeming justice and charity, by the harsh school of facts"—and he proceeds to attack "Irish Celts" as "quite unfit for self-government" (2: 199).

grandchildren better fed, better clothed, better taught than he, but his inferiors in intellect and manhood, because—whatever they may be taught—they cannot be taught by schooling to use their fingers and their wits" (17:393–94).[8] Kingsley's voyage to the West Indies is an escape from a crisis of "manhood" at home, where the "man-unmaking" forces of industrial labor have undermined the traditional basis of masculinity in independent property, and in its place inculcated a seemingly unbearable regime of discipline. The "wise Scot," "practical viceroy" of his tiny island, suffers no such disability, but he is empowered only by leaving Victorian political economy behind.

THE OTHERNESS WITHIN

Of course, the Scot with his Creole wife and "lovely brownish children" embodies another aspect of normative masculinity besides economic autonomy: sexual potency. Kingsley's unmistakably sexual "shock" at the spectacle of "superabundant animal vigour" among black women in Port of Spain reminds us that, as Stallybrass and White have put it, disgust always bears the imprint of desire. But for Kingsley, as for many Victorians in both Britain and America, products of miscegenation have a remarkable power to elicit overt expressions of desire. In *At Last*, for example, Kingsley observes Creoles dancing at a ball with English settlers, while "below—what a contrast—the crowd of white eyeballs and white teeth all grinning and peeping upward." The literal hierarchy enforces a manifold social hierarchy along racial lines, in which access to privilege is founded on European heritage.[9] Thus, for example, immediately after describing the black laborers on the

8. The opening chapter of *Westward Ho!* similarly associates manhood and "barbarism" in opposition to contemporary education, asking "whether the barbaric narrowness of [Amyas's] Information was not somewhat counterbalanced both in him and the rest of his generation by the depth, and breadth, and healthiness of his education" (5:11)—an education largely summed up as "that of the old Persians, 'to speak the truth and draw the bow' " (5:11). The contrast with another novelist is telling: whereas Dickens's attack on modern education in *Hard Times* laments the loss of imagination and sentiment, Kingsley fears the decline of virile energy and self-reliance.
9. Technically, the noun "Creole" refers to an individual of European descent born in the West Indies, but it is used throughout the period (in *Jane Eyre*, for example) to suggest figures of mixed blood. Like the tribute to the "wise Scot" with his Creole wife and "lovely brownish children," this episode, where Creoles are associated with "coloured" peoples, and with the South Sea islanders of the Bounty mutiny, makes it clear, I think, that Kingsley associated the term with miscegenation.

roof, Kingsley compares them with "coloured" peoples, who are "our kinfolk, on another ground than that of common humanity," to whom "we" are bound by "a tie more sacred, I had almost said more stern, than we are to the mere Negro" (17:309). The bond is not specified, but it can only be race: the "coloured," whether Indian or Creole, are assumed to share a consanguinity, however remote. But such a distinction is inherently unstable, and indeed the Creoles within the ball (and "above") are themselves an embodiment of transgression, a blurring of "contrast" and a confusion of hierarchies through a mingling of blood. And these women call out in Kingsley a characteristically fascinated response: "Some of them . . . so beautiful in face and figure that one could almost pardon the jolly tars if they enacted a second Mutiny of the Bounty, and refused one and all to leave the island and the fair dames thereof" (17:97). Once again Kingsley calls up the archetype of the Lotos-Eaters, this time compounding an evasion of duty by conflating it with the more active and emphatically political transgression of mutiny. But Kingsley can "almost pardon" even those violations, when they are swayed by the beauty of mixed blood, which becomes at once a sign and an extenuation of transgression.

The temptation of Amyas Leigh in *Westward Ho!* is thus reenacted throughout Kingsley's writings in the spectacle of miscegenation, which is resisted only through a discipline fraught with ambivalence. Indeed, one possible resolution of that ambivalence is to represent miscegenation as itself a mode of discipline—to construe the intermingling of blood as a civilizing force that may work to the benefit of both races. Kingsley seems to have envisioned intermarriage as one means—perhaps the only means—of elevating exhausted or "inferior" races. His preface to *Hypatia*, a historical novel set in fifth-century Alexandria, characterizes the predicament of the Western Chruch in terms of his favorite maxim: "The health of a Church depends, not merely on the creed which it professes, not even on the wisdom and holiness of a few great ecclesiastics, but on the faith and virtue of its individual members. The *mens sana* must have a *corpus sanum* to inhabit. And even for the Western Church, the lofty future which was in store for it would have been impossible, without some infusion of new and healthier blood into the veins of a world drained and tainted by the influence of Rome" (9:xii). Just such "blood" was at hand—or at the gates—in "the great tide of those Gothic nations" sweeping across Roman territory. The Syrian and Egyptian churches had been drawn "away from practice to speculation" by their distinctive intellectual gifts; "and the races of Egypt and Syria were effeminate, over-civilized, exhausted by centuries

during which no infusion of fresh blood had come to renew the stock"
(9:xv). A similar typology of racial intermingling tacitly informs *At Last*,
in which Kingsley recounts his sight of a black man in Trinidad whose
features were "altogether European of the highest type": "One could
not look at him without hopeful surmises as to the possible rise of the
Negro," who, like all races, can only rise "permanently" "by the appearance among them of sudden sports of Nature; individuals of an
altogether higher type" (17:337).[10] Miscegenation provides just the sort
of aesthetic transformation that Kingsley interprets as biological and
moral ascent—and which he savors as erotic spectacle. Conversely, marriage with "savage" blood restores a vitality to "civilized" races whose
balance of *mens sana in corpore sano* is doomed to disintegrate without
it.

These racial disciplines are clearly articulated in *Westward Ho!*, where
the ambivalence informing the "temptation" of Amyas Leigh is ultimately stabilized yet preserved in his marriage to the "savage" Ayacanora, who is apparently an offspring of miscegenation (and whose
name suggests that Kingsley, like Tennyson, had read Irving). When
Amyas first encounters Ayacanora among Indians in the forest (just
before he is "tempted of the Devil"), her exotic appearance immediately conjures up "all the strange and dim legends of white Indians,
and of nations of a higher race than Carib, or Arrowak [*sic*], or Solimo.
. . . She must be the daughter of some great cacique, perhaps of the
lost Incas themselves—why not? . . . she, unabashed in her free innocence, gazed fearlessly in return, as Eve might have done in Paradise"
(6:135–36). Like Greek sculpture, Ayacanora—by virtue of her light
complexion, apparently—offers a spectacle of disciplined sexuality: she
may return a "fearless" gaze and yet be a sign of "free innocence,"
unlike the similarly "unabashed" black women of Port of Spain, who
are a sign of "license." In fact, it turns out that Ayacanora is the long-
lost daughter of an English mariner and a Spanish woman, but for
Kingsley the Spanish ancestry seems sufficiently "tropical" to give an
innate bias to the "savagery" that has been nurtured by a childhood
in isolation from European society. Ayacanora is not like Tita, an Indian
woman who looks at her Spanish lover "devouring him with the wild
eyes of passionate unreasoning tropic love" (6:206); instead, she is by

10. Such comments, which clearly assign to Blacks an evolutionary state inferior to that
of white Europeans, are strangely ignored by apologists for Kingsley's racial attitudes,
such as Michael Banton, who claims, "There is little or no evidence of attitudes
specially associated with a dark skin colour or of any personal animus" (75).

comparison decidedly "European" in complexion, voice, and even demeanor, which—in the familiar colonialist fantasy—has prompted the
Omaguas to regard her as a priestess. But this distinction does not
exempt her from "that perilous crisis which seems to endanger the
bodies and souls of all savages and savage tribes, when they first mingle
with the white man": "For the mind of the savage, crushed by the sight
of the white man's superior skill, and wealth, and wisdom, loses at first
its self-respect; while his body, pampered with easily-obtained luxuries
instead of having to win the necessaries of life by heavy toil, loses its
self-helpfulness; and with self-respect and self-help vanish all the savage
virtues, few and flimsy as they are" (6:232–33). Like the black laborers
in *At Last*, Ayacanora here signifies indolent, "pampered" existence,
the "dreamful ease" of Tennyson's lotos-eaters, which ultimately will
be disciplined by the regimen of Victorian domesticity—a discipline
that Kingsley mystifies (typically) as a quasi-racial achievement. When
Ayacanora finally discovers that she, "the wild Indian, was really one of
the great white people whom she had learned to worship," the awareness brings a "regenerating change": "She regained all her former
stateliness, and with it a self-restraint, a temperance, a softness which
she had never shown before" (6: 245). Yet a residual difference persists
in her complexion and her self-conception: almost her last words in
the book are, "I am but a poor wild girl—a wild Indian savage, you
know" (6:359).

In part, this gesture eroticizes Victorian domesticity by incorporating
a resistant element of "savage" abandon—and thus "health"—within
its discipline.[11] At the same time, however, the persistence of the "savage" also serves—as in Tennyson's poetry—to embody profound instabilities within the regimen of manliness. Kingsley's image of "the mind
of the savage, crushed by the sight of the white man's superior skill,"

11. One might also glimpse here the dynamic that Marianna Torgovnick discovers in the
appeal of primitivism: the men who celebrate woman's civilizing mission also resent
it (63). In *At Last*, that ambivalence seems to animate even Kingsley's comment on
a palm tree: "a joy for ever, a sight never to be forgotten . . . Like a Greek statue in
a luxurious drawing-room, sharp-cut, cold, virginal; shaming, by the grandeur of mere
form, the voluptuousness of mere colour, however rich and harmonious; so stands
the palm in the forest; to be worshipped rather than to be loved" (17:103). This is
Keats refracted through Victorian domesticity, in which middle-class womanhood
serves to identify moral grandeur with a resistance to "voluptuousness." The "sharp-
cut, cold, virginal" Greek statue in a Victorian drawing-room may "shame" the more
sensual order of "mere colour," but when that purity is set against the realm of the
tropical forest it is charged with all the ambivalance of Keats's Grecian urn: it is a
"cold pastoral" indeed.

is a self-congratulatory tribute to Victorian civilization (as Wee points out), yet it is echoed throughout his writings in depictions of European male rivalries, as seen through the eyes of the weaker man. For example, the effete Spasmodic poet in *Two Years Ago*, Elsley Vavasour (author of *The Soul's Agonies*), repeatedly undergoes the "crisis" of the savage: "Impulsive men like Elsley, especially when their self-respect and certainty of their own position is not very strong, have instinctively a defiant fear of the strong, calm, self-contained man, especially if he has seen the world" (14:17). Even Philammon, the far more restrained young monk who is the hero of *Hypatia*, feels constantly "haunted" by the cosmopolitan Jew, Raphael Ben-Ezra, with his "quiet self-assured smile" and "that ease and grace, that courtesy and self-restraint, which made Raphael's rebukes rankle all the more keenly, because he felt that the rebuker was in some mysterious way superior to him, and saw through him, and could have won him over, or crushed him in argument, or in intrigue—or in anything, perhaps, except mere brute force" (9: 100). Such rivalries underscore the significance of manhood as a superb disciplinary economy, in which self-mastery confirms one's capacity for political domination. Lord Minchampstead in *Two Years Ago*, for example, is "a man born to rule self, and therefore to rule all he met" (14:260). When masculine authority inheres in self-discipline, those who are not "self-contained" feel impotent, even emasculated. And this sense of impotence is reenacted in the "perilous crisis" of the savage in *Westward Ho!* who is "crushed by the sight of the white man's superior skill, and wealth, and wisdom."

Kingsley himself by all accounts was constantly prey to inadequate self-mastery—a failing that made him seem, he feared, both "un-English" and unmanly. He suffered from recurrent spells of nervous collapse, and his contemporaries, both friends and adversaries, were struck by the extraordinary vehemence and volatility of his emotions. As John Martineau, one of his most ardent admirers, put it, "With all his man's strength there was a deep vein of *woman* in him, a nervous sensitiveness, an intensity of sympathy, which made him suffer when others suffered" (2:40). Indeed, the very insistence with which the tributes culled by his wife in her biography center on "manliness" suggests some anxiety at the discordant attributes. One need not rely on private testimony, however: Kingsley's obsessive, furious attacks on "Jesuit" effeminacy and treachery, not only in his famous controversy with Newman but throughout novels, periodical articles, sermons, and letters, have suggested to many commentators a nearly hysterical disavowal of unsettling features of his own character. Consider his summing-up of his exchanges with Newman in 1864: "I cannot be weak enough to put myself a second time, by any fresh act of courtesy, into the power of one who, like a treacherous ape, lifts to you meek and suppliant eyes, till he thinks he has you within his reach, and then springs, gibbering and biting, at your face" (Hawley 137). The echo of Caliban's outburst at Prospero's "spirits" in Act 2 of *The Tempest*—"For every trifle are they set upon me, / Sometimes like apes that mow and chatter at me, / And after bite me" (II.ii.8–10)—richly betrays Kingsley's profound sense of impotence in the face of Newman's seemingly unshakeable mastery. Indeed, Kingsley here sounds uncannily like the hysterical Vavasour of *Two Years Ago*, who likewise loses all gentlemanly self-control when confronted by the spectacle of a disciplined reserve that he cannot master, either in himself or (for that reason) in others.

But it is important not to reduce Kingsley's rhetoric of masculinity to a narrowly personal pathology. Although Owen Chadwick rightly insists that Kingsley as an individual is "typical of no one and nothing" (129), Kingsley's remarkably complex and high-strung character did make him an acutely sensitive register of larger cultural tensions. Hence the telling fact that his portrait of Vavasour, which represents a persistent type of male subjectivity in his writings, was taken by Tennyson (and a number of his circle) to be a caricature of the poet laureate himself (Martin, *Tennyson* 420–21). This might seem a paranoid ascription, given Vavasour's working-class origins (which he conceals by changing his given name, John Briggs) and his effeminate and histrionic manner, as well as Kingsley's deep and abiding admiration for Tennyson and his poetry.[12] But Tennyson's fantasy was not idiosyncratic. It recognized in Kingsley's fictional character a widely shared suspicion of the poet as a figure resistant to manly self-discipline—a notion that Tennyson's poetry, perhaps more than any other single source, had put into widespread circulation in Victorian England. (Tennyson was particularly exercised by Vavasour's opium habit—a feature which of course recalls his own lotos-eaters, as well as persistent contemporary speculation about the poet's private habits.) Kingsley's portrait of the self-destructive Vavasour, in other words, confirms the

---

12. Vavasour is most obviously derived from Shelley and the Spasmodics, but he also incorporates Kingsley's suspicions of Browning, whom he met in 1852, and who struck him as "very clever, but low-bred, effeminate, and [*arruthumos*], a man who fancies that a man can be a poet by profession—and do nothing else—a wild mistake" (quoted in Martin, *Dust of Combat* 161). Of course Tennyson likewise fancied himself a poet by profession, but Tennyson was not "low-bred," and Kingsley was an incorrigible snob.

cultural authority of an ideal of manhood as disciplined power. But as in Tennyson's tropical fantasies, the authority of that ideal is elicited through its apparent lapse—and as a pervasive, even crippling fear of failing to display adequate self-discipline.

Such anxiety, I have argued, is reflected in Kingsley's preoccupation with the "savage." But the emasculating fear of inadequate self-mastery also informs even the most "bloodthirsty" elements of *Westward Ho!*—whose immense popularity further underscores the cultural prominence of Kingsley's preoccupation with masculinity under stress. In the final quarter of the book, Kingsley's hero is possessed by a strange, extraordinary fervor as he pursues Don Guzman Sotomayor de Soto, the Spanish nobleman whose elopement with young Rose Salterne had precipitated Amyas's voyage to South America in pursuit. On his return voyage home with Ayacanora, Amyas's preoccupation sets him apart from his crew, as he alone seems oblivious to Ayacanora's erotic appeal. His sailors interpret this distinction as a mark of consummate self-discipline—and hence consummate leadership. Likening Amyas's coldness to the conduct of Sir Francis Drake putting ashore a nameless "negro lass" after her presence incited some unspecified transgression, one sailor justifies the apparent callousness by urging, "If he had not got rid of her, there would have been more throats than one cut about the lass . . . and so there would have been about this one before now, if the captain wasn't a born angel out of heaven" (6:227). If Victorian domesticity requires an angel in the house, Amyas's function here is that of the angel in the ship, who likewise regulates dangerous male passion. But the very exactitude of this parallel tends to undercut Kingsley's disciplinary paradigm, since it suggests that Amyas's conduct at this point is less a function of self-control than of lack of interest. At this point, however, Amyas's energies are entirely devoted to his longing to kill Don Guzman, ostensibly to avenge Rose's death at the hands of the Inquisition. The lust for revenge turns into a ferocity toward all things Spanish—which includes Ayacanora herself, whose heritage marks her as "one of the accursed race" (6:246)—that prompts Amyas to violently reject his mother's wish that he marry Ayacanora: "I cannot bear the thought that my children should have in their veins one drop of that poison" (6:287). Why a rage so hyperbolic—"fantastic as it may seem" (6:246)—that even Kingsley seems to have feared it would be implausible? As it underscores Ayacanora's persistent affiliation with the "savage," Amyas's rage also rather crudely prepares him to undergo a process very much like the "civilizing" of Ayacanora herself: his own "bloodthirsty" desire must be chastened, not quenched, before he can find true Christian humility and Victorian domesticity. But Amyas's vengefulness is also strikingly faithful to the homosocial structures of the narrative, within which women exist primarily to facilitate bonds between men. Tellingly, Amyas expresses little grief at the death of Rose, around whom the "Brotherhood of the Rose" was formed, since the more important function of that death is to consolidate Amyas's lust for revenge against the Spaniards in general, and Don Guzman in particular.[13] Political and religious antagonisms are submerged in an increasingly overt erotic rivalry, in which Don Guzman embodies precisely the mastery that Amyas lacks: the urbanity and self-control of the gentleman who has seen the world. Hence the exemplar of a nation ostensibly inferior on all points to the English nonetheless becomes the focal point of Amyas's existence.

There is thus a more subtle and far-reaching irony in Amyas's refusal of Ayacanora on the grounds that, as he puts it, "There's a fire burning me up, night and day, and nothing but Spanish blood will put it out" (6:288). Amyas's longing for vengeance unsettlingly conflates homocidal and sexual desire, envisioning a form of erotic gratification in the death of Guzman; only after that death can he entertain a relationship with Ayacanora. An especially vigilant sexual discipline fuels the intensification of homosocial rivalry to the pitch of homocidal rage—homosocial desire with a vengeance, quite literally. What this psychology entails, however, is that Amyas can be reconciled with Ayacanora only by murdering Guzman—which Kingsley's Christian narrative design will not allow—or by some transformation that entirely short-circuits the currents of homosocial desire that energize his longing for vengeance. An appeal to Amyas's Christian conscience would seem the obvious path to this resolution, but the episode of the forest idyll has already suggested the limited power of such persuasion in the world of *Westward Ho!* Instead, discipline can only be reasserted through physical violence, as Amyas is blinded by a bolt of lightning on board his ship in frantic pursuit of Don Guzman and the remnant of the Spanish Armada (6:345–52). Once again, as in so many similar scenes in Victorian fiction—most obviously, *Jane Eyre*—the ostensibly religious intervention is a mode of erotic regulation, which would seem to prepare Amyas to enter into an idyllic sexuality that (again as in *Jane Eyre*) at

13. Martin Green discovers in the novel a positive distaste for Rose and argues that the bonds of the Brotherhood reflect "the author's covert malevolence against Rose, and women, and sex" (217). This insight is greatly refined and generalized in Sedgwick's analysis of homosocial structures in English narrative, which is strikingly borne out by Kingsley's novels.

once resists and reaffirms Victorian erotic and social convention. Amyas's fulfillment, after all, remains associated with miscegenation, inasmuch as Ayacanora continues to call herself a "wild Indian savage." But the violence of Amyas's blinding reflects a continuing instability in the sway of Kingsleyan discipline; it releases Amyas from the maddening constraints of homosocial rivalry, but only to turn him into "a child once more," whose entrance into normative manhood in the form of marriage is yet again deferred, never to be realized within the novel.

Ultimately, then, bodily vigor is most important to Kingsleyan heroism not as an end in itself, but to the extent that it enables a man to endure greater chastisements of emotional and physical suffering. The largest plot structures of *Westward Ho!* represent such heroism through a wild vacillation between violent desire and equally violent, almost self-annihilating, restraint, which renders at fever pitch not only the conflict between savagery and civilization, but the self-division of Kingsleyan male subjectivity. The same tensions in turn inform Kingsley's remarkable preoccupation with figures of miscegenation. The woman of "mixed" blood, who incorporates the space in which the savage "mingle[s] with" the European, is an especially powerful liminal figure for Kingsley, because his racial typology codes her mixed descent as a sign of the contest between desire and reason, impulse and self-restraint, and thus of an unstable or overtly feminized masculinity. Ayacanora is but one example of this structure, which is even more prominent in *Two Years Ago* (1857), one central plot of which focuses on Marie Lavington, an American slave who has escaped to England. Although critics have followed Kingsley's introduction to the novel in treating it principally as a response to the interest in abolitionism fueled by *Uncle Tom's Cabin*, published in England just four years before, the novel more centrally develops Kingsley's long-standing preoccupation with miscegenation. In Kingsley's account, Marie is not a Negro but a Quadroon—a distinction whose social importance is underscored by the popularity of the "tragic Quadroon" in American literature of the time. In American treatments that figure typically appears in a plot that turns on the terror of social exposure, and the consequent possibility of enslavement, along with meditations on the tragic or sinister significance of miscegenation to the body politic (Aaron; Kinney 57–58). In Kingsley's novel, however, Marie's heritage figures principally to make her, like Ayacanora, at once an object of intense desire among European men and the emblem of a divided selfhood. "You do not know the craving for exhilaration, the capability of self-indulgence, in our wild Tropic blood," she cries; "Oh Sabina, I feel at times that I could sink so low—

that I could be so wicked, so utterly wicked, if I once began!'' (13:267). The stereotype is risible, but the larger context of Kingsley's writings points to its role in constructing *masculine* subjectivity. Once again Kingsley represents an irrepressible longing for "perpetual Saturnalia," now cast into an especially acute ambivalence whose sign is miscegenation: Marie's agony expresses "that strange double nature which so many Quadroons seem to owe to their mixed blood; a strong side of deep feeling, ambition, energy, an intellect rather Greek in its rapidity than English in its sturdiness; and withal a weak side, of instability, inconsistency, hasty passion, love of present enjoyment, sometimes, too, a tendency to untruth, which is the mark, not perhaps of the African specially, but of every enslaved race" (13:197). For Kingsley as for Tennyson, a manifold "otherness" articulates the internal tensions that beset an anxious masculinity.

Marie's character is an especially rich index of an array of difference that encompasses nationality, gender, and behavior, as well as race. Because of her relatively light complexion, Marie passes in Europe as an Italian diva, "La Cordifiamma." She thereby confirms the association of dark skin with "southern" blood generally, and with a temperament given to volatile passions and histrionic display, both of which reflect in turn a lack of self-discipline, which Kingsley refers to the effects of enslavement (whether political or religious, American or Roman Catholic). All of these attributes exert a profound erotic attraction for the Kingsleyan male spectator, inasmuch as they are interpreted as signs of insufficiently regulated desire. The whole array of associations is condensed in a casual, passing reference in *Two Years Ago* to "that indescribable lissomeness and lazy grace which Irishwomen inherit, perhaps, with their tinge of southern blood" (14:270). But the same network of difference is more complexly rehearsed in a passage from *At Last*, where Kingsley recalls an evening in the harbor at Grenada. There he witnessed "a tall and very handsome middle-aged brown woman" repeatedly calling to a man, and was struck by the variety of tone in her calls as "a piece of admirable play-acting" responsive to her consciousness of a male audience. "A curious phase of human nature," he comments, "is that same play-acting, effect-studying, temperament, which ends, if indulged in too much, in hopeless self-deception" and hypocrisy (17:63). The links with Marie in *Two Years Ago*, or with Pelagia in *Hypatia*, are clear enough: the female actress is the quintessence of the calculated self-display that Kingsley, along with Carlyle and Tennyson, anxiously denominate feminine—in part as a means of disavowing such theatricality in their own self-constructions. But the same emphases are uppermost in the character of Elsley Vavasour—through a logic that emerges as Kingsley proceeds to generalize further: "It is common enough among Negresses, and among coloured people too: but is it so very uncommon among whites? Is it not the bane of too many Irish? of too many modern French? of certain English, for that matter, whom I have known, who probably had no drop of French or Irish blood in their veins? But it is all the more baneful the higher the organisation is" (17:63). The sequence of "Negress," "Irish," "French," "English" articulates a familiar Victorian path from the margins of the world to England, the center of civilization, a path which also marks an ascent of "blood" and "organization." But the categories turn out to be surprisingly porous: a rhetorical structure that might seem to underscore the integrity and (self-) mastery of the English "organization" in fact depicts its shared susceptibility to a seemingly universal weakness. The apparent moral ascent is dogged by a persistent transgression that confounds secure mastery, a transgression that in fact becomes more debilitating, more "baneful," with each new incorporation into "higher" blood.

Ultimately this incursion articulates a powerful cultural anxiety, which Kingsley's writings capture with unusual force because it is experienced there as the particular and intimate burden of masculine identity. The fascination of miscegenation rehearses the constant possibility that civilization might incorporate within itself the savage it seeks to master—which for Kingsley mirrors the fear that masculine self-discipline might be susceptible to "feminine" abandon. And these possibilities explain Kingsley's peculiar investment in the private musings of Marie, when she is haunted by the fear that her African ancestry will be revealed and make her unworthy of her suitor. Looking in a mirror, she gazes

> as if her own image had been the Gorgon's head . . . [She had] no heart to tell him that in her veins were some drops, at least, of the blood of slaves. . . . Were there not in her features traces of that taint? And as she looked . . . did her eyelid slope more and more, her nostril shorten and curl, her lips enlarge, her mouth itself protrude? . . . . Her actress's fascination . . . had moulded her features for the moment, into the very shape which it dreaded. . . . Another half minute . . . and in its place an ancient negress, white-haired, withered as the wrinkled ape, but with eyes closed—in death. (*Life and Works* 13: 186)

Marie's anxiety is represented as a fear of regression—a fear which strikingly anticipates the preoccupation with atavism that, as Patrick

Brantlinger has recently observed, becomes a central presence in late Victorian imperialist fantasy (*Rule of Darkness*). But here Kingsley's typical mystification of race is also animated by the burdens of manhood: by representing Marie's fear of self-disclosure with the image of the Gorgon's head, he signals what Freud has argued is a distinctly masculine fear of castration. At this moment, at least, Marie Lavington seems transformed not into an ancestor, but into Charles Kingsley, who is contemplating his own face in a mirror, fearing that others will recognize in him a wayward, "savage" desire that he associates with "Negroid" features. The structure is closely akin to that hysterical disavowal in the attack on Newman as a "gibbering and biting" ape. Even more suggestively, Marie's brief meditation uncannily recapitulates one of the famous fever-visions in the "Dream Land" chapter of *Alton Locke*, where Kingsley's hero imagines himself as (among other things) "a baby-ape in Borneon forests": "As I looked down . . . I saw my face reflected in a pool—a melancholy, thoughtful countenance, with large projecting brow—it might have been a negro child's" (8:215–16). Susan Chitty has suggested that this passage captures Kingsley's self-loathing—"after five years of marriage he felt himself to be foul, unclean" (136)—but the identification is more complex. Once again Kingsley summons up Africans and apes to project a loathing that veils longing; under the burdens of Victorian manhood, he fearfully imagines a state of abandon that, like the realm of Tennyson's lotos-eaters, is a site at once of failure and of release.

THE PLEASURES OF ABASEMENT

I have argued that miscegenation in Kingsley's work represents a decidedly Freudian sense of the precariousness of the civilizing process, as an incessant regulation of desire that is fraught with ambivalence. But the trope also calls attention to a peculiarly complex inflection of gender that arises when such discipline is represented at an extreme intensity. The deferred gratification celebrated by Victorian political economy always exerts a feminizing influence inasmuch as it restricts male aggression and desire. Kingsley's figures of "half-savage" femininity—passionate, anguished, theatrical, mercurial—represent this gendered discipline in unstable equilibrium; indeed, the figures of Ayacanora and Marie represent the possibility that such instability in "manly" discipline may be intensified to the point that discipline becomes a program of humiliation, remarkably akin to masochism. The

fine line between conscience and moral masochism is of course a central feature of Freudian cultural theory, as of the Victorian cultural
norms out of which Freudian theory arises. But Kingsley's writings, like
the early sections of *In Memoriam*, often represent moral masochism at
an intensity at which it becomes sexualized as the abasement that characterizes so-called feminine masochism. And his work thereby calls attention to a still more complexly gendered investment in the discipline
that ostensibly regulates masculine desire.

Marie in *Two Years Ago* is again an especially suggestive figure. She
is not only the most obvious subject of violent discipline in the novel,
but *as such* she is also an agent of moral redemption for men. Her
passionate exhibition of the agonies of divided selfhood is what finally
resolves her suitor Stangrave's Carlylean crisis of vocation:

> "Yes, Marie was right. Life is meant for work, and not for ease; to labour
> in danger and in dread; to do a little good ere the night comes, when
> no man can work: instead of trying to realise for oneself a Paradise; not
> even Bunyan's shepherd-paradise, much less Fourier's Casino-paradise;
> and perhaps least of all, because most selfish and isolated of all, my own
> heart-paradise—the apotheosis of loafing, as Claude calls it. Ah, Tenny-
> son's Palace of Art is a true word—too true, too true!" (14:205)

Thus another male drifter is recalled from the "paradise" of the lotos-
eaters—or from its more aristocratic companion-space in Tennyson's
poetry, the palace of art.[14] The reclamation of male selfhood has for
Marie in turn, as for Ayacanora in *Westward Ho!*, a chastening effect,
which overcomes her histrionic, "half-savage" anguish as soon as that
anguish has exerted its disciplinary effect on the reclaimed man. In her
final appearance in the novel, after she has decided to marry Stangrave,
"her theatric passionateness had passed" (14:312–13). But like Ayacanora, Marie remains an embodiment of both difference and discipline—the latter in a quite literal sense. She retains not only the
otherness of her complexion, but the scars of a whip on her flesh. And
those scars incite Stangrave to even more fervent and erotically charged
self-discipline: "I will see in them God's commandment to me, written
not on tables of stone, but on fair, pure, noble flesh." Marie responds,
in her final words: "I glory in them now; for, without them, I never
should have known all your worth" (14:313).

---

14. The palace of art appeals to those who already enjoy the benefits of seigneurial
possession bodied forth in the lotos-eaters, but who lack a sense of vocation.

In this harrowing episode, the path to feminine fulfillment lies in abasement, in the glorification of the agony a woman suffers from a man's violence. Feminine value is mediated through self-demeaning gratitude for "worth" bestowed by men, through male sympathy for a woman's suffering at the hands of brutal male authority. That brutality is in turn extenuated, even denatured altogether, by the suggestion that it is really a form of empowerment—that through her suffering, and only through her suffering, Marie becomes an agent for the moral redemption of men. Recalling the devoted self-abasement of Tennyson's widow-wife, fixated on her desolation in section 97 of *In Memoriam*, Marie is the focal point of an even starker representation of the dynamics of power underlying the platitudes of Victorian domestic ideology. In this harsh light, that ideology constitutes a program bordering on sadism—particularly inasmuch as Stangrave continues to insist that the masters wielding the whips are themselves as much the victims of slavery as the slaves. But this insistence also replicates Kingsley's peculiar investment in Marie's predicament as a potential *masculine* subject-position. For in that configuration—in the imaginary order in which Marie's sufferings figure those of Charles Kingsley—the victim is indeed empowered, but the victim is now male, empowered through the dynamic of moral masochism. By representing himself as the subject of violent discipline, that is, Kingsley may actually reinforce male authority by replacing overt dominance with a domestic ideology that emphasizes the burdens of masculinity. In the terms of Christopher Newfield's account of Hawthorne, Kingsley's heroes thereby attain "a power of doubleness" through which they occupy both halves of the ongoing division between male domination and female submission; in the process, they obscure the power they derive from the persistent operation of that division. As Newfield puts it, being a male "at risk" thereby recovers and consolidates one's authority as a man (67).[15]

This logic in the representation of male suffering connects Kingsley's characters with a host of more familiar figures in Victorian novels—perhaps most notably, the drifting, deracinated "grey men" of Dickens's late fiction, such as Sidney Carton in *A Tale of Two Cities* and Eugene Wrayburn in *Our Mutual Friend*. Like Kingsley's heroes, these characters typically resist the dictates of masculine discipline—particularly those of an idealized domesticity—until such discipline makes

15. Newfield is principally concerned to resist the currently widespread critical gesture that takes the confounding of binary, either/or logics by the logic of "both/and" to be necessarily a subversion of patriarchal structures.

itself felt in physical violence, which brings them fulfillment by disabling them, and thereby calling out the more subtly redemptive discipline of a woman's devotion. Such characters, which are most often explained as the projection of idiosyncratic psychic burdens in the novelist, clearly reflect a larger disciplinary project that reaffirms the sway of male authority and privilege precisely by seeming to undermine it.[16] Indeed, certain formulations of ideological containment would have it that no representation of heterosexual male suffering can avoid reinforcing hegemonic masculinity.[17] As we saw in Chapter 1, however, the conclusion of *A Tale of Two Cities* suggests the more disruptive possibility also implicit in the paradoxical resolution of *Westward Ho!*: that the hero's pain or passivity may actually stand in for the domestic and erotic satisfaction it seemed designed to facilitate. In such representations, male suffering turns into a celebration of abasement, in which the hero's pain is eroticized as "feminine" (or sexual) masochism.[18]

In this regard, Kingsley's tacit identification with the sufferings of Marie in *Two Years Ago* echoes a more overtly eroticized fantasy rehearsed frequently in Kingsley's correspondence with his wife, Fanny Grenfell, particularly during their tortured (I use the term advisedly) courtship. During this period, when the two were separated not only by her family's injunction but by her own thoughts of entering a Tractarian sisterhood, Kingsley pleaded for her affection by repeatedly describing torments of unfulfilled sexual desire, which he frequently elaborated through descriptions of monastic renunciation, even flagellation.[19] These appeals obviously lend themselves to Reik's understanding of masochism as a mode of empowerment through fantasy, under which the victim, while seeming to cede authority to the woman

16. In this regard, Dickens's "grey men" figure centrally in a more general representation of repression in Dickens's novels, which is brilliantly analyzed by Kucich (*Repression in Victorian Fiction* 201–83).
17. Dollimore offers a helpful overview of theories of containment, with specific reference to sexual ideologies (*Sexual Dissidence* 81–91).
18. For an extended analysis of these categories, and their relation to male subjectivity, see Silverman (185–210).
19. "I once formed a strange project, I would have travelled to a monastery in France, gone barefoot into the chapel at matins (midnight), and there confessed every sin of my whole life before the monks and offered my naked body to be scourged by them" (Chitty 59). According to Chitty, more modest versions of this fantasy were for a time carried out in weekly episodes of self-flagellation. Clearly Kingsley well understood the appeal of the "asceticism" he denounced in Newman: hence in part the ferocity of his attacks. Hence, too, the peculiar dynamic identified by Harrington, under which athleticism and Catholicism are unexpectedly conjoined in Kingsley's writings as forms of resistance to sexuality (85).

who punishes him, is in fact casting her in a role of his own devising, and thus manipulating the relationship to the gratification of his own desires.[20] But Kingsley's romantic rhetoric is not really masochistic in a Freudian sense, inasmuch as its avowed goal is entry into a traditionally phallic heterosexual relationship, which would be codified by that most orthodox discipline of sexual life, marriage. In this context, the ruling fantasy in his letters is a traditional male domination tending more toward sadism, which is directly expressed in another feature of the correspondence, Kingsley's many graphic drawings of bound, naked women. Yet this same correspondence establishes an important structural paradigm for *Alton Locke*, inasmuch as it rehearses masochistic fantasies to an audience that is also assigned the role of disciplinarian. And in *Alton Locke* the representation of male suffering and humiliation does indeed pass into a form of abasement that offers its own libidinal gratification, and thereby disrupts the imperatives and economies of normative Victorian masculine discipline.

The focal point of this complication in *Alton Locke* is the fascinating scene in which Kingsley's hero first visits the Dulwich Gallery. Recalling his puritanical mother's iconoclasm—all pictures were in her eyes "the rags of the scarlet woman no less than the surplice itself"—Locke enters the gallery "in a fever of expectation." Yet once in the gallery— where "the rich sombre light of the rooms, the rich heavy warmth of the stove-heated air, the brilliant and varied colouring and gilded frames" underscore the strange, novel sensuousness of the world of art—what arrests Locke's gaze is not the scarlet woman, or indeed any woman:

My attention was in a moment concentrated on one figure opposite to me at the furthest end. I hurried straight toward it. When I had got half-way up the gallery I looked round for my cousin. He had turned aside to some picture of a Venus which caught my eye also, but which, I remember now, only raised in me then a shudder and a blush, and a fancy that the clergymen must be really as bad as my mother had taught me to believe, if they could allow in their galleries pictures of undressed women. I have learnt to view things differently now, thank God. I have learnt that to the pure all things are pure. I have learnt the meaning of that great saying—the foundation of all art, as well as all modesty, all

20. This dynamic is frequently assumed to be the formulation of Giles Deleuze, but it is actually taken over from Reik; indeed, Deleuze departs fundamentally from Reik only in his insistence on a fundamental incompatability between masochism and sadism— an effort, in effect, to explode the notion of "sado-masochism."

love, which tells us how 'the man and his wife were both naked, and not ashamed'. . . .

Timidly, but eagerly, I went up to the picture, and stood entranced before it. It was Guido's St. Sebastian. (7:180–81)

In its retrospective conclusion that "to the pure all things are pure," the passage obviously reenacts the hard-won accommodation of sexuality rehearsed in Kingsley's letters to his wife.[21] But this prohibition of graven images curiously exempts the male form: Locke's gaze is regulated not by iconoclastic strictures against art as such, but by gendered desire. The retrospective invocation of purity is redundant when it comes to the mesmerizing image of Saint Sebastian:

> Those manly limbs, so grand and yet so delicate, standing out against the background of lurid night, the helplessness of the bound arms, the arrow quivering in the shrinking side, the upturned brow, the eye in whose dark depths enthusiastic faith seemed conquering agony and shame, the parted lips, which seemed to ask, like the martyrs in the Revelations, reproachful, half-resigned, "O Lord how long?"— Gazing at that picture since, I have understood how the idolatry of painted saints could arise in the minds even of the most educated, who were not disciplined by that stern regard for fact which is—or ought to be—the strength of Englishmen. I have understood the heart of that Italian girl, whom some such picture of Saint Sebastian, perhaps this very one, excited, as the Venus of Praxiteles the Grecian boy, to hopeless love, madness, and death. (7:181–82)

Locke is so enraptured—"my eyes seemed bursting from my head with the intensity of my gaze"—that the sway of "discipline" can be exerted only retrospectively, through interjected understandings of "the pure" and "that strength of regard for fact" and "what I have understood"— all of which were realized only after the episode ostensibly took place.

Clearly this passage is meant to delineate a crucial threshold in Locke's life, but the structure of the transition remains unclear. Ostensibly Locke's visit to the Dulwich Gallery initiates his escape from puritan asceticism to an appreciation of art that accommodates sexuality. On this reading, the erotic martyrdom of Saint Sebastian gives therapeutic embodiment to Locke's experience of the torments of unfulfilled desire, thereby freeing him from a destructive repression. Accordingly, at

---

21. David Rosen suggestively analyzes the role of the correspondence in the formation of what he calls Kingsley's notion of "primal masculinity."

this very moment in the novel Locke is awakened from his erotic "trance" and catches sight of Lillian, who will become the great passion of his life: her providential appearance would seem to confirm his entrance into normative (hetero)sexuality. Yet Locke's response to Lillian repudiates more than his mother's puritanism. "My newfound Venus Victrix," as Locke thinks of Lillian, "beautiful, beautiful, beautiful, beyond all statue, picture, or poet's dream," is also an emblematic transcendence of art—and with it the satisfactions of an alternative discipline embodied in the image of Saint Sebastian (7:182). In that painting, erotic fulfillment inheres in mortification, and the passage describing Locke's response to that image extends and refines the erotic satisfactions of disciplined self-denial. The discipline incarnated in Sebastian, and in Locke's response to the image, is disturbingly exorbitant; it is no longer instrumental to participation in some external economy, but seems to be its own reward—and, as a consequence, threatens to subvert the libidinal economy called into play by the sight of Lillian. Hence the masochistic discipline of the painting needs to be repudiated: the homoerotic desire called out by the image of Sebastian is ritualistically cast out in favor of the assuredly heterosexual icon of Venus—an image from which Locke had just previously turned away.

But does this rejection really recuperate a normative, disciplined masculinity? Or does it further refine Locke's torments into a perverse self-abasement? After all, Locke repudiates the "idolatry of painted saints" and the male form on behalf of a woman whose social position virtually guarantees his subsequent humiliation, and whom he will ultimately come to regard as another false idol, unworthy of his devotion. Fulfillment comes only when Lillian is succeeded by Eleanor, Lady Ellerton, whose secret role as the power presiding over Locke's destiny is finally bodied forth in the figure of the veiled "prophetess" who materializes near the end of his fever dreams. Those dreams, which are themselves an extraordinary panorama of abasement, are dispelled by Eleanor's pronouncement, "Your penance is accomplished. You have learned what it is to be a man. . . . Awake!" (8:225). At this moment, Locke's relationship to women is formalized in characteristic Kingsleyan fashion, as submission to a figure of domination ("a queen rather to be feared than loved" [7:268]) who confirms his passage into manhood by means of a symbolic emasculation—a capitulation even more extreme than that of Amyas Leigh. Locke surrenders not only his self-assertion but all the markers of normative manliness—including occupation, class affiliation, and marriage. There is really no hope left for him but to begin again in the tropics, and when he dies soon after in Texas (even Locke's choice of tropical paradise is misplaced), his fate seems that of an anchorite in the wilderness.

In one light, such abasement represents a massive capitulation to an oppressive social order. In effect, Locke permanently embraces the condition that he earlier bemoaned when he consented, as he puts it, "to emasculate my poems, and become a flunkey and a dastard" by editing out their political content (8:31). Of course the renunciation has an explicit Christian paradigm, but inasmuch as Locke's renunciation represents not merely the containment but the repudiation of working-class political aspiration, Kingsley elicits the powerfully reactionary social possibilities inherent in his religious model. Yet the ideological significance of this resolution is more elusive if one sees in Locke's fate, as I have tried to suggest, the imagined subversion of a distinctly middle-class discipline—an investment signalled throughout the novel in worries over what it means to be or to become a "gentleman." On this view, Locke's "loss of self-possession" at the riot, for example, distills not only widespread fear of working-class abandon, but also the anxiety of the weak Kingsleyan hero struggling—"between disappointment and the maddening desire of influence" (8:130)—to master the masculine authority that inheres in self-disciplined power, along with the violent rage and self-abasement that may supervene if the mastery proves unattainable. In this light, Locke's emasculating journey to the tropics is not an escape from the burdens of political economy so much as the culmination of its science of renunication in a self-annihilating intensity.[22] Locke willingly embraces his suffering, it seems, less out of Christian piety than because he thereby gains a sense of autonomy—the sense that he is not submitting to the external dictates of political economy, but is instead enacting its discipline as an impulse of his own innermost being. Indeed, it may be that ascetic constructions of mas-

22. This emphasis is unfortunately obscured in the most powerful reading of the novel, that of Catherine Gallagher in *The Industrial Reformation of English Fiction.* Like most critics, Gallagher is struck by the peculiar instabilities in the characterization of Locke, but she refers them to a fundamental irresolution concerning causality, which ultimately calls into question the basic premises of literary realism: the reality of individual identity and the possibility of referentiality. This irresolution, she urges, is reflected in the fundamental "characterlessness" of Locke, who becomes little more than "a name given to a bundle of incompatible characteristics" (99) or "a consciousness of disintegration and plurality" (97). But this reading makes no allowance for the characteristic and remarkably consistent patterns of subjectivity that distinguish Kingsley's representations of embattled manhood. "Plurality," after all, is not "disintegration," and "a bundle of incompatible characteristics" may nonetheless be highly structured.

culinity owe much of their appeal to precisely this fantasy of autonomy in the face of discipline, however discipline is construed. But if Locke has indeed "learned what it is to be a man," he also thereby supports Christopher Herbert's speculations on "an essentially masochistic cultural and political unconscious" in Victorian Britain (137). "By ordering his own punishment," Reik argues, "the masochist has made himself the master of his destiny" (161). Yet in the terms of political economy, such mastery marks a catastrophic derangement of desire, through which the regimen of manhood, and Victorian schemes of progress, would collapse into the condition of the "savage."

As he exposes the self-destructive drift of the science of renunciation, Kingsley's hero also points to the complex significance of male martyrdom in Victorian discourse. The figure of male suffering occupies a powerful boundary position within the structures of Victorian gender, in which fierce attacks on the dominant culture may also articulate fantasies of self-empowerment, or in which, conversely, Victorian discipline may be registered at its greatest intensity by imagining the pleasures of self-abandon, or self-destruction. In their power to evoke the competing energies of discipline and desire within Victorian schemes of progress and manhood, Victorian tropical fantasies find their logical culmination in the figure of Conrad's Kurtz. In Kurtz's despotic, seigneurial reign in the Congo, the physical and geographical limit of Victorian discipline is the site of its self-destruction, while Kurtz himself, the ostensible paragon of the civilizing progress founded in self-denial, ultimately embraces the self-annihilating abandon of which Marlow warns him: "You will be lost" (65). In effect, Kurtz intensifies the ambivalence of manly discipline to an extreme that the speaker of *In Memoriam*, like Marlow, approaches only to "come away" (57:1). Kurtz, that is, embodies Victorian discipline at its outermost limit and utmost intensity, at the point of its dissolution, in the liminal world of Kingsley's and Tennyson's lotos-eaters.

CHAPTER FOUR

Muscular Aestheticism: Masculine Authority and the Male Body

I could wish I were an Apollo for His sake! Strange idea, yet it seems so harmonious to me!

Charles Kingsley, *Life and Works* 1:87–88

It is "the only great prose in modern English," Yeats wrote of Pater's *Marius the Epicurean* (202). Though often cited, Yeats's verdict is perplexing, inasmuch as *Marius* is of all Pater's works the most clearly responsive to the narrative and rhetorical conventions of Victorian earnestness.[1] Despite its setting in Antonine Rome, the novel enacts a familiar pattern of the Victorian *Bildungsroman*: a traditional childhood religious faith collapses under the force of contemporary skepticism, but the emotional rewards of that faith are subsequently recuperated in a secular devotion to the forces of "intellectual light" (1:127). Marius's personal qualities, moreover, confirm the age's most cherished virtues: despite his skepticism, Marius evinces "a genuine virility," "vigorous intelligence," "a cold austerity of mind," "the honest action of his own untroubled, unassisted intelligence" (1:124–25); even when he embraces the daring views of Heraclitus, Marius finds there "many precepts towards a strenuous self-consciousness in all we think and do, that loyalty to cool and candid reason, which makes strict attentiveness of mind a kind of religious service" (1:130).

---

1. Houghton, *Victorian Frame of Mind* (218–62), offers the best overview of those conventions.

Virile, vigorous, austere, honest, untroubled, strenuous, loyal, candid, strict, religious: these are adjectives far more redolent of Kingsley than of Pater. But that seems to be their point. In presenting Marius's skepticism as a form of strenuous, even religious, self-discipline, Pater implicitly responds to the many attacks on his *Studies in the History of The Renaissance* (1873). Widely denounced as a sinister invitation to hedonism, *The Renaissance* elicited a rhetoric of outrage that conjoined most norms of English life in their common vulnerability to Pater's subversive creed. Thus W. J. Courthope in 1876 denounced Pater's volume as a betrayal not only of English society, but of English masculinity: "In common, we believe, with most Englishmen, we repudiate the effeminate desires which Mr. Pater, the mouthpiece of our artistic 'culture,' would encourage in society" ("Wordsworth and Gray" 71). Although Courthope's use of the term "effeminate" echoes Kingsley's traditional usage—it is set against "manly vigour . . . healthy tone, and . . . simple dignity"—by 1876 the suspicions insinuated by the label were becoming more explicitly and dangerously associated with sexual transgression. In *Marius* and much of his subsequent career, Pater responded to those suspicions by attempting to reinscribe within the ethos of aestheticism familiar norms of Victorian masculinity, and thereby to present even spectatorship as an eminently virile self-discipline.

Pater's considerable success in this rhetorical strategy points to a neglected strand in the cultural history of British modernism: the distinctly "modern" prose that Yeats admired is directly and pervasively indebted to early Victorian rhetorics of masculinity. In this chapter I explore that genealogy by focusing on the two writers who are implicitly paired in its title, Pater and Kingsley. This may seem an unlikely conjunction, save as an exercise in parody: what figure could be more remote from Kingsley's muscular Christian than the Paterian aesthete? Yet throughout their careers both writers were centrally concerned to reclaim the male body from the antagonisms of orthodox, ascetic morality. Perhaps more than any other middle-class writer, Kingsley placed the male body into widespread circulation as an object of celebration and desire—a project recognized in the contemporary tag, "Apostle of the Flesh."[2] But Pater offers a similarly sustained attack on the war

2. Gagnier, *Subjectivities* (55–98), is a salutary reminder that the separation of mind and body perpetuated in canonical Victorian discourse is a class-bound distinction responsive to material conditions; working-class memoirs, recounting lives in which physical labor was much more central, naturally give much more, and less anxious, space to representations of the body.

between flesh and spirit, taking as the subject of *The Renaissance* the historical period that marks, in Pater's words, man's "reassertion of himself, that rehabilitation of human nature, the body, the senses, the heart, the intelligence" in opposition to a medieval tendency "to depreciate man's nature . . . to make it ashamed of itself" (31). In effacing this important continuity between the two writers, cultural histories bear witness to the extraordinary power of a gendered discourse in which Pater and Kingsley figure as virtually antithetical types of masculinity. Even Norman Vance, who in *The Sinews of the Spirit* notes "a possible meeting-point" between Paterian aestheticism and Kingsleyan manliness in the moralized Hellenism of much late-Victorian thought (185), lets slip that important insight by reaffirming the familiar opposition between, crudely speaking, the robust, bluff heterosexual and the timid, furtive homoeroticist. But the sexualized oppositions codified by late-Victorian constructions of masculinity have obscured the common invocation of the male body throughout mid-Victorian discourse as a central locus of masculine authority. The danger that Courthope and others sensed in Pater derived in large part, ironically, from his subtly insistent evocations of homoerotic satisfactions that were more obliquely at play in Kingsley's hymns to virility. (Kingsley's heroes, W. R. Greg pointed out in 1861, are "usually miracles of physical beauty. . . . They are constantly 'models'; and very often 'young Antinouses' or 'Phoebus Apollos' " [124].) By the same token, however, many contemporaries may have simply overlooked—rather than anxiously evaded or repressed—Pater's heterodoxy, precisely because the transgressive pleasures in his writings are so deftly elicited from appeals to widely shared cultural norms.

This possibility is implicit in recent accounts of Pater's writings as invitations to double reading, appeals to an audience divided (along various boundaries) into initiates and outsiders.[3] That this strategy remained so long obscure reflects an ongoing homophobia, but it is also faithful to the complexity of mid- and late-Victorian discourses of masculinity constructed within an increasingly homophobic culture. That complexity has been richly and movingly analyzed by Linda Dowling, who has traced the emergence of a late-Victorian "counterdiscourse" of male love from within mid-Victorian liberalism, whose appeal to an-

---

3. For various recent accounts of what DeLaura calls Pater's "seductive 'beckoning' to a well-disposed audience through a double suggestion" ("Reading Inman" 8), see Dowling, *Hellenism and Homosexuality* (92–99); Morgan, "Reimagining Masculinity"; Dellamora, *Masculine Desire* (58–68, 167–92); and Clements, *Baudelaire and the English Tradition* (77–139).

cient Greece as a model of cultural vitality provided an inadvertent but rhetorically powerful basis for legitimating pederasty as "the very fountain of civic health" (*Hellenism and Homosexuality* xv). In this chapter, I want to place this counterdiscourse in a more inclusive and equivocal relation to dominant discourses. Pater's influential recuperation of a homoerotic "Greek ideal" also draws on strategies of legitimation that are central to mid-Victorian constructions of the gentleman. The gentleman, as we have noted, is the most pivotal and contested norm of mid-Victorian masculinity, because it served so effectively as a means of regulating social mobility and its attendant privileges. Egalitarian understandings of the gentleman, developed in the eighteenth century in resistance to aristocratic hegemony, turned it into a norm that could be realised by deliberate moral striving, but with the rise of an ideal of deep subjectivity the calculated pursuit of gentlemanly attributes seemed, by contrast, the mark of insubstantial, because ascribed, identity. In this regard, the dilemmas of self-fashioning captured in Carlyle's rhetoric of heroism persist throughout Victorian constructions of masculine authority. But the anxiety figured in Carlyle's image of the dandy was exacerbated in the mid-Victorian decades by conservative fears that the gentlemanly ideal had become a mere status-marker, and as such accessible to aggressive, self-interested social climbers. As a way of precluding such appropriations, middle-class commentators increasingly stressed the true gentleman's entire absence of self-consciousness—an emphasis that would be brilliantly caricatured in Barrie's *Peter Pan*: "Peter did not know in the least who or what he was, which is the very pinnacle of good form" (1031). It followed that the aspiring gentleman was an oxymoronic travesty of the ideal—a type widely caricatured in late-Victorian journalism as the plebeian "gent," a lower-class version of the dandy (Cowling 280–82). This resistance subtly rejuvenated the ideal of the born gentleman, who alone was able to realize the assured autonomy that the ideal demanded. But in such apologies, inherited rank subtly yields its authority to a somatic legacy: conservative commentators increasingly represent the gentleman as an organic ideal, rooted above all in an innate, physiological sensibility. The gentleman's status thus derives from, and is made visible in, his body. That appeal is most forthright in Ruskin's famous account of the gentleman in the final volume of *Modern Painters* (1860), but it shapes a wide array of writing in the 1860s and 1870s, in which the gentleman's refinement is an emphatically aesthetic attribute. Over against earlier understandings of the gentleman as a triumph of moral discipline, we encounter the gentleman as a work of art.

In aestheticizing manhood, mid-Victorian accounts of the gentleman point to a convergence of Kingsleyan muscularity and the aestheticism that Pater derives (via German Hellenism) from the model of classical Greece. In both discourses, the properly ordered male body functions as a ground of authority opposed to the claims of abstract rationality—whether it be political economy, Tractarian theology, or philosophical reflection generally. The gentleman thereby underscores the social ramifications of the aesthetic in codifying what Terry Eagleton has called "the body's long inarticulate rebellion against the tyranny of the theoretical" (13). More narrowly, the ideal testifies to the enduring relevance of Carlyle, since Pater, Kingsley, and Ruskin all invoke the impulses of the virile body in opposition to a self-baffling "speculation." One of the enabling conditions of the late-Victorian "counter-discourse" of male desire is thus widely and variously diffused in Victorian culture in "manly" praise of the male body as an object of aesthetic delight, a celebration that culminates in the rhapsodies of Victorian athleticism. And as that body is made the focal point of a comprehensive ascetic discipline, Pater's aestheticism becomes richly susceptible of description as an eminently "manly" project.

As an apologetic design, Pater's appeal to discipline might seem extraneous to his critical program, even a rearguard effort to efface the most subversive implications of his Hellenism. More generally, it might seem an effort to obscure that broad cultural antagonism between, in Matthew Arnold's well-worn dualism, Hebraism and Hellenism. Yet from the very outset of his career, Pater's appeal to Greece urges a rethinking of that distinction, inasmuch as "the Greek ideal" represents, not an escape from ascetic discipline, but a reconfiguration of it. Certainly Pater's project is more overtly indebted to a Goethean ideal of *Bildung*, which emphasizes subjective response and openness to experience in a manner that is subtly antagonistic to the energetic self-restraint of Victorian "character" (Collini 101–3). Yet Pater locates *within* the dynamics of *Bildung*—and thus, implicitly, within Arnoldian "culture"—the familiar anatagonism of Hebraism and Hellenism. As Kingsley's aspirations expose crucial tensions in the Pauline legacy, so Pater wrestles with a tension within Hellenism: the challenge of reconciling an invigorating susceptibility to new experience with a sense of stable, coherent selfhood. His appeal to Greece, that is, constantly comes up against Carlyle's recognition of 1826: "Few men have the secret of being at once determinate (*bestimmt*) and open; of knowing what they do know, and yet lying ready for farther knowledge" (*Notebooks* 77). In its largest reverberations, this dilemma conjoins the alternative models of romantic self-fashioning so resonantly evoked by Keats: the egotistical sublime is set against negative capability. But these possibilities are complexly and urgently interrelated in the anxious social strategies of mid-Victorian masculinities. Kingsley's "strange idea" of becoming "an Apollo for His sake" (*Life and Works* 1:87–88) sums up the paradoxes of a discourse of masculinity under which the rejuvenated chivalry of Carlylean earnestness joins hands with a prototype of emergent homosexual identity in the "New Chivalry" of the 1890s.

EXCAVATING WINCKELMANN

Pater's earliest surviving essay, "Diaphaneitè" (1864, but first published in *Miscellaneous Studies*), initiates his lifelong appeal to models of masculine identity derived from ancient Greece. But it does so within a complex (and largely neglected) engagement with the example of Carlylean heroism. In "Diaphaneitè," Pater sketches a "character" that is "like a relic from the classical age, laid open by accident to our alien modern atmosphere" (251). The diaphanous character is "classical" in its consummate harmony and integrity, but Pater's understanding of the ancient world is obviously refracted through Carlyle's insistence that self-consciousness is a mark of disease—a diagnosis to which Pater alludes in his opening paragraph: "As if dimly conscious of some great sickness and weariness of heart in itself, it [the world] turns readily to those who theorise about its unsoundness" (247). Inasmuch as the serene autonomy of the diaphanous character rebukes both that "unsoundness" and those who theorise about it, Pater's ideal reproduces the impact of the Carlylean hero. Indeed, Pater insists that the integrity of such characters renders them "revolutionist," and as such their very existence incites violent hostility. "Poetry and poetical history have dreamed of a crisis," he writes, "where it must needs be that some human victim be sent down into the grave. These [those who possess the diaphanous "character"] are they whom in its profound emotion humanity might choose to send" (253). As throughout his writing, most notably the late *Imaginary Portraits*, Pater associates cultural renewal with the violent sacrifice of the agents of change. Here he seems to imagine a Dionysian ritual sacrifice shading into a Christ-like atonement reminiscent of Carton's fate in *A Tale of Two Cities*. And indeed, Pater calls on a revealing "poetical history" to illustrate the sacrifice he envisions:

"What," says Carlyle, of Charlotte Corday, "What if she had emerged
from her secluded stillness, suddenly like a star; cruel-lovely, with half-
angelic, half-daemonic splendor; to gleam for a moment, and in a moment be extinguished; to be held in memory, so bright complete was she,
through long centuries!" (253)

Writing from the secluded stillness of Brasenose College, the young
Oxford don looks to Carlyle's *French Revolution* for a model of his vocation. But he finds that model not in Mirabeau, nor in what he calls
the "dim Blackguardism" of Carlyle's Danton, but in Charlotte Corday.[4] At the very outset of his career, Pater envisions an ideal critical
sensibility as a spectacle, and conceives of its triumph in a manner
uncannily like that of Sydney Carton.

But Pater also elicits more openly the stresses of gender informing
Carlyle's and Dickens's representations of heroism as the self-conscious
object of a public gaze. In "Diaphaneitè," as Carolyn Williams has
pointed out, Pater evokes a "paradoxical union of sheer passivity with
'unconscious' activity" (179). But the same conjunction is central to
the Victorian ideal of domestic womanhood, as well as to the paradox
of Carlylean heroism—recalling not only Sydney Carton on the scaffold
but the representation of Carlyle in Madox Brown's *Work* as one of
those who, "seeming to be idle, work, and are the cause of well-
ordained work and happiness in others." Whereas Carlyle recoils from
this conflation of feminine "influence" and masculine heroism, Pater
concertedly blurs the boundary between them. He boldly appropriates
for his enterprise a powerful emblem of gender disturbance: a woman
of decisive and murderous action, whose crowning achievement was to
become an unfathomable star-like spectacle of heroic self-sacrifice,
cruel-lovely, half-angelic, half-demonic. The title and governing trope
of "Diaphaneitè" reinforce this identification. "Diaphaneite" may at
first suggest an ideal of transparency, an effort to dispel the secrecy
that so fascinates Dickens. In this light, Pater seems to be extending
Carlyle's celebration of sincerity as the first attribute of the hero. "The
artist and he who has treated life in the spirit of art," Pater writes,

---

4. As Donald Hill kindly confirmed for me, "dim Blackguardism" is one of Pater's cre-
ative misquotations; although the phrase "dingy blackguardism" appears in part 1,
book 4, chapter 4 ("The Procession"), in the paragraph in which Danton is first
mentioned, it refers to Camille Desmoulins. Pater's phrase profoundly distorts Carlyle's
generally admiring view of the "huge, brawny Figure" of Danton (*French Revolution* 1:
143), but thereby suggests the vigor of Pater's effort to distance himself from Carlylean
heroism.

"desires only to be shown to the world as he really is; as he comes nearer and nearer to perfection, the veil of an outer life not simply expressive of the inward becomes thinner and thinner" (249). But Pater here concedes much greater authority to the audience than Carlyle does; the leading "desire" is not so much fidelity to an inner self as it is the presentation of that self to "the world." Furthermore, although the "veil or mask" that divides inner and outer life might disappear at some utopian vanishing point, that veil also defines the very interiority that is the basis of Pater's self-construction as a critic. In a world without masks, there would be no "inward" life at all; nothing would be held in reserve, because there would be nothing to withhold. In practice, whatever transparency Pater imagines for his critical persona tends to be that of what he calls "receptivity," which denotes the transparency of a one-way mirror, allowing "the transmission from without of light that is not yet inward" (251).

Pater in his earliest surviving essay thus associates his critical enterprise with icons of gender transgression; more precisely, he emphasizes the construction of a critical subjectivity as a masculine appropriation of traditionally feminine attributes. And that strategy is central to "Winckelmann" (1867), the earliest of the essays that would form *The Renaissance*, in which the concerns sketched in "Diaphaneitè" are developed into what has been called "the first rallying cry . . . of the new aesthetic hellenism" (Jenkyns, *Victorians* 222), as well as one of the central documents in an emergent ethos of male-male desire. In "Winckelmann," Pater discovers in Greek sculpture an image of man "at unity with himself, with his physical nature, with the outward world," because he had not yet begun to pursue "a perfection that makes the blood turbid, and frets the flesh, and discredits the actual world about us" (*Renaissance* 177). "The Hellenic ideal," as Pater calls it, is closely akin to Kingsleyan "health": both writers celebrate the vitality of an "unperplexed" mind, which has not been baffled and enervated by the quest for an ascetic "perfection" that would denigrate the body. This parallel reflects the pervasive influence of German Hellenism in Victorian thought: both Pater and Kingsley are heirs to Winckelmann's insistence that the Greeks had united physical and intellectual perfection. But Pater is the more canny and self-conscious participant in this tradition. He situates his account of Greek sculpture within an intellectual history that offers a genealogy of Kingsleyan (and Carlylean) "health": Pater historicizes the German romanticism that Carlyle so influentially popularized in England, by going back to the wellsprings of the tradition—through Hegel and Goethe to Winckel-

mann, and thence to "the Hellenic ideal" in its earliest incarnations
in Greek sculpture. Pater thereby presents his own critical program as
a discourse of the body that exemplifies and extends what he calls "the
Hellenic tradition."

Pater evokes that tradition through a complex figurative strategy,
which sustains a virtuoso meditation on a single trope in "Diaphaneitè"
(1864): the diaphanous temperament as "like a relic from the classical
age, laid open by accident to our alien modern atmosphere" (251).
Whereas "relic" might suggest merely "survival," "laid open by accident" turns the relic into something more palpable, a buried physical
artifact unexpectedly exposed to view. This suggestion reinforces the
visual register in the title, "Diaphaneitè": the character Pater wishes to
evoke is not merely a psychological and critical triumph, but an embodied, aesthetic harmony. In "Winckelmann" this fusion of disparate
categories becomes the distinctive feature of "the Greek ideal." Following Hegel's *Aesthetik*, Pater urges that the Greek mind was uniquely
able to think concretely; hence Greek thought could be represented
transparently, and without residue, in Greek sculpture. The leading
attributes of that sculpture, *Allgemeinheit* and *Heiterkeit*, breadth and serenity (Pater borrows the terms from Hegel), equally describe the
Greek mind: they are at once psychological and formal qualities. Consciousness itself is thus rendered an aesthetic achievement; the Greeks
both define and solve "the eternal problem of culture" as "balance,
unity with one's self, consummate Greek modelling" (182)—phrasing
that further fuses moral, psychological, and physical attributes. The
body as represented by the Greek sculptor is not only a triumph of
sensuous form, but a consummate moral and psychological achievement. This is the triumph that Pater wishes to reclaim for, and in the
person of, the modern critic. "Diaphaneitè" evokes an embodied critical "character"; in "Winckelmann," Pater transfers this achievement
to the German critic, not only by analogy, but by direct (though unacknowledged) quotation from the earlier essay. It is now Winckelmann's "nature" that is "like a relic of classical antiquity, laid open by
accident to our alien, modern atmosphere" (175). Once again, "relic"
denotes not merely a survival, as in most accounts of Winckelmann's
"pagan" temperament, but a concrete artifact—an ambiguity that is
faithful to an ideal under which temperament is always incarnated as
physical form, "consummate Greek modelling."[5] In this light, however,

---

5. The identification is underscored by a further self-quotation: the "colourless, unclas-
    sified purity of life" that Pater had attributed to the diaphanous character reappears

Winckelmann's appearance as "a relic of classical antiquity" associates the critic's life with previous discoveries of the physical relics of Greek art, events that confirm and extend the authority of "the Hellenic tradition." Singular as it might seem, Winckelmann's anachronistic paganism is no more (and no less) wonderful than the fortuitous recoveries of other Greek "relics" throughout Western history. Hence his influence on the young Goethe: in Winckelmann (according to Pater), the challenge of culture is incarnated "as in a fragment of Greek art itself, stranded on that littered, indeterminate shore of Germany in the eighteenth century" (182). Like those relics, Winckelmann is not merely an intellect, but an embodied spirit, a being who uncannily resembles those bodies in Greek sculpture that triumphantly incarnate mind in material form.

Appropriating the critical commonplace (popularized by Goethe) that Winckelmann was an instinctive, anachronistic pagan, Pater recasts that identity as a tradition in which his own reception of Winckelmann participates. As Pater's response to Winckelmann (and thence to other "relics" of classical antiquity) echoes Winckelmann's response to earlier "buried relics," so Pater's essay takes its place in a series of critical encounters that constitute the authority of the Greek ideal as a tradition renewed and extended with each rediscovery of a "relic" of Greek culture. Winckelmann's response to Greek sculpture "reproduces for us the earlier sentiment of the Renaissance," that liberation of the senses and the understanding "when, in the midst of a frozen world, the buried fire of ancient art rose up from under the soil" (146). That response is echoed in turn in Winckelmann's influence on the young Goethe, for whom "he defines, in clearest outline, the eternal problem of culture—balance, unity with oneself, consummate Greek modelling." (The ambiguity of "he" again underscores an ideal fusion of mind and form: the pronoun most immediately refers to Winckelmann, but it equally applies to any male form in classical sculpture.) And so in turn this "type" of culture comes to Pater himself through the conjoint influence of Winckelmann and Goethe; his response is further testimony to "the authority of the Hellenic tradition, its fitness to satisfy some vital requirement of the intellect" (158).

By appealing to tradition as the basis for his critical authority, Pater is in effect constructing his own version of the Tractarian apostolic succession. Like Newman, that is, he envisions intellectual authority as

---

in "Winckelmann" as an attribute of the Panathenaic frieze in the Elgin marbles (167).

a homosocial continuum across history, in which past and present are linked by a masculine relay of charismatic power, power that is communicated through a palpable "contact" with its embodiments—whether those be apostles of Christ or relics of Greek sculpture. Having divined "some unexpressed pulsation of sensuous life" in Greek poetry, Winckelmann "suddenly . . . is in contact with that life, still fervent in the relics of plastic art" (146). To be sure, the trope of "an underground life" seems to owe more to the romantic vulcanism of Byron (an influence likewise registered in Matthew Arnold's "buried life") than to Newman. Yet Carlyle's *Past and Present* offers a vivid precedent for configuring an apostolic succession in just this way. In describing Abbot Samson's ceremonial exhumation of the body of Saint Edmund, Carlyle not only narrates but reenacts a laying on of hands that, in perpetuating the influence of the saint's holiness, links audiences across the centuries (J. Rosenberg 124). Samson's touching of Edward's relics is transmitted through the recently unearthed works of Jocelyn the scribe, whose power to communicate across the ages is a recurrent motif in "The Ancient Monk"; as Carlyle bears witness to the power of Jocelyn's record, so he communicates it in turn to his own (unknown) audience, on whom he seeks to work a similar influence: "Stupid blockheads, to reverence their St. Edmund's dead Body in this manner? Yes, brother;—and yet, on the whole, who knows how to reverence the Body of a Man? It is the most reverend phenomenon under this Sun". (*Past and Present* 122). The passage evidently had the desired influence on Pater: at the very end of his career, in *Plato and Platonism*, he borrows Carlyle's words to evoke the enduring power of Plato's writing. It is a measure of Plato's artistry, Pater argues, that his account of the torchlight procession at the opening of *The Republic* can evoke such a vivid image across more than two millennia: "that old midnight hour, as Carlyle says of another vivid scene, 'shining yet on us, ruddy-bright through the centuries'" (*Plato and Platonism* 128). The other "vivid scene" is that of Edmund's exhumation: "that old midnight-hour, shining yet on us, ruddy-bright, through the depths of seven hundred years" (Carlyle, *Past and Present* 122). A quarter century after "Diaphaneitè," it is Carlyle who still exemplifies for Pater what it is to be "held in memory . . . through long centuries."

Pater attempts to formalize this memorializing power in his account of the Hellenic tradition, which like Newman's apostolic succession represents intellectual authority as an elite possession defined in opposition to the claims of "abstract theory." Winckelmann's Hellenism, Pater argues, is epitomized in an intuitive, aesthetic "tact," a "native tendency . . . to escape from abstract theory to intuition, to the exercise of sight and touch" (147); he grasps Hellenic art "not through the understanding, but by instinct or touch" (176). "Philosophy can give us theoretical reasons why not poetry but sculpture should be the most sincere expression of the Greek ideal. By a happy, unperplexed dexterity, Winckelmann solves the question in the concrete" (147). As John Stuart Mill objected, such appeals to intuition or instinct are inherently conservative inasmuch as they disallow countervailing appeals to theory or logical argument. They thereby reinforce the appeal to tradition, which likewise instantiates hegemonic authority in aesthetic form, as "a kind of lawfulness without law" (Eagleton 58). For both Pater and Newman, the melding of intuition and tradition solidifies the social integrity and authority of an elite society, annexing historical continuity to extend the sway of a contemporary brotherhood. Whatever the subversive dynamics of Pater's aestheticism, there is a powerfully conservative, antihistorical bias in his appeal to the Hellenic tradition, which not only insists on Hellenism as "the standard of taste . . . fixed in Greece, at a definite historical period" (159), but anchors its operation in the aristocratic virtue of intuitive "tact."

But such constructions of tradition may also be turned toward the future and enlisted as what Carolyn Williams has called a "prophetic conservatism" (183). In excavating Winckelmann, Pater literalizes the Shelleyan trope with which Carlyle heralds the authority of the contemporary man of letters: he "[rules] . . . from his grave after death, whole nations and generations. . . . What he teaches, the whole world will do and make" (*Heroes* 383–84). We have already glimpsed a very similar tribute to heroic authority in Dickens's *Tale of Two Cities*, which seems to have powerfully affected Pater—not least in mediating Carlyle's construction of revolutionary heroism.[6] Throughout his early writings, Pater urges a form of revolution by tradition: authority is figured as a return to origins, the recovery of a lost or forgotten past. Thus in both "Diaphaneitè" and "Winckelmann," critical authority is manifested as a Platonic *anamnesis*, in words Pater adapts from the *Phaedrus*: "the reminiscence of a forgotten culture that once adorned the mind; as if the mind of one [lover and philosopher at once], fallen into a new

---

6. Memories of *A Tale of Two Cities* may well have shaped the narrative structure of *Marius*, which concludes with the hero taking the place of another man (his friend and triumphant rival for the hand of the widow, Cecilia) facing martyrdom for his Christian faith. In this light, the novel's closing meditation on the ironies of Marius's "martyrdom"—for a faith in which he does not believe, and through death by fever rather than execution—offer a mordant commentary on Dickensian heroism.

cycle, were beginning its progress over again, but with a certain power
of anticipating its stages" (*Miscellaneous Studies* 250).[7] "The Hellenic
tradition" in this sense survives as both a historical continuum and a
collective unconscious, which is remembered—recalled and reembod-
ied—in the lives of its "enthusiasts." The "revolutionism" of the diaphanous character, Pater explains, is that of one "who has slept a
hundred years" and has inexplicably reawakened, to bring the past into
startlingly direct, even coercive, influence over the present (250). The
parallels with Dickens's Dr. Manette, similarly buried by repressive authority and "recalled to life" with shattering effects, are irresistible. In
his early writings, Pater likewise imagines himself as one liberated from
a kind of living death. "On a sudden the imagination feels itself free";
this is how "Winckelmann" sums up the Renaissance encounter with
relics of Greek art (147). But Pater's criticism is also in an important
sense the work of a Dickensian "resurrection-man." In promulgating
the Greek ideal, the Hellenic enthusiast liberates others by liberating
himself; in this regard, "Winckelmann" reinforces the parallel between
the diaphanous character and Sydney Carton. In "Winckelmann," Pater formalizes a structure of secular redemption: in excavating Winckelmann, and insisting that he, like other relics of the Greek ideal, is
"still red with life in the grave," Pater at once remembers and reenacts
Winckelmann's career, commemorating both Winckelmann and the
larger tradition in which he participates. Pater thereby accords to
Winckelmann something very close to the ritualized commemoration
for which Carton longs at the close of *A Tale of Two Cities*.

But of course Pater also thereby envisions for himself, as well as for
Winckelmann, an enduring posterity, and a form of surrogate paternity.
In presenting himself as an agent of "the Hellenic tradition," he not
only claims for his criticism a potent intellectual authority, but imagines
for himself a secular afterlife such as Carton envisions in the ritual
commemorations of his heroism by the descendants of Lucie Darnay.
Such imagined redemption is evidently responsive in part to the di-
minishment of traditional Christian faith. Carton exemplifies the pursuit of a "subjective immortality," in Comte's phrase, that would
replace the lost consolation of the Christian afterlife. In this light, one
might compare Pater's praise of Winckelmann, or Carton's vision of

7. Pater's rephrasing of the passage in "Winckelmann" provides the bracketed phrase,
a translation of the Greek *philosophēsas pote met' erōtos*, which stands alone in "Diaphaneite." Dowling follows William Shuter in suggesting that Pater coins the phrase "lover
and philosopher at once" in place of the "unspeakably explicit" phrasing of *Phaedrus*
249a, which uses the term *paiderastēs* (*Hellenism and Homosexuality* 94).

his own commemoration by subsequent generations, to the elaborate festivals of remembrance that Comte stipulated for his "religion of humanity."[8] But both Dickens's novel and Pater's criticism locate in such structures of commemoration a patriarchal authority separate not only from Christianity but from marriage and paternity. Indeed, Pater consistently substitutes for the traditional consolations of the marriage plot—fictional and otherwise—the satisfactions of an imagined homosocial tradition. Marius is an exemplary Paterian hero as the last of a family line, whose lack of kinship directs attention to an alternative filiation: he bequeathes to an imagined posterity not a dynastic but a cultural legacy, the "inheritance" of tradition, which has been augmented by his own small but exemplary contribution.[9]

As it serves to authorize both individual and collective masculine identity, Pater's construction of "the Hellenic tradition" strikingly resembles the invention of tradition associated with the Victorian cult of the public school, which also celebrated a homosocial order affirmed through various cultic signs, such as the school tie and blazer. These secular rituals were central to a widespread, and ultimately successful, effort to reshape masculine social authority by reconfiguring the traditional ideal of the gentleman, which was turned into a badge of distinction accorded to anyone who displayed the marks of a public-school education. But conservative critics protested this compromise as a mechanical notion of "gentlemen to standard," to which they opposed a renewed ideal of the born gentleman (Castronovo 62). Ruskin in particular boldly referred the gentleman's prerogatives to an innate, organic sensibility. In volume 5 of *Modern Painters* (1860), in the chapter titled, "Of Vulgarity," he declared, "A gentleman's first characteristic is that fineness of structure in the body, which renders it capable of the most delicate sensation; and of structure in the mind which renders it capable of the most delicate sympathies—one may say, simply, 'fineness of nature' " (7:345). The gentleman, in short, is "well bred, in the sense that a horse or dog is well bred" (7:343). In founding the gentleman's status on an innate sensibility akin to that of the Shelleyan poet, Ruskin offers a strikingly exact precedent for Pater's celebration of a "tact" rooted in the body itself. Indeed, Pater may well have taken

8. As Gerald Monsman points out, a verbal account of the Old Mortality society at Oxford, for which Pater wrote "Diaphaneitè," refers to a still earlier presentation to the society in which Pater addressed "subjective immortality" ("Old Mortality").

9. Gilbert's account of *A Tale of Two Cities* analyzes the trope of resurrection as a form of resistance to genealogy and history (259). Gent offers an overview of the trope as a widespread Victorian tribute to the artist's power of creation.

the term from Ruskin, who in *Sesame and Lilies* (1865) invokes it as the
quality that crucially distinguishes the gentlemanly from its antithesis,
vulgarity: "the essence of all vulgarity lies in want of sensation. . . . of
all that, in deep insistence on the common, but most accurate term,
may be called the 'tact' or touch-faculty of body and soul"—a faculty
Ruskin sees most powerfully embodied in the "pure woman" (18:80).[10]
For Ruskin as for Pater, an exquisitely embodied sensibility affirms the
authority of sensation and feeling against the tyranny of "the diseased
habit . . . the hardened conscience," as Ruskin puts it; the body thereby
becomes a basis for membership in a male elite not defined by formal
social ties. Ruskin's account of the gentleman, moreover, captures the
important social utility of such an appeal. By defining the gentleman
in terms of bodily instinct, the ideal can be insulated from the anxious
self-fashioning, and thus the disabling self-consciousness, that Carlyle
embodies in the figure of the dandy.

Ruskin's account of the gentleman is unusually shrewd in recognizing and resisting appropriations of the norm in the service of social
mobility. Samuel Smiles, for example, whose enormously popular hand-
books of masculine self-fashioning grew out of a series of lectures to
working men in Leeds, emphasized the importance of "strict self-
control" in the formation of the gentleman (Travers 184, 112). Ruskin,
who was completing *Modern Painters* when Smiles's *Self-Help* was published in 1859, objected that "self-command . . . is rather a way of im-
itating a gentleman than a characteristic of him; a true gentleman has
no need of self-control; he simply feels rightly on all occasions. . . . [I]t
is to be noted that great powers of self-restraint may be attained by very
vulgar persons when it suits their purposes" (7:349). Ruskin's logic
resembles that informing Kingsley's more anxious celebrations of the
gentleman, in which worries over social climbers are subsumed in a
more inchoate repudiation of self-consciousness. Kingsley's muscular
Christianity represents (among other things) an effort to cut the Gor-
dian knot of self-consciousness by celebrating a willed truncation of
reflection, which tends to glorify impulsive action. In *Westward Ho!*, for
example, Kingsley stresses the scheming and tortured apologetics of
the Jesuits in order to celebrate by contrast Amyas Leigh's vigorous
habit of "just doing the right thing without thinking about it" (*Life
and Works* 5:65). The conservative social logic of this imperative

10. Joseph Bizup explores the Ruskinian gentleman as an important model in Pater's
Marius, where characters are emphatically distinguished by their relative capacity for
sensory and emotional, and hence moral, "receptivity."

emerges most clearly in *Alton Locke*, where Kingsley's hero insists that the working man who wishes to move up in rank can only become "a sham gentleman" (7:162). "Be natural, and you will be gentleman-like"—which is apparently the best he can hope for (8:5).

Such bluster may seem remote from Pater's rhetoric. But "Winck-elmann" also develops what Mill called Carlyle's "anti-self-conscious-ness" stance—a stance that Pater engages, characteristically, by historicizing it. In "Winckelmann" Pater tends to present the Greek ideal as the product of a willed truncation of self-consciousness: Greek thought "had advanced to a particular stage of self-reflexion, but was careful not to pass beyond it" (164). This "delicate pause" is in turn recapitulated in the "happy instinct" by which Winckelmann compre-hended Greek sculpture, and which seems to be reenacted with each recovery of the "relics" of Greek thought. At the same time, however, "Winckelmann" offers a second, broadly Hegelian scheme of history, under which the development of art marks an intensification of, rather than an escape from, self-consciousness. Because these competing his-tories are offered as forms of *Universalgeschichte*—a world history pat-terned on the model of an individual life—their interplay captures tensions that centrally structure Paterean self-fashioning. And those tensions are precisely congruent with the conflict articulated in the more mundane debate over the nature of the gentleman, and of ascetic discipline generally. Can Winckelmann's recovery of Greek culture be emulated through concerted intellectual discipline, or is it available only as the "happy gift of nature" of "Diaphaneitè" (149)?

One strand of Pater's argument evokes Winckelmann's conception of ancient Greece only to reject it, in accordance with a broadly He-gelian logic, as an intellectual state from which we are irrevocably es-tranged. Greek sculpture in this light endures as an emblem of our distance from Greece, not as an ideal for the present. The conclusion of "Winckelmann" in particular outwardly endorses a familiar roman-tic teleology: Winckelmann is a splendid anachronism, but the modern mind cannot entrust its intellectual deliverance to the fortuitous erup-tion of buried fire or "happy instinct." Only as the Greek ideal is avail-able in a conscious intellectual tradition can it assist the eminently "perplexed" modern mind in its effort to solve "the eternal problem of culture." It is in this regard that Winckelmann is "infinitely less" than Goethe, "and it is chiefly because at certain points he comes in contact with Goethe, that criticism entertains consideration of him" (181). For it is Goethe, above all, who confirms a redemptive teleology in the history of art, in which the disruption of the Greek mind's

"happy limit" of consciousness becomes a fortunate fall. "It was necessary that a conflict should come, that some sharper note should
grieve the existing harmony, and the spirit chafed by it beat out at last
only a larger and profounder music" (178). In Goethe's art, this more
profound music is realized as a fusion of Greek "blitheness and repose" with the deeper "inwardness" that is the legacy of the middle
ages: "a union of the romantic spirit, in its adventure, its variety, its
profound subjectivity of soul, with Hellenism, in its transparency, its
rationality, its desire of beauty—that marriage of Faust and Helena, of
which the art of the nineteenth century is the child" (181). This is a
familiar narrative; in M. H. Abrams's influential account in *Natural Supernaturalism*, it is the definitive romantic scheme of history. Yet Pater's
imagery of the Greek ideal's recrudescence tells a very different story.
Figures of that recovery as the eruption of buried fire, or the exhumation of a body "red with life in the grave," represent the medieval
world as a bleak suspension of intellectual vitality, a dark, frozen night
of the mind that is abruptly dispelled by the encounter with Greek
relics. Indeed, when Pater describes the Greek ideal, he similarly departs from Hegel's account of the mind's inexorable growth towards
self-awareness: "The Greek mind had advanced to a particular stage of
self-reflexion, but was careful not to pass beyond it" (164). With "was
careful," Pater unexpectedly attributes to the Greek mind a willed curtailment of self-consciousness, as if it had presciently glimpsed its de-
mise in a future state of development and prudently arrested its
advance at a "happy limit."

This inconsistency is echoed in Pater's confused account of the relation between Christian spirituality and art. Throughout the essay Pater insists on the antagonism between Christianity's "uncompromising
idealism" and "the artistic life, with its inevitable sensuousness": "It is
hard to pursue that life without something of a conscious disavaowal
of a spiritual world" (177, 264).[11] Just three pages later, however, he
strikingly reverses himself: "Pagan and Christian art are sometimes
harshly opposed, and the Renaissance is represented as a fashion which
set in at a definite period. That is the superficial view: the deeper view
is that which preserves the identity of European culture. The two are
really continuous; and there is a sense in which it may be said that the
Renaissance was an uninterrupted effort of the middle age, that it was

---

11. This is the bold language of the 1873 text. In subsequent editions, Pater was more
    circumspect: "Christianity" became "Christian asceticism," and "It is hard to pur-
    sue" was changed to "It has sometimes seemed hard to pursue" (177).

ever taking place" (180). The notion of the Renaissance continuously unfolding during the Middle Ages is sharply at odds with earlier images of the medieval world as a long night of the mind. But Pater needs to affirm "the identity of European culture" if that culture is to be available to the modern observer. This follows from the structure of Pater's *Universalgeschichte:* if "European culture" lacks a coherent identity—if, that is, its history is one of intractable self-division rather than dialectical progression—that incoherence will be mirrored in the individual mind. The belated modern observer will find it impossible to "solve" the eternal problem of culture, except by the fortuitous, anachronistic recovery of the Greek ideal exemplified by Winckelmann. Yet even as Pater affirms the identity of European culture, his explanation belies his claim: "the sense in which it may be said" that the middle ages and the Renaissance were continuous turns out to be, once again, the continuity of night and day. "The medieval spirit too had done something for the new fortunes of the antique. By hastening the decline of art, by withdrawing interest from it and yet keeping unbroken the thread of its traditions, it had suffered the human mind to repose itself, that when day came it might awake, with eyes refreshed, to those ancient, ideal forms" (181).

Pater's conflicting schemes of history in "Winckelmann" reflect a shaping ambivalence in his writings—one that confirms unexpected affinities with Kingsley by calling attention to their shared legacy of Carlylean romanticism. The tradition Pater constructs in "Winckelmann" seems to exclude Carlyle, but that patriarch is ever present as the mediator of Goethe's example—a mediation tellingly signaled when Pater perpetuates Carlyle's influential misquotation of Goethe's account of culture, "*Im Ganzen, Guten, Wahren resolut zu leben*" (182).[12] In this context, Pater's evocation of the tormented "inwardness" of medieval art eroticizes Carlyle's analogous insistence on the burdens of self-consciousness. Moreover, the Paterian observer follows a Carlylean prescription inasmuch as he struggles through the cultivation of self-consciousness to escape from the burdens of self-consciousness.[13] Pater's celebration of the "unperplexed" Hellenic ideal thus shares with Kingsleyan "health" not only similar aspirations but the crucial

12. As Donald Hill points out in his invaluable edition, Goethe's words are "*Im Ganzen, Guten, Schönen / Resolut zu leben*" ("Generalbeichte"); Pater follows Carlyle's immensely telling substitution, in both "Schiller" and "Death of Goethe," of "Wahren" for "Schönen" (Pater, *Renaissance* 439–40).

13. Hartman, "Romanticism and Anti-Self-Consciousness," offers a helpful overview of this structure in Romantic literature.

model of Carlylean "health." To be sure, as we will see in the next chapter, Pater far more than Kingsley dramatizes the fascination of Carlyle's "abyss" of self-scrutiny as at once exhilarating and treacherous. That appeal is anatomized in the incessant dualisms of his writings—pagan and medieval, classical and romantic, Dorian and Ionian, centrifugal and centripetal—and embodied in his various *Imaginary Portraits*, the protagonists of which are typically torn by the claims of "rival religions," as the conflict is phrased in *Marius the Epicurean*. Yet Pater's idiosyncratic appropriation of Hegel invariably collapses the dialectical structure of Hegelian history. For Pater, the objective embodiment that constrains Hegel's *Geist* remains, emphatically, the spirit's supreme need.

This conclusion underscores Pater's enduring affinities with Winckelmann. Although he relies on the descriptive categories of Hegel's history of art, Pater ultimately repudiates those "theoretical reasons" that Winckelmann likewise disdains. He will not accept the crucial axiom that consciousness possesses a transcendent dimension that finds its ultimate realization in a realm independent of the finite, material present. Unlike Hegel, that is, Pater follows Carlyle in yearning to recapture some equivalent of that "happy limit" to self-consciousness embodied in Greek sculpture—even as he savors the turbulent, brooding "inwardness" of romantic art.[14] Even the "Conclusion" to *The Renaissance* can be usefully read as the mapping of a Carlylean strategy, which seeks to recover some latter-day equivalent of the "happy limit" of Greek thought. In the "Conclusion," Pater deploys a mastery of "modern thought" in order to destroy the authority of that thought, to insist on the emptiness of "theories" as anything more than stimuli to an ideal of "success in life" which leaves them behind. As it dismisses the economic reverberations of "success," moreover, Pater's exhortation is faithful to Carlyle in offering labor as its own reward. For Paterian observation is indeed a labor. "To burn always with a hard gem-like flame," as Pater famously defines "success in life," is the goal of a remarkably strenuous hedonism; it in fact gestures towards a pagan asceticism that owes as much to Carlyle's (comparatively) Christian discipline as it does to the "modern thought" of contemporary science (188–89). See, for the night cometh, wherein no man may see—thus Pater's "Conclusion" in effect rewrites the injunction of John 9:4,

---

14. DeLaura, *Hebrew and Hellene* (202–22), carefully analyzes the tensions in Pater's argument in "Winckelmann," although I think he gives too much weight to the influence of Arnold.

which animated so much of Carlyle's social gospel and thereby became perhaps the fundamental imperative of high Victorian earnestness.[15] Even in this most notorious of Paterian manifestos, then, both the rhetoric and psychological economy of Pater's aestheticism develops the structures of Carlylean earnestness, a genealogy it shares with Kingsley's muscular Christianity. From the very outset of his career, Pater like Kingsley follows Carlyle's lead in resisting abstract and metaphysical questions as, at best, "unprofitable" to an ideal of "success in life" organized around a discipline of the body.

PLATONIC ENTHUSIASM

From the very outset of his career, then, Pater's aestheticism draws on well-established models of masculine authority that had wide currency in contemporary social and cultural commentary. Yet at the same time Pater daringly exposes the compatibility of those models with powerfully transgressive organizations of intellectual and emotional life. In calling attention to the centrality of the male body in "the Hellenic tradition," Pater not only associates aesthetic understanding with a homoerotic "temperament," but—as Linda Dowling has emphasized—still more boldly reminds his readers that a pederastic eros had shaped their very notion of "culture." Winckelmann's "romantic, fervent friendships with young men," Pater urges, are evidence "that his affinity with Hellenism was not merely intellectual, that the subtler threads of temperament were inwoven in it" (*Renaissance* 152). Indeed, such friendships were essential to his achievement: by "bringing him into contact with the pride of human form, and staining his thoughts with its bloom," they "perfected his reconciliation to the spirit of Greek sculpture" (152). Winckelmann's reliance on sensuous "dexterity" consistently recalls Ruskin's appeal to the root sense of "tact" as a sexually charged touch, through which the German critic "fingers those pagan marbles with unsinged hands, with no sense of shame or loss" (177). Winckelmann's erotic sensibility thus becomes integral to the Hellenic tradition. As the male body becomes at once an aesthetic spectacle, an object of desire, and a medium of understanding, Pater appropriates Plato to authorize Winckelmann's "enthusiasm"—enthu-

---

15. Pater's debt to Carlyle, though frequently noted in passing, has not been studied at length, although Dellamora (62–67) offers a suggestive account of "Diaphaneitè" that stresses Pater's revision of Carlylean masculine anxiety.

siasm "in the broad Platonic sense of the *Phaedrus*" (152). If "broad
Platonic sense" hints at obfuscation, Pater's classically trained readers
would have recognized in "enthusiasm" not merely a state of mind but
a central dynamic of the pederastic relationship (Dowling, *Hellenism and
Homosexuality* 96). And this erotic association likewise charges Pater's
claims that Winckelmann's Greek "temperament" radiates from his
entire being: "The quick, susceptible enthusiast, betraying his temperament even in appearance, by his olive complexion, his deep-seated,
piercing eyes, his rapid movements, apprehended the subtlest principles of the Hellenic manner, not through the understanding, but by
instinct or touch" (154).

Pater thus constructs in "Winckelmann" not only a model of homoerotic desire, but a history that authorizes its pleasures. In Pater's
Universalgeschichte, the recovery of Greek relics comes to define a recurrent episode in the collective history of Europe, which is reenacted
in the experience of every Hellenic "enthusiast." "Renaissance" denotes not only a moment in European culture, but an archetypal psychological structure that organizes an elemental human desire:

> Filled as our culture is with the classical spirit, we can hardly imagine
> how deeply the human mind was moved, when, at the Renaissance, in
> the midst of a frozen world, the buried fire of ancient art rose up from
> under the soil. Winckelmann here reproduces for us the earlier senti-
> ment of the Renaissance. On a sudden the imagination feels itself free.
> How facile and direct, it seems to say, is this life of the senses and the
> understanding, when once we have apprehended it! Here, surely, is that
> more liberal mode of life we have been seeking for so long, so near to
> us all the while. How mistaken and round-about have been our efforts to
> reach it by mystic passion, and monastic reverie; how they have deflow-
> ered the flesh; how little have they really emancipated us! Hermione
> melts from her stony posture, and the lost proportions of life right them-
> selves. (146–47)

It may be hard to imagine "how deeply the human mind was moved"
by the unearthing of Greek relics at the Renaissance, but it is not hard
to guess the depths of Pater's own response, which transforms those
relics into a volcanic fire unrestrained by human intervention.[16] Suddenly "the imagination feels itself free." The words are charged with

---

16. The power Pater attaches to that transformation is richly underscored by its association with the concluding act of *The Winter's Tale*, which is where "Hermione melts
from her posture."

both exhilaration and pathos, particularly in light of what Billie Andrew Inman has recently discovered about a suppressed sexual scandal that nearly destroyed Pater's career at Oxford in the 1870s ("Estrangement"). Here, a decade earlier, Pater daringly insinuates the subversive power of an erotic liberation in likening the recovery of buried Greek relics to the opening of "an ancient plague-pit" from which "all the world took the contagion of the life of nature and of the senses" (180). And that exhilaration resonates throughout Pater's characterization of the Hellenic tradition as "an absorbed, underground life" throughout Western culture—a life that, alone among the other intellectual forces within that culture, "from time to time . . . has started to the surface" (158). The Hellenic tradition is "underground" in a literal sense, in buried, concrete artifacts, but also in the figurative sense of "neglected"; in a further, psychological sense, reminiscent of Arnold's "buried life," the trope identifies a yearning or drive latent or repressed within the mind. That connotation in turn takes on physiological overtones through the association of such "life" with a biological vitality: the relics of Greek art are "red with life in the grave," and at their unearthing communicate that vitality to the beholder as a veritable "contagion."

As Pater identifies his critical response with that of Winckelmann, then, he boldly affiliates himself with Winckelmann's anathematized "temperament," by means of which the Greek ideal is most fully and intimately understood. In this regard, "Winckelmann" is an extremely important document in late-Victorian constructions of a homosexual identity. But we cannot understand the significance of such constructions unless we recognize their manifold affinities to more orthodox structures of masculine identity. "Suddenly the imagination felt itself free" might equally be invoked, after all, to describe Alton Locke's encounter with the image of Saint Sebastian in the Dulwich Gallery— which reminds us that both Kingsley and Pater define their critical enterprises as a resistance to forms of Christian asceticism. In the process, moreover, both writers repeatedly attack the "mystic passion, and monastic reverie," in Pater's terms, that would discredit the sensual vitality of ancient Greece:

> The spiritualist is satisfied as he watches the escape of sensuous elements from his conceptions. . . . But the artist steeps his thought again and again into the fire of colour. To the Greek this immersion in the sensuous was indifferent. Greek sensuousness, therefore, does not fever the blood; it is shameless and childlike. But Christianity, with its uncompromising ide-

alism, discrediting the slightest touch of sense, has lighted up for the artistic life, with its inevitable sensuousness, a background of flame:—*I did but taste a little honey from the end of the rod that was in mine hand, and lo! I must die.* (177; 264 [1873 text])

Daring as such antagonism to Christianity might seem, if one recasts "Christianity" as "the Romish priests," the passage has many parallels in Kingsley's writings.[17] Kingsley's characters repeatedly seek precisely the sexual "serenity" that enables Wincklemann to handle pagan marbles "with unsinged hands." Still further, "Winckelmann" represents yet another Victorian effort to define a dissident masculinity in terms of an elite group identity, membership in a form of brotherhood, which is often difficult to distinguish from a secret society. When Pater refers to Winckelmann as an enthusiast "betraying his temperament even in appearance," he may seem to anticipate late-Victorian medical taxonomies of homosexuality as a mode of deviance whose sign is the very countenance of the deviant. But one might just as plausibly see this passage as the development of the more comprehensive and inchoate social semiotics that we have been tracing throughout this study, which seeks various equivalents of the "sign" by means of which Thomas Arnold longed to recognize kindred spirits. Winckelmann's appearance, that is, represents a mark of elite intellectual affiliation—and hence a claim to intellectual authority—much like that encrypted in the countenance of Ruskin's gentleman, or in the body of Kingsley's muscular Christian. In the Hellenic "enthusiast," the sign of intellectual distinction, which in Tractarian reserve had been a concerted social strategy, has been recast as a physiological inheritance.

In stressing these affiliations I do not wish to obscure the distinctiveness of Pater's self-presentation in "Winckelmann," nor—in particular—to minimize the daring it required to identify his desires with Winckelmann's. But in order to understand the coercive power of the norms within and against which Pater wrote, we need to recognize the extent to which they continue to shape our own categorizations of the period by effacing important continuities among disparate masculinities. Richard Jenkyns, for example, has discovered in Pater's evocations of Greece a "not altogether pleasing" image of the writer as "a middle-

17. Thus a letter of 1851, for example, offers a lengthy attack on the view Kingsley associated with "the Romish and neo-Platonist anthropology," that man is "but a spirit accidentally connected with, and burdened by an animal," and hence that "the ideal of man . . . is to deny, not himself, but the animal part which is not himself, and to strive after a non-human or angelic state" (*Life and Works* 2:267).

aged gentleman loitering wistfully at the edge of the playing fields"
(*Victorians* 225). Some might indeed elicit that impression from a reverie over the image of Socrates at Salamis, where, "then sixteen years
of age, the loveliest and most cultivated lad in Athens, undraped like
a faun, with lyre in hand, was leading the chorus of Athenian youths."
But these are not Pater's words, they are Kingsley's, from his late essay
"The Stage as It Was Once" (*Literacy and General Lectures* 26).[18] That
they might easily be confused should remind us that Kingsley, too, frequently engages in a virtually pagan exultation over the spectacle of
the virile body. The gentleman at the edge of the playing fields, after
all, was frequently a man who had been, and perhaps continued to be,
an immensely vigorous, "manly" participant in games. This is an obvious enough fact, but it continues to be effaced by the homophobic
oppositions that straightjacket the homosocial continuum, in Eve Kosofsky Sedgwick's helpful term.

John Addington Symonds, whose life was so complexly ordered and
tormented by such oppositions, also was able to capture with particular
suggestiveness the continuum that they disrupted. His 1893 essay on
Edward Cracroft Lefroy, a clergyman and author of a collection of
markedly homoerotic verse, *Echoes from Theocritus* (1885), calls attention
to the striking compatibility of "Muscular Christianity" with the Paterian ideal of "a rare and exquisite personality." Lefroy had attacked
both Pater and Symonds in print in 1877, when Lefroy was an undergraduate, and the two older men were campaigning for the Professor-
ship of Poetry at Oxford. But Symonds had come to recognize in Lefroy
"a fellow Arcadian" (Reade 30) and shaped his praise accordingly.
"Muscular Christianity," Lefroy argued, in a passage Symonds quotes,
"includes all that is brightest in Hellenism, and all that is purest in

18. Ironically, Jenkyns quotes J. A. Symonds's more drily expository account of the same
episode, in *Studies of the Greek Poets*, in order to elicit a specifically "homosexual"
preoccupation from the fact that Symonds "dwell[s] so much upon the poet's adolescence" (*Victorians* 217). Kingsley's tribute to faun-like male beauty might be more
profitably pondered in light of Linda Dowling's careful and incisive speculations
about the construction of a "homosexual" code of allusion among writers connected
with Oxford in the 1860s and 1870s, including Pater. The central term in that code,
Dowling suggests, is the Greek *poikilos*, "dappled" or "pied," which is the term ha-
bitually applied to the skin of a fawn, particularly as it is part of the regalia of Bacchus
("Ruskin's Pied Beauty" 5–6). Although it is doubtful that Kingsley consciously par-
ticipated in this network as Dowling sketches it, the conjunction reminds us of how
a shared classical education (in every sense of the term) gave middle-class men both
experience of and a ready language for vicarious homoerotic pleasures, however
consciously articulated.

Hebraism" (*Key of Blue* 94). But it was Lefroy himself who embodied these excellences, Symonds argued. Lefroy's "sympathy with youthful strength and beauty, his keen interest in boyish games and the athletic sports of young men . . . were connected in a remarkable way with Hellenic instincts and an almost pagan delight in nature" (89). "What I have called his spiritual apperception of sensuous beauty was the outcome of a rare and exquisite personality. It has the translucent quality of a gem, beryl or jacinth, which . . . retains one flawless colour. This sympathy and absolute sincerity of instinct is surely uncommon in our perplexed epoch" (109–10). That last tribute might have been lifted almost verbatim from "Winckelmann," which is built around the opposition of modern "perplexity" and the perfectly "unperplexed" instinct and sincerity of a pagan devotion to sensuous form. Yet in Symonds's account Lefroy's "pagan delight" flows directly from what Lefroy himself called "Muscular Christianity."[19]

Granted their manifold points of affinity, how have the writings of Pater and Kingsley lent themselves to such persistent and emphatic opposition? The most obvious feature is the relative openness with which Pater acknowledges the homoerotic pleasures afforded by the spectacle of the virile body. Pater, like Winckelmann, celebrates beauty and grace in the male body, whereas Kingsley typically reserves those attributes for the female. Thus Pater emphasizes the delicacy and grace of the male figures in the Panathenaic frieze, whereas Kingsley stresses their incarnation of physical power; Kingsley is careful to stress "the awful yet tender beauty of the maiden figures from the Parthenon and its kindred temples" (*Health and Education* 69–70), but Pater clearly shares Winckelmann's view that the supreme beauty of Greek art "is rather male than female," and as such can only be fully appreciated by those who share Winckelmann's "enthusiasm" (*Renaissance* 152). When Pater likens the recovery of Greek art to the opening of "an ancient plague-pit," he seems to cast a gibe not only at medieval Christianity, but at contemporary constructions of a moral hygiene that identified sexual discipline with effective sanitation, and hence might find the erotic freedom of Greek art "unhealthy" (Mort 19–64). Kingsley was one of the leading participants in such constructions—his invocations of Greek sculpture frequently appear in his writings on sanita-

19. The gem as an emblem of an exquisite sensibility figures prominently in commentary on the gentleman throughout the 1860s, which increasingly emphasizes the aesthetic appeal of the ideal: J. F. Stephen, writing in *Cornhill Magazine* in 1862, goes so far as to explicitly sever "the perfect gentleman" from any form of religious or moral value, arguing that his "dispositions" are valued solely for their beauty ("Gentlemen" 331).

tion—and he acknowledges such objections to Greek sculpture when he insists on its paradoxical conjunction of freedom and discipline: "a self-possession and self-restraint so habitual and complete that it had become unconscious, and undistinguishable from the native freedom of the savage" (*Health and Education* 69). Such a response, however, echoes Pater's in suggesting how powerful a vehicle of sublimation Greek sculpture was to the middle-class Victorian spectator. Both writers find in Greek sculpture the image of the body at once free and disciplined, naked and restrained. Where they differ is in Pater's more canny recognition of the erotics of such sublimation:

> It has been sometimes said that art is a means of escape from "the tyranny of the senses." It may be so for the spectator: he may find that the spectacle of supreme works of art takes from the life of the senses something of its turbid fever. But this is possible for the spectator only because the artist, in producing those works, has gradually sunk his intellectual and spiritual ideas in sensuous form. He may live, as Keats lived, a pure life; but his soul, like that of Plato's false astronomer, becomes more and more immersed in sense, until nothing which lacks the appeal to sense has interest for him. . . . [T]he artist steeps his thought again and again into the fire of colour. (176)

It is this "fire" of the senses—its moral daring underscored by the invocation of Keats, in 1867 a byword for sensuality—that Winckelmann, like the Greeks, experiences "with unsinged hands." In thus insisting on the powerful sensuality in artistic creation, Pater acts as the prism (to use his own imagery) that would decompose the "clear white light" of Greek sculpture into its constituent elements of "colour"—in particular, the color of blood, which recurs throughout "Winckelmann" as an emblem of both action and desire. Thus we are never allowed to forget the powerful erotic investments in the Greek ideal, which Kingsley typically displaces in his celebration of an all-embracing "health."

Pater's strategy suggests, however, that what may have seemed dangerous in his early essays was not their specifically homoerotic component, so much as their readiness to expose the work of sublimation informing contemporary discourse of both art and manhood. Pater's early work largely refuses to invest observation with any overt structure of traditional ethical discipline—a discipline that would have (among other things) outwardly regulated the erotic pleasures of spectatorship, and subordinated them to the demands of action, in a manner akin to

Kingsley's strategy in *Alton Locke*. Over against Kingsleyan calls to strenuous physical activity and exercise, Pater seemed to offer only detached,
passive contemplation, "the exercise of sight and touch" evoked in
"Winckelmann." Even in "Winckelmann," moreover, this enterprise is
associated with a rhetoric of arcane wisdom and cultic experience (subsequently elaborated, even more daringly, in "Leonardo da Vinci")
that was further provocation to a Kingsleyan rhetoric of bluff, democratic "manliness." Yet it is on this point that the Carlylean legacy again
figures centrally in Pater's writing. In the degree to which Pater's ideal
of "success in life" is derived from a Carlylean psychological economy,
his own "exercise" is susceptible to description in a rhetoric of earnestness. Through such description, Pater could forestall contemporary
suspicion of gender deviance while at the same time underscoring his
affinities with Hellenic "enthusiasm." He was able to present aesthetic
contemplation as a strenuous discipline closely akin to, perhaps precisely congruent with, that discipline which shaped both the subjects
and the techniques of Greek art.

 A hint of this rhetoric appears in "Winckelmann," in Pater's account
of both Greek sculpture and "the eternal problem of culture"—which
are in effect the same achievement. The "generality" of Greek sculpture, Pater insists, "has nothing in common with the lax observation,
the unlearned thought, the flaccid execution" of some art denoted
"general" (he is evidently thinking of Rossetti's criticism of "Sir Slo-
shua" Reynolds) but arises instead from a culture "minute, severe, constantly renewed, rectifying and concentrating its impressions" (170).
Repeatedly Pater describes the sculptor's work as one of "purgation":
"All that is accidental, all that distracts the simple effect upon us of
the supreme types of humanity, all traces in them of the commonness
of the world, it gradually purges away" (172). This discipline is to be
emulated by those in the modern world who would seek Goethe's life
im Ganzen; the aspiring intellect must grapple with "every divided form
of culture" in the construction of a perfectly disinterested vitality: "It
struggles with those forms till its secret is won from each, and then lets
each fall back into its place, in the supreme, artistic view of life. With
a kind of passionate coldness, such natures rejoice to be away from and
past their former selves" (183). "Passionate coldness" neatly distills
the ascetic vitality that both Pater and Kingsley discover in Greek sculpture, as well as the qualities evoked in the capacity "to burn with a
hard, gem-like flame."

 Pater's first major essay thus subtly insists on a paradox that was to
organize much of his later, and what might seem more conservative,

rhetoric of masculinity. The breadth and serenity of Greek sculpture (and hence of culture at large) may seem mere "insipidity," a standing affront to Victorian ideals of "character"—a norm to which Pater wickedly alludes in suggesting that the male form in Greek sculpture is "characterless." Yet, Pater argues, that achievement is nonetheless the consummation of a rigorous discipline. In his later writings Pater increasingly locates a model for such discipline in Greek *askesis*, a concept that suggestively unites physical and mental exercise in a discipline that, like Kingsleyan muscularity, is also erotically charged. It is in these writings that Pater's romantic Hellenism most fully merges with the discourse of late-Victorian athleticism. In "Lacedaemon" (1892), reprinted in *Plato and Platonism*, Pater looks to Spartan discipline as a fundamentally aesthetic exercise, precisely congruent in its mental regime with the self-discipline sustained by the Paterian beholder. "Why this loyalty to a system, so costly to you individually . . . ?" is the question Pater poses to the Spartan ephebe (232). The question is enforced in the "Conclusion" to *The Renaissance*, where Pater had urged that *any* "theory or idea or system which requires of us the sacrifice of any part of" the world of experience "in consideration of some interest into which we cannot enter . . . has no real claim upon us" (189). In "Lacedaemon," however, Pater has discovered a profound congruence between the late-Victorian cult of athleticism and his own enterprise: his imaginary Spartan ephebe responds, "To the end that I myself may be a perfect work of art, issuring thus into the eyes of all Greece." (*Plato and Platonism* 232). In the rigors of Spartan discipline Pater can find a technology of the self, in Foucault's phrase, that confirms a gratifying sense of authority through the aesthetic discipline of one's mind and body. As Linda Dowling points out, Pater in "Lacedaemon" thereby deftly "appropriate[s] the language of cultural legitimation in such a way as to authenticate the proscribed" ("Ruskin's Pied Beauty" 5)—the unnamed pederasty that centrally structures Spartan discipline—by couching it in a rhetoric absolutely fitted to the most "manly" Victorian schoolmaster.[20] Spartan discipline, in Pater's ac-

---

20. That legitimation is more overt in Charles Kains-Jackson's essay, "The New Chivalry," published in *The Artist* of 2 April 1894, three months before Pater's death. In urging an "exaltation of the youthful masculine ideal" as an ideal more "spiritual" that that of the old chivalry, because removed from mere procreation, Kains-Jackson turned to Spartan discipline as exemplum and authority: "As in Sparta so once more, will the lover be the 'inbreather,' . . . the beloved the 'listener' . . ." (Reade 316). As he aligns his program with the imperatives of Malthus, Kains-Jackson suggests the man-

count, "ethically . . . aimed at the reality, aesthetically at the expression, of reserved power, and from the first set its subject on the thought of his personal dignity, of self-command, in the artistic way of a good musician, a good soldier" (*Plato and Platonism* 221). Or a Paterian writer, one might add, for the discipline thus evoked is not only that of Marius, but of "the male conscience" evoked in the essay, "Style": "His punctilious observance of the proprieties of his medium will diffuse itself through all he writes with a general air of sensibility, of refined usage . . . Hence a contention, a sense of self-restraint and renunciation, having for the susceptible reader the effect of a challenge for minute consideration. . . . Surplusage! he will dread that, as the runner on his muscles" (Pater, *Appreciations* 14–15, 19).

To be sure, Pater's sympathy with the Spartan project is characteristically hedged: "Lacedaemon" concludes by stressing the mystery of the motives underlying "that exacting discipline of character." But Pater returns to just such a discipline in "Emerald Uthwart" (1892), an imaginary portrait that readers have long recognized as a companion piece to "Lacedaemon." In "Lacedaemon" Pater repeatedly draws analogies between Spartan training and a Victorian public-school education; in "Emerald Uthwart," he depicts a contemporary English schoolboy who seems the almost wholly passive recipient of "influences," shaped like the young Spartans in perfect compliance to "the lightest touch, of the finger of law" (*Plato and Platonism* 79). At school Uthwart is "the plain tablet, for the influences of the place to inscribe" (*Miscellaneous Studies* 179); through such inscription he is impressed with a "sense of responsibility to the place" (185) that reproduces the young Marius's "sense of responsibility . . . to the world of men and things" (1:18), just as the fascination of young Marius's reserve is echoed in the young Uthwart's "soldier-like, impassible self-command" (184), which arrests the gaze of all around him. Here, however, Pater more obviously locates the model of his ephebe's fashioning in the Hellenic ideal embodied in Greek sculpture. Even as the influences of his school shape the "unmeaningly handsome facial type" into a more complex expressiveness, Uthwart retains a seemingly perfect psychic equilibrium: all these influences leave "the firm, unconscious simplicity of the boyish nature still unperplexed." Here is the world of Greek sculpture uncannily reconstituted in the modern world as the apparent

---

ifold array of sexualities that might be authorized by Victorian rhetorics of masculine discipline.

goal of Paterian discipline. "It would misrepresent Uthwart's wholly unconscious humility to say that he felt the beauty of the askesis . . . to which . . . as under a fascination he submissively yields himself" (182). Yet the achievement is destroyed in a moment when, with the exuberant daring of a young soldier, Uthwart violates military law—"almost the sole irregular or undisciplined act of Uthwart's life" (199). Within the program of Paterian discipline, what would otherwise seem merely a wayward irruption of desire reenacts the transgression of the Greek mind's "happy limit"—a curtailment that Pater at once longs to recover and at the same time suggests is an impossible, self-destructive repression. As William Shuter has noted, the very aesthetic perfection Uthwart embodies also makes him a sacrificial victim ("Arrested Narrative" 23).

"Young Apollo," Uthwart is called; but, the narrator objects, he "was more like a real portrait of a real young Greek, like Trypho, son of Eutychos" (Pater, *Miscellaneous Studies* 191). That model refers us once again to the critical authority of Greek sculpture, which in "Emerald Uthwart" as in "Lacedaemon" seems perpetuated in the rhapsodies of Victorian athleticism. In "The Age of Athletic Prizemen" (1894) the fusion of these two discourses seems complete: for Pater as for Kingsley the heroic athletes of Greek art are superbly reincarnated as cricketers on the banks of the Thames. Like Kingsley, Pater looks to the celebration of the body in both English youth and Greek art as an aesthetic triumph that affirms a consoling theology. "Man with them was divine, inasmuch as he could perceive beauty and be beautiful himself," as Kingsley phrases it in "The Stage as It Was Once" (*Literary and General Lectures* 52), and the "work" of the Greeks in every sphere was to assert "the dignity of man." Pater initially finds in heroic sculpture a more specific triumph: its celebration of youth, he argues, is "a sign that essential mastery has been achieved by the artist. . . . For such youth, in its very essence, is a matter properly within the limits of the visible, the empirical world; and in the presentment of it there will be no place for symbolic hint" (*Greek Studies* 282). But what might seem a narrowly technical achievement encapsulates the governing impulse of Pater's aestheticism: from his earliest writings Pater presents his vocation as a programmatic extension of empiricism, which would confine and focus the mind's activity "within the limits of the visible, the empirical, world." Hence the seeming paradox that Pater's acutely self-conscious discipline could find not merely a stimulating beauty but an emblem of its largest aspirations in the perfectly unconscious perfection of the Discobulus, which embodies "all one has ever fancied or seen, in old

Greece or on Thames' side, of the unspoiled body of youth, thus de-
lighting itself and others, at the perfect, because unconscious, point of
good-fortune, as it moves or rests just there for a moment, between the
animal and spiritual worlds" (*Greek Studies* 288). One could hardly find
a more eloquent contribution to the late-Victorian celebration of athleticism—even, surprisingly, to the pronounced anti-intellectualism
that animates it: "It is of the essence of the athletic prizeman . . . not
to give expression to mind, in any antagonism to, or invasion of, the
body; to mind as anything more than a function of the body, whose
healthful balance of functions it may so easily perturb;—to disavow that
insidious enemy of the fairness of the bodily soul as such" (286).

   Of course, one might see Pater's description as a quiet parody of
Kingsleyan muscularity, inasmuch as it evacuates any hint of mind in
fetishizing the athletic body—removing the *mens sana* from the *corpore
sano.* Pater is in league with the "insidious enemy," after all, inasmuch
as his description will not allow us to forget the mind that the sculpture—like youth itself—excludes. But what he is constructing here is
yet another representation of the Greek mind's "happy limit," which
like the achievement of the athlete is a delicate, precarious balance
"just there for a moment, between the animal and spiritual worlds."
In fact, the sculpture embodies at least three time schemes: the brief
moment of stasis in the athlete's motion; the point of equilibrium between youth and maturity, between "the animal and spiritual worlds;"
and "the delicate pause in Greek reflection" that marks the Greek
mind's happy limit in the history of human consciousness. By presenting the psychic equilibrium of the Hellenic ideal in such emphatically
temporal terms, Pater seems to renounce any possibility of recovering
it, to ironize the nostalgia informing his rapturous gaze. Once again,
however, Pater's response to Greek sculpture reproduces the divided
aspirations of his own vocation. In the very moment of his success the
athlete may be unconscious, yet his achievement in all its significance,
Pater reminds us, is the product of a sustained, concerted discipline.
"The athletic life certainly breathes of abstinence, of rule and the keeping under of one's self. And here in the *Diadumenus,* we have one of
its priests, a priest of the religion whose central motive was what has
been called 'the worship of the body'" (295). Such discipline is obviously reproduced in the ascetic discipline of those who commemorate
it, the sculptor and Pater himself, who consistently presents his vocation
as an assertion of rule dedicated to the worship of the body, as the
focal point of a delight in the visible, sensuous world. The Discobulus,
Pater notes, is full of "learned involution," yet that quality is entirely

"subordinated to the proper purpose of the *Discobolus* as a work of art, a thing to be looked at rather than to think about" (288). Once again the refinement of self-consciousness is deployed to the aim of arresting reflection, and such is the aspiration of Pater's own criticism. The notion that art is "a thing to be looked at rather than to think about" may seem a bizarre notion in light of Pater's own practice in *The Renaissance*, yet it echoes the premise of "The School of Giorgione," that art "is always striving to be independent of the mere intelligence, to become a matter of pure perception" (108). Even in his famous reverie on the Mona Lisa, Pater seeks to evoke hidden depths of intention and meaning in order ultimately to return us to the surfaces of an image with an enriched appreciation for its immediate, primary appeal as "a thing for the eye." If the Diadumenus is a priest in the worship of the body, so, too is Pater: "the Hellenic tradition" invoked in "Winckelmann," after all, is an apostolic succession in which Pater himself figures as but the most recent in a long series of disciples. In this regard not merely the discipline but the crowning achievement of the athletic prizemen is reproduced by the sculptor's labors, and by those of the critic who re-creates and extends the example of both in subsequent generations.

Pater's late reveries thus may be seen to address a central tension within neoclassical aesthetics, under which the beautiful male body may serve as "both an ideal object of desire" and "an ideal subject with which the male spectator can identify" (Potts 11). This "radical disjunction," as Alex Potts calls it, is such only through the proscription of homoerotic desire, which Pater works to subvert by subtly yet insistently conjoining the twin appeals of the beautiful male body. From this vantage, it no paradox that the cricketer or quoit-player "under the eternal form of art" thus becomes at once the object and emblem of Paterian longing. And only in recognizing this significance can we appreciate the extraordinary valedictory with which Pater closes "The Age of Athletic Prizemen":

> Take him, to lead you forth quite out of the narrow limits of the Greek world. You have pure humanity there, with a glowing, yet restrained joy and delight in itself, but without vanity; and it *is* pure. There is nothing certainly supersensual in that fair, round head, any more than in the long, agile limbs; but also no impediment, natural or acquired. To have achieved just that, was the Greek's truest claim for furtherance in the main line of human development. He had been faithful, we cannot help saying, as we pass from that youthful company, in what comparatively is

perhaps little—in the culture, the administration, of the visible world; and he merited, so we might go on to say—he merited Revelation, something which should solace his heart in the inevitable fading of that. We are reminded of those strange prophetic words of the Wisdom, the *Logos*, by whom God made the world. . . . "I was by him, as one brought up with him; rejoicing in the habitable parts of the earth. My delights were with the sons of men." (*Greek Studies* 298–99)

In one sense, this emphatic historical framing distances Pater from the achievement he celebrates; certainly the invocation of Christianity seems to hedge his allegiance to the Hellenic ideal, in a far cry from "Winckelmann." But it is not so much the Greek ideal that has been revalued as Christianity—with the result that Pater's meditation on Greece, despite its characteristically wistful and hesitant rhetoric, startlingly recalls Kingsley's liberal and muscular Christianity. The satisfactions of "pure humanity" incarnated in the athletic body, satisfactions defined through renunciation of the "supersensual," are sanctified, becoming the vehicle of a grace that will redeem those who have proven their worthiness simply through a devotion to "the visible world." In Pater's reverie, the Greek athlete has realized the youthful Kingsley's "strange idea": he has become "an Apollo for His sake."

CHAPTER FIVE

Gentleman, Dandy, Priest: Masks and Masculinity in Pater's Aestheticism

I have grown to love secrecy. It seems to be the one thing that can make modern life mysterious or marvellous to us. The commonest thing is delightful if only one hides it.

Wilde, *The Picture of Dorian Gray*

Shortly after Walter Pater's death, Henry James wrote to Edmund Gosse that Pater "has had . . . the most exquisite literary fortune: i.e. to have taken it out all, wholly, exclusively, with the pen (the style, the genius) and absolutely not at all with the person. He is the mask without the face." Pater's dedication to his craft, in James's account, is crowned by a vanishing act that frustrates the surveillance of popular journalism: "And there isn't in his total superficies," James continues, "a tiny point of vantage for the newspaper to flap its wings on" (*Letters* 3:492).[1] In imagining the newspaper as a bird of prey, James captures the increasingly acute pressures of Victorian publicity that Alexander Welsh has analyzed in *George Eliot and Blackmail*. Indeed, James may well have known (through Edmund Gosse) that Pater's Oxford career had been shadowed by blackmail in the 1870s, when he was threatened with the exposure of compromising letters written to an undergraduate

---

1. Tintner helpfully collects James's comments on Pater; Freedman offers a penetrating analysis of Pater's importance to James's aestheticism.

(Inman, "Estrangement").[2] In this context, James's remark invites an approach to Pater's notorious reticence and obliquity—as well as James's own—as a concertedly defensive reaction to hostile surveillance, a strategy for shielding himself from the mechanisms of Victorian power.

But masks may be deployed to seduce as well as to defend. Indeed, James's remarks point to both possibilities. In his rendering, Pater eluded the engines of publicity by entirely submerging his person in a persona, thereby turning himself, in effect, into an aesthetic creation. He wrote himself out of the newspapers' view and into the gaze of his readers as another and emphatically theatrical self, a mask. In pointing this out, however, James himself participates in the fascinated surveillance: masks are recognizable as such only to an audience schooled in the arts of obliquity, an audience ready to discern a disjunction between surface and depth. Pater's mask thus depends on the complicity of his readers—on their readiness to suspect that every surface is a mask. And in this regard Pater's achievement, as James understood it, solicits the very hermeneutic of suspicion it seems designed to frustrate. Who or what does "the mask" conceal? Such is the axiomatic response of contemporary readers schooled in what Althusser has called symptomatic reading. Allon White has incisively studied the rise of modernist narrative technique as a response to the burdens of such a hermeneutic of suspicion. But James's tribute to Pater hints at a further rhetorical possibility, one which has been overlooked by recent criticism approaching secrecy and obliquity through a Foucauldian lens. Secrets, after all, exist to be shared as well as exposed. The refusal to allow for this basic fact—and the social structures that follow from it—is a central weakness of Foucauldian machinery, a weakness closely akin to its refusal to allow for reciprocity of vision. (As Martin Jay has pointed out, in "The Empire of the Gaze," in twentieth-century French thought *le regard* does not assume the alternative meaning of "caring" or "esteeming" that distinguishes its English cognate.) A sense of shared secrecy, as we noted in Chapter 2, is often central to establishing or reinforcing social bonds, particularly those which define a subgroup within a larger society: hence the widespread Victorian fascination with secret societies or brotherhoods, not only as paranoid constructions, but as appealing forms of an imagined solidarity. Indeed, as the reception of Tractarianism makes plain, the mere assertion, or intimation, that one *has* a secret may be offered to an outsider as an enticing

2. Gosse had recounted the episode to A. C. Benson, one of Pater's early biographers; hence the likelihood that James knew of it.

invitation to participate in such a community. And that strategy will have particular force when the audience is trained in a "common sense" that is at once social and literary: a hermeneutics of suspicion.

Just such a hermeneutics governs the code of robust manliness most vividly represented in the writings of Charles Kingsley. In the previous chapter I stressed the affinities between Pater's rhetoric and Kingsley's, affinities that rest on their shared preoccupation with the male body as a potential ground of intellectual and social authority—a preoccupation that is central to contemporary constructions of the gentleman. In this chapter I deal with a more familiar image of Pater: the "decadent" prose stylist, the high priest of fin-de-siècle aestheticism. And yet I hope to show that this icon is informed by Victorian reconfigurations of the ideal of the gentleman: that Pater constructed one of the founding rhetorics of British modernism by subverting from within a Kingsleyan discourse of masculine identity. Pater's effort to reinscribe norms of masculinity within the ethos of aestheticism—to present even spectatorship as an exercise in eminently virile self-discipline—is founded on his habit of envisioning his critical activity under a public gaze, as a mode of performance. In pursuing that strategy, he structures his aestheticism through the social forms and psychology that it ostensibly repudiates, those of Victorian gentility. And by "aestheticism" I refer to the patterns of activity embodied both in and by Pater's writings: not only the social forms they represent, but their strategies of representation. What seems most innovative and even daring in Pater's prose—and in much of the literary technique it influenced—can be usefully viewed as a form of mask, a peculiarly theatrical reticence and ostentatious reserve, that is grounded in the social decorum and discipline of middle-class Victorian life. Even Pater's most famously "purple" rhetoric, the rhapsody on Leonardo's Gioconda that became Yeats's notorious opening selection in his *Oxford Book of Modern Poetry*, employs a strategy of representation that blurs distinctions between aesthetic representation and social presentation; aesthetic understanding comes to be understood on the model of intimate knowledge of another person.

The boundary between those two categories, which Pater concertedly obscures throughout his works, is most thoroughly confounded in a late, unpublished draft of an essay titled "The Aesthetic Life." In this work, while sketching a distinctly contemporary incarnation of the Paterian spectator, Pater at one point refers to an imagined aesthetic ephebe as "the new Gioconda," "modernity made visible." As this arresting equation might suggest, Pater draws on the social forms of middle-class Victorian masculinity by eliciting the dandyism—a paradoxical element of transgressive performance—latent within those forms. This is his great legacy to Wilde, who draws so heavily on Paterian rhetoric in his own models of masculine self-fashioning. But Pater's aestheticism, with its more overt continuities with earlier Victorian rhetorics of masculinity, thereby underscores the volatile and perpetually contested character of "manliness," and in many regards epitomizes the tensions I have been exploring throughout this book. The discipline of the aspiring gentleman, Pater recognizes, depends on a fundamentally theatrical strategy of self-presentation, yet such theatricality is emphatically repudiated in the specifically middle-class, Victorian constructions of the ideal of the gentleman. The aspiring gentleman thus shades into the dandy, who occupies a social space that Victorian discourse typically reserves for the feminine; hence the consistency with which various programs of self-consciously masculine discipline are attacked as forms of effeminacy. As we saw in Chapter 2 this is a paradox acutely registered in hostility to the Oxford Movement: it is no accident that Courthope's 1876 attack on Pater echoes Kingsley's denunciation of Newman as both unmanly and un-English. Yet Pater finds in Tractarianism a model for his vocation, not merely in the suspicions that it incited, but in the fact that an elite order devoted to "otherworldly" values could nonetheless exert an extraordinary social influence through the quality that Weber would later call charisma. The priest is thus joined with the dandy and the gentleman as a means of embodying new forms of masculinity and social authority amid the decline of an aristocratic order. As a result, the familiar appropriation of religious forms and vocabulary in the discourses of aestheticism can be seen as something other than a banal deification of art: in Pater's works a specific religious paradigm articulates particular *social* possibilities. Pater's aesthete unites the figures of gentleman, dandy, and priest as he attempts to construct new forms of charisma through an active solicitation of hostile surveillance. Whatever the burdens of that surveillance, it offered Pater new rhetorical strategies and hence new forms of social authority—most notably, an ideal of the critic's vocation as a mode of seduction.

AUTHORITY IN RESERVE

Throughout his writings, Pater explores the relations of aesthetic experience and religious ritual, in the process constructing an implicit

genealogy of his own aestheticism as an outgrowth of religious observance. Thus in *Marius the Epicurean*, the protagonist as "boy-priest"
grows into an aesthete who envisions his vocation as "a new form of
the contemplative life," "an ordered service to the visible world."
Whatever the autobiographical context of this narrative, it encapsulates
a larger intellectual genealogy, in which the rise of modern aesthetics
appropriates and transvalues earlier theological discourse.[3] But the continuum of religious and aesthetic discourse has a special urgency within
the apologetic design of *Marius*, where it serves as a social and moral
paradigm. In a footnote added to the third edition of *The Renaissance*
(1888), Pater explained that "this brief 'Conclusion' was omitted in
the second edition of this book, as I conceived it might possibly mislead
some of those young men into whose hands it might fall. On the whole,
I have thought it best to reprint it here, with some slight changes which
bring it closer to my original meaning. I have dealt more fully in *Marius
the Epicurean* with the thoughts suggested by it" (186). In urging a
strenuous discipline to redirect young men who might have been "mis-
led," *Marius* is deeply indebted to the model of the Christian gentleman enshrined in Stanley's *Life of Thomas Arnold*, and to a degree in
more recent memoirs of the Oxford Movement, which had begun to
proliferate in the wake of Newman's *Apologia*. Like both Arnold and
Newman, Pater in *Marius* associates religious belief with a comprehensive regimen of self-discipline, which is set against the suspicion that
Marius's skepticism is really "a languid, enervating, consumptive nihil-
ism . . . a precept of 'renunciation,' which would touch and handle and
busy itself with nothing" (1:135). Tellingly, Pater envisions the adversary in the language of Kingsley's attacks on Tractarian "Manicheanism." And indeed Pater's language at times reads as if it had been lifted
from a Victorian schoolmaster's exhortation. Thus he argues, for example, that the New Cyrenaicism is "not so properly the utterance of
the 'jaded Epicurean,' as of the strong young man in all the freshness
of thought and feeling," who pursues that "clear-eyed intellectual consistency, which is like spotless bodily cleanliness, or scrupulous personal
honor" (2:16). The hyperbolic insistence on purity and vigor suggests
the rigors of Kingsleyan gender surveillance, which likewise informs the
chapter sardonically titled "Manly Amusement," which closes the first
volume of the novel. The "manly" amusement is that of the Roman

---

3. On the genealogy of aesthetics, see Abrams, "Kant and the Theology of Art." A
   precisely analogous process is plotted in Pater's unfinished *Gaston de Latour*, set amid
   the religious wars of sixteenth-century France.

amphitheater, which is tolerated by all of Roman society—including
the otherwise enlightened Marcus Aurelius—except for Marius: "It
amounted to a tolerance of evil," he concludes (1:240). In this baldly
sententious episode, Marius's fastidiousness represents a triumph at
once aesthetic, ethical, and religious: his acutely sensitive eye impels an
ethical advance beyond the stoicism of Aurelius, which in turn points
toward the supercession of pagan religion by Christianity. But these triumphs are united in the conformity of Pater's hero to a Victorian ideal
of masculine conduct: it is Marius, not the "manly" brutes around him,
who displays the conscience of the Victorian gentleman. Marius alone is
guided by "that decisive conscience at first sight" (1:241), which has
developed out of the sensibility of the boy priest, and "to offend against
which, brought with it a strange feeling of disloyalty" (1:156).

A revulsion against blood sports is thus submerged in an all-
embracing ethos of manliness, understood as "a responsibility towards
the world of men and things" (1:18). That ethos clearly derives from
the early Victorian reconfiguration of masculinity, under which the
highest virtue of manhood is not martial valor but moral courage. Marius's experience at the amphitheatre exemplifies what Thomas Hughes
in *The Manliness of Christ* calls "one of the most searching of all trials
of courage and manliness," when individuals must "stand by what ap-
proves itself to their conscience as true . . . against all disparagement"
(31). But the very title of Hughes's volume reflects not only the immense social authority of "manliness" but a correspondingly acute contest in defining the norm. When Samuel Smiles in *Character* likewise
celebrates moral courage, he reminds us that "manliness" thus conceived is an attribute available to both men and women: moral courage,
he urges, is "the highest order of manhood or womanhood" (140).
This is likewise true of Thomas Arnold's association of manliness with
moral and spiritual discipline. Over the course of the century, however,
this conception of manhood was increasingly challenged by the Kingsleyan equation of manliness with physical vitality and hearty simplicity
in word and deed—a construction more responsive to the rigors of
Victorian economic life, and most influentially celebrated in the Victorian cult of athleticism. The divergent emphases—broadly speaking,
those of *arete* and *thumos*—exist in uneasy conjunction throughout the
period, but by 1870 the divergence has passed into open antagonism:
hence the need Hughes felt to defend even the manliness of Christ.
To those for whom manliness is above all hearty, unguarded sponta-
neity, self-restraint is liable to seem devious; to celebrants of physical activity, self-discipline may seem passive and effeminate, even self-

annihilating—as in Kingsley's fierce attacks on "Manicheanism" (New-some, *Godliness* 195–239; Girouard 232–48). This is the conflict that Newman, who felt the great burden of both forms of suspicion, iden-tified in his 1843 sermon, "Wisdom and Innocence." "The world," Newman writes there, mistrusts innocence as "craft" because "sobriety, self-restraint, control of word and feeling have about them an air of being artificial, because they are not natural; and of being artful, be-cause artificial." Thus self-restraint, he continues, "is the first thing which makes holy persons seem wanting in openness and manliness" (*Sermons* 299–300).

Pater's Marius, then, hearkens back to an older discourse of manli-ness, within which Newman is especially important. In particular, New-man's example calls attention to a persistent but unremarked attribute of Pater's characters, their *reserve.* Given the prevalent image of those characters as intensely isolated beings, reserve is an unexpectedly sig-nificant attribute, since it functions only in a social context. One can be quiet in solitude, but reserve must be displayed; it characterizes a subject in relation to an audience. "Why this reserve?—they asked, con-cerning the orderly, self-possessed youth, whose speech and carriage seemed so carefully measured" (1:127). Thus his schoolfellows observe with fascination the young Marius, as he in turn will be fascinated by the reserve of the young Roman officer, Cornelius: in both instances a "carefully measured" demeanor embodies the resources of self-discipline. Of course, such reserve may be a defensive posture, a means of shielding oneself from hostile scrutiny. But Pater presents it through-out his writings as a deeply seductive quality, because reserve is the index of one's powers of self-control—and hence of a potential to con-trol others. The appeal is that of what he elsewhere calls Plato's "in-tellectual astringency," for example, "enhancing the sense of power in one's self, and its effect upon others, by a certain crafty reserve in its exercise" (*Plato and Platonism,* 283). We may recall Kingsley's tribute to the man "born to rule self, and therefore to rule all he met" (*Life and Works* 14: 260). When reserve is acknowledged as an index of self-regulating power, it lends unexpected social authority to otherwise un-prepossessing demeanors, such as "the somewhat sombre habitude of the avowed scholar." So it is that reserve gives to Marius "a peculiar manner of intellectual confidence, as of one who had indeed been initiated into a great secret" (1:157).

The appearance of Marius's reserve among the Roman gentry would have had for Pater's contemporaries a fairly specific counterpart in re-cent social history: it mirrors the early Victorian emergence of increas-

ingly somber norms of decorum in both manners and dress, which
helped to codify the growing social authority of the upper middle class
(Davidoff and Hall 401–10). "The sober discretion" of Marius's
thoughts, "his sustained habit of meditation," although "it never inter-
fered with the perfect tone, 'fresh and serenely disposed,' of the Roman
gentleman, yet qualified it as by an interesting oblique trait, and fright-
ened away some of his equals in age and rank" (1:157). Marius, in
short, incarnates a new form of the gentleman, whose self-discipline is a
claim to authority greeted with an uneasiness closely akin to that which
Newman experienced: "the world" mistrusts outwardly religious men,
Newman asserts, because they are a mystery, because it senses "that it
has not fathomed them, that there is some secret to be found out" (Sermons 300).[4] Pater's characters, however, also recall Newman's capacity
to transform suspicions of secrecy into a source of fascination.

Through the dynamics of reserve, Marius's arresting social presence
is grounded, paradoxically, in what is most intensely private in his experience: "In spite of, perhaps partly because of, his habitual reserve
of manner, he had become 'the fashion,' even among those who felt
instinctively the irony that lay beneath that remarkable self-possession,
as of one taking all things with a difference from other people, per-
ceptible in voice, in expression, and even in his dress" (1:212). This
tribute to the seductive power of Marius's reserve closely echoes accounts of Newman's influence over Oxford undergraduates. Yet the
"self-possession" of Marius's reserve rests on, and in turn seems to
reinforce, the "irony" wrought by a radically skeptical epistemology,
the very epistemology that is rehearsed throughout Pater's writings as
a means of enforcing a gulf between mind and the external world. As
Pater explains it in Marius, his hero has "the air of one who, entering
vividly into life . . . yet feels all the while, from the point of view of an
ideal philosophy, that he is but conceding reality to suppositions,
choosing of his own will to walk in a day-dream, of the illusiveness of
which he at least is aware" (1:213). Critics typically point to this skepticism, particularly as it is set forth in the famous "Conclusion" to The
Renaissance, to explain what seems the extraordinary social isolation of
the Paterian spectator: after all, what substantial communication could
one expect under the reign of "modern thought," where every mind

4. The transition is more specifically embodied in the reserve of Marius's friend Cornelius, the Roman centurion whose "secret" is his Christian faith, and who thus
reproduces the influence of Evangelicalism in early Victorian decorum. Marius, by
contrast, represents the social discipline of Victorian life detached from any specific
theology.

is "keeping as a solitary prisoner its own dream of a world" (188)? Yet in *Marius the Epicurean* this same affirmation of a radical, solipsistic privacy, even as it calls into question the very substance of the social world, becomes incarnated in Marius's physical presence as an almost mesmerizing social authority.[5] It is Marius's epistemology, of all things, that makes him "the fashion."

Marius's ostensible rejection of worldly concerns thus turns out to confirm a very worldly hierarchy. This might seem an idiosyncratic fantasy, were it not largely true to Pater's own life: the notoriously reserved Oxford don was indeed transformed into a cultural icon. But of course the seeming paradox shapes many social incarnations of "ideal philosophy" in varieties of priesthood; in this regard, Pater's influence recapitulates in muted form earlier responses to Newman. In both cases, a strikingly "otherworldly" intellectual allegiance is embodied (or at least intimated) in the extension and intensification of everyday social decorum into a mode of virtuoso discipline. Paterian "reserve," like its Tractarian counterpart, seems to transform everyday life into ritualized activity. Yet the forms of both men's triumphs also bear witness to a collective fantasy of the Victorian middle classes. When Marius becomes "the fashion" on the basis of "his habitual reserve of manner," he epitomizes a central episode in the history of nineteenth-century public life. His reserve exemplifies what Richard Sennett in *The Fall of Public Man* has called the "discipline of silence" enforced by midcentury urban decorum in England and France. Silence in public became a norm, Sennett argues, in response to the "profound self-doubt" generated by the rise of what one might call social symptomatics, which assumed that one's public presence could involuntarily disclose one's private character. As silence shielded spectators from potentially embarassing self-revelation, however, it also functioned as a mark of social rank, delimiting the "respectable" classes from their inferiors, who exhibited less self-control. Thus silence that was narrowly defensive in its original impetus could be turned into a mode of self-assertion. Pater insists on just such a dynamic when he would have us regard "reserve" as the mark not of insecurity but of a richly intellectual self-confidence. He thereby enacts what Sennett calls "the fantasy of authority" among the anxious but silent middle-class public. The spectator has become a performer, whose authority resides in a capacity at once to show and to

5. This is a further point of contact between Newman and Pater, whose "Conclusion," as DeLaura remarks, in many respects echoes Newman's famous sermon "The Individuality of the Soul" (*Hebrew and Hellene* 309).

control one's feelings (Sennett 195–218). Indeed, since that outward control is what confirms one's possession of a "compelling self," the logic Sennett describes points to the paradox that selfhood is affirmed through self-repression.

This paradox has been developed with great subtlety and suggestiveness by John Kucich, who argues that Victorian novels frequently represent repression as a means of constructing richer and more eroticized domains of subjectivity. From this point of view, repression draws its social authority in Victorian culture not from conformity to outward social norms but as "a sign of deeper resources of subjectivity . . . of superior inward libidinal depth" (*Repression in Victorian Fiction* 269–70). Paterian "reserve" appeals to an onlooker for just such recognition of more complex and hence more compelling subjectivity, which would lend authority to a socially marginal public self. In this sense the extraordinary prominence of grave, subdued, reserved figures in Pater's writings is not merely a function of psychic exigency, but a social strategy—which is one reason why Paterian figures persist through much fin-de-siècle poetry and fiction. In such figures, Pater is constructing a form of Weberian charisma, or what Gustave le Bon calls *prestige*: "a faculty independent of all titles, of all authority, and possessed by a small number of persons whom it enables to exercise a truly magnetic fascination on those around them, although they are socially their equals and lack all ordinary means of domination" (Barrows 173). The assertion of psychic autonomy may thus come to articulate a new social authority, which makes itself felt through "fascination."

The construction of masculine charisma, as we have seen, figures centrally in Carlyle's rhetoric of heroism, and in contemporary reception of Newman and Thomas Arnold, which was in large part shaped by Carlyle's influence. But the same dynamic is likewise invoked by the persistent shadow of Carlylean heroism, the dandy—another eminently middle-class appeal to a charismatic authority that would displace the influence of wealth and inherited rank. Such authority is also crucial to yet another Victorian secular priesthood, that of the professional man. Indeed, we might see *Marius* as a subtle articulation of the cultural logic that connects the professional and the priest. The dandy and the professional man are linked by their shared affiliation with the ideal of the gentleman, which—as we saw in Chapter 1—centrally depends on an appeal to "disinterestedness," including a professed disdain for economic self-interest. The dandy mystifies the economic relations informing the ideal of disinterestedness, which helped to secure

professionals the status of gentlemen, and thereby to encourage a rapid
growth in the prestige and authority of the professions—which in turn
secured for the successful professional a great deal of worldly interest.
Like the Paterian aesthete, the professional defines himself through
the possession of a knowledge or talent in some degree arcane, the
value of which depends not on the market, but on the professional's
power of persuasion, which tends to be charismatic. Common to both
is a frame of value that is in some degree "otherworldly"—*umbratilis*,
in the term with which Pater evokes "the sort of mystic enjoyment
[Marius] had in the abstinence, the strenuous self-control and *ascesis*"
(1:25) with which "the boy priest" performed his religious offices.
Such an ideal of exalted renunciation became an especially appealing
image of literary life in the 1890s, and thus helps to explain the influence of Pater's narrative on aspiring writers—not only Yeats but Ernest
Dowson, who paid tribute to Marius's example by titling a poem "Amor
Umbratilis" (Thornton 91). In imagining one's life as "otherworldly"
devotion, a writer might find consolation for a dearth of economic
reward; by the same token, however, the ideal might be invoked to
obscure the professional's (or the poet's) complicity with the marketplace.

To be sure, Marius seems to have little talent suited to Victorian
exchange; he has only the fascinating sensibility intimated in his reserve. Yet Pater makes this sensibility the basis of something very much
like a profession. Such is the worldly force of Marius's otherworldliness
that he is summoned to Rome to become private secretary to the em-
peror—largely on the basis, it seems, of his captivating reserve (1:158).
This is a traditionally aristocratic career pattern, of course, but its structure persists amid the Victorian transfer of patronage from individuals
to professional bodies, or to the state; that persistence is encapsulated
in the career of Matthew Arnold, who left employment as private secretary to Lord Lansdowne to assume the newly created post of inspector
of schools.[6] Marius's reserve, moreover, reflects the professional's elaboration of the psychology of Victorian gentility. It is not simply that
Marius is an unabashed elitist, who enjoys the sense that his intellectual
life is a mystery to the vulgar. His reserve also enacts a paradox at the
heart of bourgeois self-presentation in Victorian life: it makes a badge
of personal and professional distinction out of the very quality that

6. Larson (220) stresses the "traditional or precapitalist" components of nineteenth-
century professionalism.

seems designed to efface individuality in social life. Precisely by holding
in reserve one's merely or singularly personal identity, one establishes
that one is worth knowing.

"THE ART OF GOING DEEP": INTIMACY
AND FASCINATION

As it manifests the indwelling presence of intellectual power devoted
to disinterested ends, reserve helps to secure the Paterian aesthete's
status as a gentleman, and thus to legitimate a life devoted to spectatorship—more generally, a life whose relation to the world of action
and exchange is at best problematic. Pater's novel in this light represents a social as well as a psychological and intellectual continuity between the "boy-priest" and the adult Epicurean. Jonathan Freedman
has recently stressed the extent to which aestheticism served its adherents in both Britain and America as a means of upward mobility, and
goes so far as to argue that aestheticism is "the highest form of professionalism, when that is conceived as the claim of possessing a particular, esoteric form of knowledge, and the generally fervent assertion of
a vocation to impart that knowledge" (55). Yet the association of aestheticism and professionalism is complicated by Pater's habitual appeal
to the singularity of individual temperament, whose "knowledge" resists any program of standardization.[7] This singularity is manifested in
Marius's power to capture the gaze of onlookers, a power that is something more and other than respectable. The logic of Marius's influence
is precisely captured in Jules Barbey D'Aurevilly's account of Brummell's "empire . . . over his contemporaries": "The genius of irony suf-
fices, for it gives a man that sphinx-like air which interests as a mystery
and troubles as a danger" (55). Like D'Aurevilly's dandy, Marius fascinates, and that uneasy compound of desire and suspicion elicits the
inherent tension in Victorian constructions of the gentleman that we
have been tracing throughout this book. ("I didn't say I liked it,
Harry," Wilde's Dorian Gray tells his aristocratic mentor; "I said it
fascinated me. There is a great difference" [Picture of Dorian Gray 241].)
Whereas conservative commentators emphasized the gentleman's
unself-conscious ease and straightforwardness, others stressing the egalitarian character of the ideal argued that it could be realized through

---

7. Small, Conditions for Criticism, stresses Pater's resistance to the growing professionali-
zation of academia and letters.

"an application of the discipline of civilization to every motion and activity" (Curtin 116). Pater quietly embraces this intractable hint of perfomance in the aspiring gentleman, who emulates Trollope's Lord Fawn of *The Eustace Diamonds* in envisioning himself "in the eye of the British public" (2:247). Pater thus points to a logic more flamboyantly enacted by Wilde: in a reversal of earlier valuations, the gentleman is seen as a fundamentally theatrical being, whose "nature" is emphatically a pose. But Pater also thereby makes plain that what Jonathan Dollimore has called Wilde's "transgressive desire" is enacted *through* "conformity to rule," not against it; it is enacted through Wilde's insistent staging of the contradictions that beset the ideal of the gentleman in Victorian culture.

The Wildean paradox of the theatrical gentleman, then, is more quietly at work in Marius's gentlemanly reserve. But the appeal of that reserve mirrors the appeal that Pater discovers in art—and it is through this aspect of his works that Pater bequeathed to Wilde not only a social strategy but an entire rhetoric of seduction. Leonardo's art in particular, like the reserve of the Paterian beholder, fascinates because it seems a public withholding of private experience, which by virtue of being withheld is assumed to be singular, strange, even forbidden. "More than those of any other artist," Pater writes in "Leonardo da Vinci" (1868), Leonardo's works "seem to reflect ideas and views and some scheme of the world within" (*Renaissance* 77); in his art, traditional subject matter becomes "a cryptic language for fancies all his own," which everywhere hints at "something far beyond the outward gesture or circumstance" (97, 93). Hence Leonardo seems to be "the possessor of some unsanctified and secret wisdom," and "fascination is always the word descriptive of him" (78, 85). It is crucial to the talismanic power of Pater's Leonardo that his art is enigmatic—and that Pater's style works to reinforce this effect. When Pater claims, for example, that Verrocchio's achievement "awoke in Leonardo some seed of discontent which lay in the secret places of his nature," the phrasing reinforces the sense of unfathomable depth in Leonardo's art (81). "Some seed of discontent in his nature" would be sufficient to evoke the requisite note of mystery, but the apparent redundancy of "secret places" buries the elusive seed more deeply. As one speculates on the source of Leonardo's discontent, hidden in the rich soil of his "nature," it recedes still further into more remote and inaccessible "secret places."

This calculated enticement is frequently cited as one of the seminal instances of symbolist technique in English prose. Yet its congruence

with Marius's reserve suggests that Pater's rhetorical strategy is informed by a similar norm of social decorum. More precisely, Pater's
evocation locates in Leonardo's art just such a "luxuriously disruptive
auto-erotic experience" as Kucich has described in the workings of
Victorian repression. And in this regard the unlikely conjunction of
Pater's Gioconda and the aspiring gentleman's demeanor undercores
the paradoxical structure of transgression inscribed within the gentleman's discipline. Insofar as it incarnates a fundamental theatricality,
the self-presentation exemplified in Marius's reserve invites suspicion
from both Victorian and modern audiences. Pater clearly exploits such
suspicion in the Leonardo essay, where his rhetoric of secrecy and
transgression seems designed to excite the surveillance of a potential
blackmailer. In Pater's rhetoric, however, the threat of exposure is
turned into a concerted enticement. He claims our interest by intimating his possession of "strange" and "sinister" secrets about Leonardo's art (and hence the artist) that he never fully discloses. Such
ostentatious reticence is in one sense a gesture of fidelity to the surfaces
of Leonardo's art: to explain those images, to decipher their "cryptic
language," would violate the integrity of their mystery. But what is offered as fidelity to a specific image, or to the drama of understanding,
is also a gesture of seduction on the part of the critic. Pater's technique,
that is, not only describes but attempts to reproduce the erotic "fascination" of Leonardo's art.[8]

Such foregrounding of the critic's activity, which we have already
noted in "Winckelmann," follows from a cognitive norm that locates
the significance of cultural artifacts in the discovery of an informing
"temperament" or "personality." This emphasis is a widespread romantic legacy, of course, but Pater is distinctive in stressing the erotic
dimension of its appeal, for which he finds authority in Plato. In *Plato
and Platonism*, his account of what he calls Plato's "animism" clearly
identifies a leading impulse of his own criticism: "the instinctive effort
to find *anima*, the conditions of personality, in whatever pre-occupied
his mind" (169). Indeed, that effort is rehearsed in the central claims
of *Plato and Platonism*, where Pater equates Platonism with a distinctive
"temper," and argues that the "trial-task of criticism" in regard to
Plato is to "reproduce the portrait of a *person*" (125). He concludes

8. Welsh stresses the extent to which the blackmailer's threat to publish a secret generates an intimacy with his or her victim that can be sustained only so long as the
blackmailer fails to carry out the threat—so long, that is, as the secret remains shared
but not public knowledge. This is one version of the larger "paradox of secrecy"
analyzed by Bellman.

that "the *formula* of Plato's genius, the essential condition of the specially Platonic temper, of Platonism," is that of the lover, "carrying an elaborate cultivation of the bodily senses, of eye and ear . . . into the world of spiritual abstractions . . . filling that 'hollow land' with delightful colour and form, as if now at last the mind were veritably dealing with living people there, living people who play upon us through the affinities, the repulsion and attraction, of *persons* towards one another, all the magnetism, as we call it, of actual human friendship or love" (140). In "Style," Pater similarly evokes the quality of "soul" in literature, which appeals especially to readers "to whom nothing has any real interest, or real meaning, except as operative in a given person" (*Appreciations* 26). The Platonic "formula" holds equally for "the lover of strange souls" who is captivated by the fascination of Leonardo's art (*Renaissance* 78). And within this dynamic of magnetic "repulsion and attraction," reserve has a central and special function. (Again we hear echoes of Newman's insistence on "the personal element" in knowledge.) When knowledge is both a function of personality and modeled on the knowledge of a person, mystery is something beyond a temporary obstacle or enticement to knowledge, to be dispelled by the attainment of truth. Instead, mystery remains a permanent and essential element of the experience of understanding. In the words of "Style," the quality of soul in art offers "the completeness of a personal information," yet "it does but suggest what can never be uttered" (*Appreciations* 26).

In his aestheticized version of Platonic eros, Pater subtly but insistently aligns hermeneutics with a quest for human intimacy, yet at the same time suggests that such intimacy can only be experienced through the distancing enforced by aesthetic mediation. Throughout *The Renaissance* he looks to art for *intimité*, which is what he calls "expression" at its most intense. *Intimité* is "the seal on a man's works of what is most inward and peculiar in his moods and manner of apprehension," the culmination of an artist's effort "to bring what was hidden and unseen to the surface" (56). But "expression," as Pater uses the term, does not denote the communication of a particular message or mental state; instead, it refers to the capacity of an object or image to communicate affect to a beholder. Typically, expression is associated with a pronounced intricacy or subtlety of form, which generates a sense of psychic energy informing material fact—what Pater calls "that intimate impress of an indwelling soul." But the effect remains curiously impersonal—as, for example, in Pater's account of the work of fifteenth-century Tuscan sculptors: "The whole essence of their work is *expression*, the passing of a smile over the face of a child, the ripple of the air on a still day over the curtain of a window ajar" (50). Whatever the nature of the effect, it evidently depends on a residue of mystery or opacity. In a work possessing *intimité*, there is always more than meets the eye. Indeed, the quality resides in the very power of an image to suggest some realm of interiority. As "the seal . . . of what is most inward and peculiar" in a work of art, expression is a public stamp of identity that nonetheless seals up a portion of that identity as intractably private, "hidden and unseen." In this regard, what Pater designates "expression" or *intimité* closely resembles what Walter Benjamin calls *aura*. "Experience of the aura," Benjamin writes, "rests on the transposition of a response common in human relationships to the relationship between the inanimate or natural object and man. The person we look at, or who feels he is being looked at, looks at us in turn. To perceive the aura of an object we look at means to invest it with the ability to look at us in return" (*Illuminations* 188). For Benjamin, contrasting the experience of aura to the "shock-experience" of modern life recorded in the poetry of Baudelaire, aura gives structure to experience through an element of ritual; aura is "the unique manifestation of a distance" that is essentially ceremonial in character. Indeed, Benjamin famously refers aura to a cultic conception of art that will inevitably be dispelled by mechanical reproduction. Pater, on the other hand, notoriously struggles to reclaim the cultic significance of the artwork. But Benjamin's account of aura clearly delineates the tension that more diffusely but insistently structures Pater's responses to art. The pursuit of *intimité* offers the spectator an enticing sense of contact with a companionable spirit, but that reward is derived only from what remains "essentially distant," in Benjamin's terms—from an object that is ultimately "inapproachable."

The delicate equipoise of distance and desire that distinguishes *intimité* is enacted in the insistent figuration of surface and depth in Pater's art criticism. Although the essay on Leonardo is the most obvious example, the place of the dynamic in Pater's aestheticism is most suggestively set forth in a late, unpublished manuscript titled "The Aesthetic Life," which recasts the rhetoric of "Leonardo da Vinci" into a comprehensive program of aesthetic education. In this unfinished essay, Pater urges that compensation for the outward dreariness of contemporary England may be obtained through a vigilant refinement of observation that will encompass "the reception of life as a whole." In such "reception," Pater writes, "everywhere, so to speak, he will seek the face the face [*sic*] of man the image of a personal soul, the companionship of that of human soul made visible" (34). Here, it seems, is precisely the pursuit of aura—aura understood as the ability to place even impersonal artifacts within an imagined human history. In such reception, the object of one's "companionship" is tellingly ambiguous, poised between "soul" and the "image" of soul. "Soul" is made available, it seems, only in aesthetic form; it is manifested in the human face, but only when that face is contemplated as a material object, as if it were a portrait. As "soul" makes its presence felt, however, and thereby confirms the expressive character of aesthetic form, it also entices the spectator into imagining the transaction as unmediated contact with another mind. It is the power of Pater's *intimité*, as of Benjamin's aura, to seduce the spectator into surrendering aesthetic detachment and regarding the sense of "intimate presence" in an artwork not as formal effect but as an indwelling psyche. Yet the effort to approach that presence, to fathom the image, so to speak, explodes the distance on which its existence depends. Hence Pater's famous insistence in "The School of Giorgione" (1877) that painting "must be before all things decorative, a thing for the eye, a space of colour on the wall . . . this, to begin and end with" (*Renaissance* 110). "The Aesthetic Life" rephrases this imperative as a prescription for the observer, who should approach "the entire scene of human action experience" [*sic*] as "a portrait to interpret, to get behind, but only that he may return to the face of it, its momentary message to the eye, with finer and fuller sense of the particular visible fact" (35). In this program, the observer's vigilant distancing and aestheticizing of experience is enforced not only by the paradigm of the portrait, but—more remarkably—by the tacit elision of any distinction between "a portrait" and "the face of man," which Pater had previously urged as the paradigmatic object of observation. In another logic that would have a powerful resonance for Wilde, portraits are to be contemplated as faces, and faces as portraits, or masks.

Pater's evocation of art dwells insistently in this unending circle—or, alternatively, in a constant wavering of distance figured as the play of surface and depth. This tension is but one facet of the insistently agonistic structure of the Leonardo essay, the most prominent facet of which is what Pater calls Leonardo's "struggle between the reason and its ideas, and the senses, the desire of beauty" (88). Although the conflict outwardly corresponds to Leonardo's dual vocations as scientist and artist, Pater subtly eroticizes Leonardo's "curiosity." Matthew Arnold had recently given renewed critical currency to "curiosity" in "The Function of Criticism at the Present Time," which Pater had heard delivered as a lecture at Oxford. Pater, however, dislocates the Arnoldian definition of the term as a disinterested play of the mind. Instead, the central dualisms of "Leonardo da Vinci" hearken back to the more volatile binaries of Augustine's *Confessions*, which distinguishes between "the pleasure of these eyes"—Pater's "desire of beauty"—and "the lust of the eyes," which Augustine, too, calls "curiosity." Augustinian curiosity is "another form of temptation more manifestly dangerous" than the desire of beauty, because it seeks out not only beautiful forms, but "the contrary as well, not for the sake of suffering annoyance, but out of the lust of making trial and knowing them": "For what pleasure hath it, to see a mangled carcase that will make you shudder? and yet if it be lying near, they flock thither, to be made sad, and to turn pale . . . From this disease of curiosity, are all those strange sights exhibited in the theatre. Hence men go on to search out the hidden powers of nature, (which is besides our end,) which to know profits not, and wherein men desire nothing but to know" (238–39). Both of Leonardo's vocations represent a virtual apotheosis of such transgressive desire: he is "a bold speculator, holding lightly by other men's beliefs, setting philosophy above Christianity" (*Renaissance* 77), "the possessor of some unsanctified and secret wisdom" (78), "the sorcerer or magician" (84), the scientist who "penetrated into the most secret parts of nature" (86), and the artist whose image of Medusa is suffused with "the fascination of corruption" (83). The depths Leonardo seeks to fathom are a realm of forbidden knowledge, of "strange," "secret," "sinister," "unsanctified" experience.

Pater implicitly anatomizes precisely this feature of his own criticism when he describes Leonardo's achievement as the outgrowth of two "elementary forces," "curiosity and the desire of beauty" (86). The fusion of these two forces, Pater argues, produced the distinctive beauty of Leonardo's art, but they more often came into conflict because curiosity "tended to make him go too far below that outside of things in which art really begins and ends" (88). In seeking to fathom the secrets of beauty, curiosity threatens to dissolve it. But of course Pater displays just this curiosity in his response to Leonardo's enigmatic images: he responds to "the power of an intimate presence" in those images by attempting to fathom them, thereby displaying what he calls "the art of going deep, of tracking the sources of expression to their subtlest retreats" (81). Thus the essay on Leonardo emphatically violates his own prescriptions in "The School of Giorgione." In stressing the enigmatic interiority of Leonardo's images, evoking in them hidden depths harboring "cryptic fancies," Pater exemplifies precisely the activity he attacks in the later essay as "the false generalisation of all art into forms of poetry" (103). His rhetoric subverts the integrity of aesthetic form, that is, by approaching the image as the vehicle of some idea or sentiment it does not fully embody. Yet the "thing for the eye" exerts its attraction precisely as it arouses just such a sense of interiority, and thus entices the spectator into an effort to "get behind" it.

Pater's rhetoric aims to evoke a similar effect in his readers. His rhetoric of secrecy and dangerous wisdom, that is, evokes a curiosity that is checked—but not suppressed—by the refusal to fully disclose what pearls (if any) he has brought up from his own diving in the deep sea of Leonardo's images. This gesture underscores the character of expression, as Pater understands it: an expressive image cannot be opaque, but neither can it be transparent. Like other forms of intimacy, the *intimité* of art is a structure threatened equally by silence and disclosure. But Pater's criticism reproduces that quality by evoking a world of secrets that it fails to disclose. It aims to transfer to the mediation of the critic the "fascination" of Leonardo's art, under the spell of which a reader would respond to the critic's own writing as a repository of forbidden wisdom associated with an enigmatic "soul."

Such a strategy may not seem very specific to Pater: to take only one instance, a similarly ostentatious intimation of forbidden experience is central to the appeal of the Byronic hero. But as Pater connects Leonardo's psychomachia to a particular hermeneutic stance, he links his descriptive techniques to the rise of a central interpretive strategy in Victorian literature and society. In its preoccupation with hidden or recondite meanings, Pater's essay on Leonardo, written in 1868, participates in the obsession with secrecy and exposure that distinguished the exactly contemporary vogue of the sensation novel, whose popularity Alexander Welsh has suggestively linked to the rise of a culture of information. In the same decade, however, hidden meanings took on a different form of cultural authority in another literary development—the growing acceptance of Robert Browning as a major poet. A typically hostile review of *Men and Women* in 1856 attacked as "pure impertinence" the publication of poems "the interpretation of which is a private occurrence, or a conversation to which the public is not admitted."[9] "The public is not admitted": the critic interprets a failure of comprehension as the result of a form of social exclusion, in which the public is belittled by their tantalizing glimpse of a private world

---

9. G. Brimley, *Fraser's Magazine*, January 1856 (Litzinger and Smalley 169).

that remains inaccessible. By 1864, however, with the publication of
Dramatis Personae, the same mystery has become an honorific quality:
mystery has become *difficulty*, which distinguishes any literary work possessing significant meaning. The shift in opinion—and the imagery
central to the debate—is anticipated in a dissenting review of 1856 by
George Eliot: if Browning's reader "finds the meaning difficult of access," she urges, "it is always worth his effort—if he has to dive deep,
'he rises with his pearl.'"[10]

Browning's acceptance, in short, required and in turn reinforced the
authority of a particular manner of reading, in which one approached
the literary work—and human character—as an enigmatic surface to
hidden depths of meaning. It is in this context that Pater in "Winckelmann" instances "Dis Aliter Visum," from *Dramatis Personae*, as a
model of romantic art. In Browning's monologue (which Pater refers
to by its subtitle, *Le Byron de nos Jours*), characters "not intrinsically
interesting" take on new significance through Browning's elaborate
mediation: "what a cobweb of allusions, what double and treble reflexions of the mind upon itself, what an artificial light is constructed and
broken over the chosen situation" (171). The celebration of obliquity,
intricacy, and refinement—qualities figured as glancing, prismatic
lights—may seem characteristically "Paterian," but it is an increasingly
prominent note in criticism of both literary and visual art in the 1860s.
A *Saturday Review* article of 1865, for example, decried representations
of human eyes in both literature and art as objects "to read like a riddle
or a cuneiform inscription" rather than as "essentially things to ad-
mire" (Cowling 97). The distinction tellingly echoes Kingsley's exas-
perated response two decades earlier to the "lawless allegorizing" of
Tractarian exegesis. But for those who relished such difficulty, the satisfaction of grasping the meaning of a difficult work brought with it
the sense of admission into an exclusive community—a response that
united the Pre-Raphaelites with those more respectable devotees of the
official Browning Society. Swinburne made the appeal most boldly, in his
William Blake (1865): in looking to literature for "the high and subtle
luxuries of exceptional temperament," he urged that such "bread of
sweet thought and wine of delight is not broken or shed for all, but for a
few only. . . . The sacramental elements of art and poetry . . . [are] reserved for the sublime profit and intense pleasure of an elect body or

10. [Mary Ann Evans], *Westminster Review*, January 1856 (Litzinger and Smalley 174). For
an account of the shift in views of Browning as the focal point of a change in literary
criticism in the 1860s, see Woolford.

church" (85).[11] With this claim, the search for "deep meanings" bears out Kingsley's worst fears: the cultural vanguard of England, celebrating an art accessible only to an elite few, openly declares itself a priesthood subversive of both Christianity and an orthodox morality of art. But the same response was echoed by less daring critics, who also were gratified by the belief that in comprehending "deep" art one confirmed a correspondent depth in oneself. As George Eliot put it, "What we took for obscurity in him was superficiality in ourselves" (Litzinger and Smalley 174–75).

When Pater calls Leonardo an expert in "the art of going deep," and finds in his supreme artifact, the Gioconda, "a diver in deep seas," he signals the dependence of his rhetoric on just such a mode of reading. He is appealing, that is, to a reader who expects to encounter difficulty, and who looks for meaning in that which is hidden, secret, or arcane—a reader, in short, who has mastered what Althusser calls symptomatic reading. But Pater's reserve in regard to Leonardo's secrets also encourages the reader to respond to Pater's own works in precisely the way that he responds to Leonardo's: as a seductive veil to the secret, seemingly unfathomable depths of an exquisite sensibility. And this public withholding of private information works in turn to enforce a charismatic authority in the author. This is the sociological dynamic first seized upon by Georg Simmel:

> That which we can see through plainly to its last ground, shows us therewith the limit of its attraction.... If the utmost attractiveness of another person is to be preserved for us, it must be presented to us in part in the form of vagueness or impenetrability. This is the only substitute which the great majority of people can offer for that attractive value which the small minority possess through the inexhaustibility of their inner life and growth. (Simmel, "Secrecy" 461–62)[12]

Here is another construction of charisma in terms that clearly link Marius's reserve to Leonardo's art. Like Benjaminian *aura*, this charisma is

---

11. Swinburne's prose style had a crucial influence on Pater's early writings (as, according to Swinburne, Pater acknowledged); the debt is especially marked in comparing the Leonardo essay with Swinburne's "Notes on Designs of the Old Masters at Florence," which appeared in the *Fortnightly Review* of July 1, 1868. But Swinburne's episodic, desultory commentary—which in structure derives from Royal Academy reviews—Pater transforms into a new kind of critical portraiture.

12. Bartley recalls the outraged reactions to his discussion of Wittgenstein's homosexuality in a biography of the philosopher. "*Indefiniteness is essential*: the taboo and the temptation must be there together," he concludes of Wittgenstein's charismatic influence; once the mystery was gone, "it was 'just sex'" (193–96).

endangered equally by silence and by disclosure, or (in visual terms) by opacity and by transparency. The normative, intermediate state of "vagueness," of reserve or a form of veiling, is necessary to sustain what Simmel calls *nescience,* the condition of ignorance regarding another mind. But this impenetrability, Simmel reminds us, is something more than a resistance to surveillance: it is the intractable residue of mystery that is essential to charismatic influence, and thus to the seductive pleasures that Pater derives from art—and hopes to extend in turn to his reader.

Of course a treatment of secrecy and obliquity along Foucauldian lines would see in this very strategy a capitulation to the disciplinary order of Victorian discourse: the very fascination we enjoy in reading "Leonardo da Vinci," one might argue, normalizes life under hostile surveillance. D. A. Miller, for example, argues in *The Novel and the Police* that secrecy in the Victorian novel is "radically empty," because it embodies a character's vain effort to affirm autonomy in the face of a disciplinary order that the subject internalizes in the very act of keeping secrets. Hence the closely guarded secrets of Dickens's characters, for example, frequently turn out to be mere clichés, the platitudes of the society against which the characters are struggling to defend themselves. Miller finds this irony anatomized in *The Picture of Dorian Gray,* in a remark of Basil Hallward the painter: "I have grown to love secrecy. It seems to be the one thing that can make modern life mysterious or marvellous to us. The commonest thing is delightful if only one hides it." Here, Miller urges, Wilde exposes "the misleading common sense that finds the necessity of secrets in the 'special' nature of the contents concealed" (195).

But this reading exposes a curiously puritanical strain in Foucauldian tactics. What Wilde has done is not to mock "common sense" but to neatly anticipate Simmel's account of the relation between secrecy and charisma. In his insistence that there are no innocent pleasures, Miller reproduces a very Victorian suspicion of theatricality. But Wilde's appeal to his audience's "common sense" typically follows Pater's practice in calling on secrecy not to demystify, but to fascinate. After all, to the audience that *assumes* every secret is special, the mere assertion—or intimation—that one *has* a secret becomes a source of fascination. That claim offers the reader or observer a sense of proximity to the subject's private life, a sense of intimacy that feeds on the prospect of acquiring further, and perhaps more "special," knowledge. But of course Miller's own suave rhetoric in his essay, "Secret Subjects, Open Secrets," is just such an exercise in enticement. By everywhere intimating one's possession of secrets that are never disclosed, the author invites an audience to invest his or her achievement with secrets of its own, secrets that may be far more "special," more "mysterious or marvellous," than anything the author actually possesses, or might convey in less arcane forms. Wilde himself acknowledges this strategy more tendentiously: "What Dorian Gray's sins are no one knows. He who finds them has brought them" (*Letters* 266). But that refusal also sustains the "vagueness or impenetrability" that, as Simmel notes, is essential to fascination. In Wilde as in Pater, the rhetoric of fascination appeals to the reader to acknowledge "the utmost attractiveness," as Simmel puts it, in both the character and the author. Pater's most famous prose is in this sense an exercise of reserve: it is offered as the index of (again, in Simmel's terms) an "inexhaustibility of . . . inner life and growth," which solicits a response like that of Marius's youthful audience, who regard his reserve as a sign that he has been "initiated into a great secret" (*Marius* 1:157).

CRITICAL INITIATION: AESTHETICISM AS RITUAL

Pater's rhetorical strategies thus reinforce the manifest themes of his work by urging readers to experience his own influence on the model of the "fascination" of his personae: as a form of initiation. The critic himself begins to displace the traditional artifact as the centerpiece of cultic authority. Leonardo, Pater claims, surrounded himself with young men "capable of being initiated into his secret" (*Renaissance* 86). But Pater's own writings likewise beckon to the reader with the promise he discovers in Wordsworth's poetry:

> He meets us with the promise that he has much, and something very peculiar, to give us, if we will follow a certain difficult way, and seems to have the secret of a special and privileged state of mind. And those who have undergone his influence, and followed this difficult way, are like people who have passed through some initiation, a *disciplina arcani*, by submitting to which they become constantly able to distinguish in art, speech, feeling, manners, that which is organic, animated, expressive, from that which is only conventional, derivative, inexpressive. (*Appreciations* 41)

The appropriately attentive and devoted reader of Wordsworth is initiated into a secret society, whose wisdom is manifested in a technique

of beholding that embraces not only art but all forms of human experience susceptible of aesthetic apprehension—"speech, feeling,
manners." If the reader finds a similar reward in reading Pater, his
works will take their place in the hallowed transmission of the same *ars
aesthetica* that informs Wordsworth's poetry. That arcane tradition
would be fulfilled in the transformation of life itself into a ritualized
beholding—which is precisely the promise codified in Marius's "New
Cyrenaicism," where Marius envisions his life as "an ordered service to
the visible world."

Here is an alternative version of the structure of apostolic succession
that Pater sketches as early as "Winckelmann." Once again, the critic's
authority is grounded in a charismatic tradition whose members constitute a body akin to a secret society or religious cult. And similar
structures are invoked throughout Pater's writings, which are full of
descriptions of secret societies, both imagined and historical. In addition to the Orphics of *Greek Studies*, and the Pythagorean brotherhood
and Sparta in *Plato and Platonism*, early Christianity in *Marius* derives
much of its appeal from its structure as an extended secret society.
Indeed, so powerful is the appeal of that structure that when Marius
hears Fronto's appeal to the idea of "humanity" as a moral ideal, he
immediately envisions this abstraction as "some vast secret society"
(2:11). Like the other secret societies Pater evokes, this is not the paranoid fantasy of a hidden enemy, which so often surfaces in late Victorian literature and journalism. Instead, it represents—as it had for
many Tractarian enthusiasts—a utopian vision of community seen from
the margins of society. The particular secrets that bind together such
societies necessarily remain obscure: they seem to designate a particular
state of mind or mode of existence rather than a body of discursive
lore, and hence are not to be revealed, only experienced. In this sense,
a form of secret society is implicitly constituted in virtually all of Pater's
accounts of the reception and transmission of artworks or cultural
traditions. The prototype of such accounts is "the Hellenic tradition"
constructed in "Winckelmann," a tradition that is animated by, and in
turn legitimates, an elite community of "enthusiasts" linked by their
shared devotion to "the Greek ideal." But of course this same model
suggests that Paterian secrecy is inevitably homoerotic, and that his
rhetoric of secrecy and secret societies marks a calculated affiliation
with homoerotic subcultures that still remain shadowy in recent social
and literary histories of Victorian England.[13] Certainly the highly-

13. Dowling's exemplary *Hellenism and Homosexuality* has the great advantage of dealing

charged rhetoric of transgression in "Leonardo da Vinci" suggests that the "secret" into which Leonardo initiates young men is as much sexual as artistic. And Pater's trope of arcane wisdom thus invites the fin-de-siècle celebration of art as an irrevocable initiation into dangerous experience, as in the trope of "the fatal book" (Dowling, "Pater").

But Pater's prose does not exhaust the potential significance of secrecy in late Victorian discourse. Homoerotic desire is but one structure that may be articulated through an appeal to secrecy, which operates within a more comprehensive, more inchoate construction of charismatic masculine authority that we have been tracing throughout Victorian rhetorics of masculinity. As it is associated with both elite understanding and a capacity for self-regulation, a rhetoric of secrecy may be deployed as above all else a claim to power. And the potential threat posed by such a claim seems acknowledged in the gendered norm of communication that fiercely proscribes secrecy or obliquity. "Manly" writing or speech is clear, direct, and forthright: in the words of James Fitzjames Stephen in 1862, "the great characteristic of the manners of a gentleman, as we conceive them in England, is plain, downright, frank simplicity . . . the outward and visible sign of the two great cognate virtues—truth and courage" ("Gentlemen" 336). Hence the hermeneutic of suspicion that Newman analyzes in his sermon, "Innocence and Wisdom": "the world," disturbed by the secrecy of those who withdraw from its scrutiny, interprets the transgression as a subversion of manliness. As one element in the rise of a social hermeneutics of suspicion, the discipline of masculinity would eliminate any hint of disjunction between surface and substance; even as it enforces the habit of emotional reserve, the ideal of the gentleman presumes that one has nothing to hide. But it is important not to conflate gender deviance with sexual transgression. A sufficiently rigorous paranoia, after all, can discover transgression in any gesture of self-witholding or intimation of secrecy. As such gestures solidify male communities, however, they call attention to, and hence arouse anxiety over, the unstated and unstable boundaries that structure the homosocial continuum. The hostility aroused by collective male secrecy underscores the intensity of the fears that organize relations between men; it marks, in Sedgwick's phrase, "the coming to visibility of the normally implicit terms of a coercive double bind" (*Between Men* 89). By the same token, however, such hostility is a treacherous guide to the historian

with such a subculture in the unusually self-conscious, expressive, and (relatively) visible community of the University of Oxford.

who sees in male secrecy a necessary index of transgressive sexual desire. In itself, that hostility can only confirm gender heterodoxy—and thus the powers of social control that may be mobilized by appeals to gender.

Exposed to a mid-Victorian hermeneutic of gender, the figures of gentleman, dandy, and priest begin to circulate among one another, as each incites suspicion of "effeminacy." We have been glancing at the circulation of these figures throughout this book, but it takes on special clarity in relation to the particular society that Pater alludes to when he describes Wordsworth's "difficult way." The *disciplina arcani* was a central concept in Tractarian theology, and became a focal point of public controversy precisely because, by authorizing a special "reserve" in the communication of truth to "the profane and uninstructed," it raised suspicions of deviousness and falsehood. Hence Newman devoted an appendix of his *Apologia* to explaining this concept of an economy of truth, which he had described in *The Arians of the Fourth Century* as "this self-restraint and abstinence . . . in the publication of the most sacred doctrines of our religion" (49–50). Marius's reserve exemplifies the translation of such self-restraint into a social strategy, which divides the world into initiates and outsiders, while calling attention to Marius as one "in possession of a great secret." And the implicit elite joined by the discipline of secrecy defines a social space that frequently informs Pater's representation of his own vocation. "All disinterested lovers of books," he contends in "Style," will look to literature as "a refuge, a sort of cloistral refuge, from a certain vulgarity in the actual world" (*Appreciations* 18). Although this trope might suggest a rather simple-minded escapism, or simply an immersion in art, it takes on more literal significance when Pater continues, "A perfect poem like *Lycidas*, a perfect fiction like *Esmond*, the perfect handling of a theory like Newman's *Idea of a University*, has for them something of the uses of a religious 'retreat.'" A religious retreat associated with the name of Newman is a far cry from the palace of art. It may be a refuge, but it also circumscribes an elite society constructed around an ascetic discipline. That discipline is registered most palpably in the form of ritual, which (as Simmel first poined out) forms one of the central attractions and organizing structures of a secret society. Ritual enforces in its participants an "energetic consciousness of their life. This life substitutes for the organically more instinctive forces an incessantly regulating will; for growth from within, constructive purposefulness" (Simmel, "Secrecy" 478).[14] From the time of his attack on

14. The appeal of social exclusivity joined with the energetic consciousness of danger

Coleridge's organicism in "Coleridge's Writings" (1866), his earliest published essay, and his accounts of the Greek sculptor in "Winckelmann," Pater associates his vocation with just such models of incessantly self-regulating will, which in his later works he highlights as *askesis*. Such discipline is the burden of Marius's reserve, which is offered as a direct outgrowth of the boy's solemn participation in religious ritual. Pater's hero in *Gaston de Latour* likewise develops his passionate observation out of his boyhood calling as a priest. Indeed, the remarkable prominence of ritual throughout Pater's writings— most thoroughly studied by Richard Stein—is reflected in the many contemporary tributes to the "hieratic" character of his prose. As "a new form of the contemplative life," then, Marius's New Cyrenaicism identifies something more than the displacement of divinity by works of art. Pater is appealing to the discipline of ritualized devotion as a means of giving shape and solemnity to a life of aesthetic experience— of realizing aestheticism as what Foucault has called a technology of the self.

A self-regulating will seems absolutely normative in Victorian rhetorics of masculinity. Yet when the discipline it enforces crosses an elusive boundary that demarcates a realm of ostentation, or theatricality, or calculated social role—when, that is, discipline is manifested as public ritual—contemporary observers typically attack it as a form of effeminacy. This is the burden of Kingsley's heated attacks on the "fastidious, maundering, die-away effeminacy" of the Tractarians, which conflate the priest with the dandy (*Life and Works* 1:260). Yet the very terms of Kingsley's attack also concede, as we saw in Chapter 2, a powerful resemblance between Tractarian "foppery" and many versions of the gentleman's good form.[15] This association of religious ritual with a kind of dandyism agitated even more sympathetic observers. Samuel Wilberforce, bishop of Oxford and founder of the college for Anglican clergy at Cuddesdon, wrote in 1858,

> Our men are too peculiar—some, at least, of our best men. . . . I consider
> it a heavy affliction that they should wear neckclothes of peculiar con-

---

certainly helps to explain Wilde's fascination with various forms of secret societies, including the Catholicism with which he flirted throughout his life. Pater, according to his early biographer Thomas Wright, regularly attended ritualist services at the all-male congregation of St. Austin's Priory in Walworth, South London, founded by a maverick Anglican "Order of St Augustine" in 1872.

15. The vehemence, as many critics have pointed out, is a measure of Kingsley's early attraction to the movement; even after he repudiated its "Manicheanism" he conceded "a solemn and gentlemanlike earnestness which is most beautiful."

struction, coats of peculiar cut, whiskers of peculiar dimension—that they
should walk with a peculiar step, carry their heads at a peculiar angle to
the body, and read in a peculiar tone. I consider all this as a heavy af-
fliction. First because it implies to me a want of vigour, virility, and self-
expressing vitality of the religious life in the young men. (Newsome,
Godliness 208)

Once again one catches unexpected echoes of Baudelaire's claim that
the dandy's discipline rivals that of "the strictest monastic rule." As
both dandy and priest resist participation in economic life, and—perhaps more important—as they seem to display a theatrical self-
consciousness, they intrude on a position that in Victorian life is
reserved for the feminine.[16] Hence the character of contemporary attacks on critics who adopted a similar stance—not only Pater but Matthew Arnold, whose conception of culture was frequently decried as a
form of dandyism. While social turmoil on every side cries out for re-
medial action, Frederic Harrison objected, "over all sits Culture high
aloft with a pouncet-box to spare her senses aught unpleasant."[17]

"VIRILE CONSCIOUSNESS": MANLINESS IN ART AND LIFE

The logics of self-display informing masculine discipline impose a
special burden on the apologetic design of *Marius*. As Pater stresses the
fascination aroused by Marius's reserve, he must at the same time place
Marius's masculinity beyond suspicion. That challenge informs Pater's
careful separation of Marius from the dandyism of Aurelius's decadent
brother Lucius Verus, a second-century Wilde whose "more than wom-
anly fondness for fond things" gives rise to a cult devoted to "minute
details of attire and manner" (1:195–96). In a more concerted strategy,
however, Pater calls on an emphatically gendered rhetoric to locate
Marius's virility entirely apart from outward demeanor, in the very
strength of his intellect. Marius is guided by a "singularly virile consciousness of the realities of life" (1:43), "virile apprehension of the
true nature of things, of the true nature of one's own impression, first

16. Psychoanalytic accounts of Pater's Gioconda overlook this social affiliation between
    the aesthete and a dangerous femininity, which is helpfully stressed by Gagnier, *Idylls
    of the Marketplace* (67–81), who examines affinities between dandies and women in
    late Victorian society.
17. Frederic Harrison, "Culture: A Dialogue," *Fortnightly Review*, November 1867 (re-
    printed in Dawson and Pfordresher 233).

of all!" (1:155). As in "Manly Amusement," moral awareness is masculine awareness, and its language is the language of earnestness. Here,
however, Pater implicitly reinforces Victorian gender norms with the
ancient Greek dichotomy of masculine form and feminine matter
(Lloyd 1–18). This is an increasingly explicit formulation in his later
writings, especially in *Plato and Platonism*, where a conception of "manliness in art" is offered as the type and basis of a comprehensive masculine ethos:

> Manliness in art, what can it be, as distinct from that which in opposition
> to it must be called the feminine quality there,—what but a full con-
> sciousness of what one does, of art itself in the work of art, tenacity of
> intuition and consequent purpose, the spirit of construction as opposed
> to what is literally incoherent or ready to fall to pieces, and, in opposition
> to what is hysteric or works at random, the maintenance of a standard.
> (280–81)

The maintenance of a standard: this is, of course, precisely what is at
stake in Marius's appeal to his conscience in "Manly Amusement," and
also what seems to be incarnated in the "carefully measured" self-
discipline of Marius's reserve. More generally, however, masculine self-
awareness and rational form are affirmed not only *within* writing, but
in the very *act* of writing, since writing imposes logical structure on the
random, incoherent flux of experience. Accordingly, throughout Pater's later career, writing figures as a consummately masculine intellectual labor, the imposition of form on recalcitrant material: in the terms
of the essay, "Style," the writer requires not only an austere "self-
restraint" (a phrase repeated several times) in dealing with language,
but "a full, rich, complex matter to grapple with" (*Appreciations* 16).
Or, in the terms of *Marius*, "the male element, the logical conscience
asserted itself now, with opening manhood—asserted itself, even in his
literary style, by a certain firmness of outline, that touch of the worker
in metal, amid its richness" (1:156).

Such tributes to the painstaking literary craftsman are frequently
cited as Pater's contribution to a "decadent" cult of style. But they are
equally an engagement with Victorian discourses of masculinity. Although we have noted a rhetoric of self-purifying asceticism in Pater's
earliest writings—in, for example, the celebration of "purgation" and
"passionate coldness" in "Winckelmann"—the rhetoric begins to be
emphatically (and conventionally) gendered only after the attacks on
his "effeminate desires" in the mid-1870s. In linking ascetic discipline

to traditional appropriations of rationality as a distinctly masculine attribute, Pater formulated a rhetoric that was especially appealing to the male Victorian writer and professional, who "had far more difficulty than the businessman in laying claim to a positive male image such as that of the civilized hunter" (Stearns 112–13, 135). Not surprisingly, Pater's discovery of manhood in the appreciation of exacting prose has found a sympathetic audience among male readers. Indeed, the continuing success of Pater's rhetorical self-construction has been vividly (albeit unwittingly) confirmed by the anthropologist David Gilmore, who recently quoted Pater's description of "manliness in art" as the epitome of a trans-cultural norm of "manhood" understood as "a mythic confabulation that sanctifies male constructivity" (113, 226). If one considers Pater's description in historical context, however, his role as a spokesman for manhood is rich in irony. Pater's account of "manliness" is formulated in tacit response to suspicions about his own masculinity; it appears in a book devoted to Plato, whose writings were for Pater and late-Victorian culture a central locus of transgressive male sexuality; and Pater defines "manliness" in terms that his own early writings seem to confound. "The maintenance of a standard," after all, is precisely what Pater seems to renounce at the outset of his career, inasmuch as the phrase suggests an evaluation of art against certain aesthetic norms, rather than a self-delighting surrender to "experience." Yet the shaping authority of an artistic standard is already implicit in "Winckelmann" and the "Conclusion" as a program of ascetic self-fashioning, in the *psychological* ideal of organizing life as "a hard gem-like flame." Pater's emphatic gendering of the act of writing works to translate this discipline of self-fashioning into more familiar terms of artistic production.

To effect this transformation, however, Pater must revise the ethos of spectatorship that presides over the "Conclusion." "Not the fruit of experience, but experience itself, is the end," he famously declares, but an artwork is "experience itself" only from the spectator's vantage. For an artist engaged in material production, the completed work is emphatically the fruit of experience, which is created through the very dynamic of deferral and instrumentality that Pater repudiates—along with so much else—under the banner of "experience itself." The spectator's achievement is similarly normative in the charismatic appeal of Marius's reserve: it is Marius's very being, after all, not his artistic production, that fascinates his audience. And yet Marius, like his creator, harbors more traditional artistic ambitions—and thus comes to recognize "a kind of inconsistency" in the desires that govern his life. On the one hand, Marius pursues "the ideal Now" as an immersion in the pleasures of immediate sensation, which would be compromised by any subordination of one form of pleasure, or one moment, to another. At the same time, however, Marius longs for "something to hold by" amid the Heraclitean flux of impressions, for a means of fixing and enhancing the pleasures of "experience itself." In a narrow sense, the conflict distinguishes two forms of spectatorship: one that embraces a specific aesthetic or criteria of evaluation—"the maintenance of a standard"; another that upholds what is in effect an ideal of the innocent eye. But inasmuch as conventional artistic production rests on some form of aesthetic, the "kind of inconsistency" Marius acknowledges ultimately embraces a conflict between spectator and artist.[18]

In a sense, this "inconsistency" restates a conflict noted in the previous chapter between Keats's "negative capability" and the "egotistical sublime" that he associated with Wordsworth and Milton. Pater throughout his writings represents a version of this distinction as a competition between "rival religions" whose claims divide the allegiance of his heroes. Thus, for example, Marius ponders his intellectual predicament as he looks forward to his first vision of the early Christian mass: "The thirst for every kind of experience, encouraged by a philosophy which taught that nothing was inherently great or small, good or evil, had ever been at strife in him with a hieratic refinement, in which the boy-priest survived, prompting always the selection of what was perfect in its kind, with subsequent loyal adherence of his soul thereto" (2:107). As throughout the novel, the specifically religious dilemma is also a moral, aesthetic, and—in marked departure from Keats—gendered opposition. For Marius, to embrace Christianity would be to affirm an aesthetic standard—the selection of what was perfect of its kind—and thereby also to give content to the boy-priest's inchoate "sense of responsibility," which impels and directs his masculine self-discipline. On the other hand, the refusal of such a principle would entail that he remain an undisciplined spectator, whose experience is a "literally incoherent"—and therefore feminine—assemblage of discrete, random moments. By thus gendering the encounter with Christianity, Pater raises the stakes in Marius's, and his own, career: if "the spirit of construction" is not triumphant in Marius's activity, if he

18. On the tensions in Pater between spectatorship and artistic production, see Poirier, 30–31, and McGowan, 420–26.

fails to realize a coherent ethos of religious "responsibility," then by
Pater's own criteria his vocation represents a triumph of "the feminine
quality."

In witnessing the Christian mass, Marius would seem to have arrived
at his quest's end. Here, it seems, is "the seeing of a perfect humanity,
in a perfect world," of which he has long dreamed. Throughout his
pilgrimage, he had set such seeing "above the *having*, or even the *doing*,
of anything. For, such vision, if received with due attitude on his part,
was, in reality, the being something, and as such was surely a pleasant
offering or sacrifice to whatever gods there might be, observant of him"
(2:218). Yet in thus summing up his quest, Marius already has surren-
dered the artist's discipline. He directs his energies instead toward the
cultivation of a "due attitude"—a "being" rather than a "having" or
"doing"—that, like his distinctive reserve, will in itself present a re-
warding spectacle to imagined observers. Not surprisingly, then, even
Marius's experience of the Mass ultimately remains but one beautiful
"vision" among many. Yet from this apparent failure of commitment
Pater elicits a triumph of self-discipline. Marius approaches perfection
not in the realization of any single vision, but through his powers of
reception, his "general capacities of vision," which are confirmed precisely by his refusal to embrace any single vision as an object of his
allegiance. The ultimate triumph of his sense of responsibility lies in
the innocent eye—but an innocent eye presented as the culmination
of incessant discipline. Hence the paradoxical claim that Marius's "unclouded receptivity of soul" has "grown so steadily through all those
years" precisely by remaining *unchanged*: his "unclouded and receptive
soul" is leaving the world "with the same fresh wonder with which it
had entered the world still unimpaired" (2:224).

In fundamental respects, the resolution of *Marius* remains faithful
to the imperatives of "Winckelmann." In the terms of that essay, Marius's "unclouded and receptive soul" marks another imagined recuperation of "the delicate pause in Greek reflexion": the strenuously
self-effacing ideal of the mind as *tabula rasa* is faithful to the "passionate
coldness" that distinguishes both Greek sculpture and the culture it
embodies. Thus Marius imagines himself once again in a posture of
perfect receptivity, preserving "the house ready for the possible guest;
the tablet of the mind white and smooth, for whatever divine fingers
might choose to write there" (2:224). Here is the culmination of Marius's reserve, of the self-discipline that sustains it, and of the insistence
on purity that is central to Pater's rhetoric of earnestness: Marius's
crowning moral and aesthetic achievement is a radical self-effacement.

As in "Winckelmann," culture is available only to the observer who refuses to embrace any one "form" of "the life of culture" as an adequate embodiment of that life. To be sure, Marius's "receptivity" still seems directed to "some possible further revelation," and in this light many commentators have read the novel as an episode in the Victorian literature of honest doubt. But Marius's deathbed meditation articulates a more skeptical logic: "Surely, the aim of a true philosophy must lie ... in the maintenance of a kind of candid discontent, in the face of the very highest achievement" (2:220). The Cyrenaic ideal of "disinterested" beholding has hardened into a "discontent" that refuses to acquiesce in any image as the embodiment of an ideal standard. Thus Pater reproduces the peculiarly open-ended and objectless dynamic of the romantic quest, in which finality is failure, by suggesting that a conventionally feminine posture of passive expectancy is the assertion of a strenuously masculine discipline. "The maintenance of a standard" is affirmed in the conclusion that all earthly standards are inadequate. Such are the rigors of Marius's "new form of the contemplative life," in which the only form of artistic production will be the worshiper's very being.

The same paradox is recapitulated (as we saw in the previous chapter) within Pater's account of the authoritarian, indeed brutal masculinist ethos of Sparta in *Plato and Platonism*. The fantasy of authority articulated in Marius's reserve is echoed in his account of Spartan discipline: renunciation and self-effacement become modes of self-assertion, in which an aesthetic organization of one's being confirms the gratifying sense of power. The evocation of Sparta likewise embodies the "desire for predominance" that Marius detects in his friend Flavian, and which Pater repeatedly associates with the soldier. In *Gaston de Latour*, for example, Pater describes his hero's effect on his fellow priests: "It was part of their precocious worldliness to recognise, to feel a little afraid of, their new companion's intellectual power" (38)— a "power" that is closely connected with a delight in "every incident of soldiering": "Half-clerical, they loved nevertheless the touch of steel. . . . In mimicry of the great world, they had their leaders, so inscrutably self-imposed:—instinctively, they felt and underwent that mystery of leadership, with its consequent heats of spirit, its tides and changes of influence" (34). Here a Paterian delight in intellectual mystique is harnessed to a markedly Carlylean hero-worship. Out of this unlikely but pervasive conjunction in Pater's writings grows the more complex preoccupation with Spartan *askesis* as the apotheosis of the manly discipline that unites gentleman, dandy, priest, and soldier.

"Ethically it aimed at the reality, aesthetically at the expression, of reserved power, and from the first set its subject on the thought of his
personal dignity, of self-command, in the artistic way of a good musician, a good soldier" (*Plato and Platonism* 221). And the triumph of
such discipline is once again the male body: under "the Pythagorean
philosophy of music, of austere music, mastering, remoulding, men's
very bodies," the young warriors emerge from their "severe schools . . .
like some perfect musical instrument, perfectly responsive to the intention, to the lightest touch, of the finger of law" (72).

John Buchan, along with other contemporaries, singled out "Lacedaemon" as the mark of "a real change of attitude" over the course
of Pater's career. "The discipline of the ritualist was changing to the
discipline of the thinker. . . . The soul is no longer a mirror but a fire"
(Seiler 404). But such praise uncritically embraces Pater's own late
rhetoric, which obscures the continuity between ritual and *askesis* as
varieties of the discipline of self-fashioning announced in "Winckelmann." "If we mean to mould our lives to artistic perfection": this is
how Pater poses the challenge of culture (*Renaissance* 185). One might
say, then, that Marius envisions *himself* as Mallarmé's "poème dégagé
de tout appareil du scribe." But that aspiration only underscores the
powerful ascetic impulse in Pater's aestheticism. Mallarmé's dream, as
we saw in Chapter 1, is itself an outgrowth of the suspicion of rhetoric
that agitates the Carlylean hero; it is an extension of the ascetic regulation that connects Paterian self-fashioning with the literary program
sketched in "Style." Marius's self-delighted contemplation of himself
as a *tabula rasa*, that is, shares with Mallarmé's dream both an impulse
toward form and a rejection of all form as worldly and hence death to
the spirit. In this regard, the conclusion of *Marius* bears out Geoffrey
Harpham's more general claim that asceticism is the distinctively "cultural" element in culture (Harpham xiv–xv). As such, however, the
aspirations of the Paterian critic generate a profound gender dissonance. On the one hand, Marius's self-regulation is presented as the
product of a resolutely "virile" consciousness and executive will. Yet
the ideal is not only bound to a renunciation of action; it culminates
in a traditionally feminine position, in which textuality is inscribed in
the body (Gubar). This is the logic that Yeats recognized in his sum-
mary assessment of Pater (which pointedly reverses Buchan's): whatever
the fascination of Pater's prose, Yeats concluded, his ideal of culture
"can only create feminine souls. The soul becomes a mirror not a bra-
zier" (*Autobiography* 323).

WILDE AND THE NEW GIOCONDA

I have emphasized the extent to which Pater locates the fulfillment of his discipline in a realm of self-fashioning apart from, and prior to, the conventional "manliness" of writing. In this sense, he remains faithful to the Platonic "temper" he analyzes throughout his writings. And it is this understanding of aestheticism as a technology of transgressive selfhood that marks Pater's most important legacy to Wilde. Of course the fact of Pater's influence on Wilde is a commonplace, but most sustained analyses of it go little beyond identifying verbal echoes, or pointing to a cult of art. More important affinities tend to be obscured by facile contrasts of "temperament," in which the almost pathologically reticent don is set against the histrionic self-promoter. And yet *Dorian Gray* can be seen as a sustained exploration of Paterian self-fashioning, which is insistently preoccupied with the perplexity that informs the irresolution of *Marius*. Once the artwork has been displaced by the observer, and the pursuit of "culture" is identified with a process of self-fashioning, where does one find the guiding principle, the *technē*, that would order that program? Wilde will suggest that the only bounding order to a potential infinitude of "selves" lies in history itself. But in this regard he gestures toward a resolution that Pater had already anatomized—and in a form that points directly to a modernist poetics of history.

Long read as a moralizing account of aristocratic "decadence," *Dorian Gray* in fact represents a triangle of men caught up in an eminently middle-class struggle for charismatic "influence," an authority that derives not from the marketplace but from the seemingly irresistible—and hence dangerous—"fascination" of an exquisite personality. This is the project of the dandy, of course, but also of the Paterian critic, and Wilde's protagonist emphatically reaffirms the persistent Victorian continuum between the dandy's social authority and the critic's intellectual authority. Like Marius, Dorian mesmerizes spectators by an outward elegance that is the index of psychic mystery; indeed, the main difference between the two characters is Dorian's more overt ambition, which recalls the "desire for predominance" that distinguishes Pater's Flavian. Dorian "desired to be something more than a mere *arbiter elegantiarum*. . . . He sought to elaborate some new scheme of life" (101). The "new Hedonism" that he embraces as such a "scheme" is appropriated almost entirely from Pater—even to the point of borrow-

ing Pater's exact phrasing in the "Conclusion": "It was to have its
service of the intellect, certainly; yet it was never to accept any theory
or system that would involve the sacrifice of any mode of passionate
experience. Its aim, indeed, was to be experience itself, and not the
fruits of experience. . . . [I]t was to teach man to concentrate himself
upon the moments of a life that is itself but a moment" (101).

Yet Wilde's appropriation of Pater's manifesto underscores its persistent incoherence. As in most Victorian models of self-discipline, Paterian "concentration" of self is experienced first of all as an
energizing and enrichment of psychic depth. In this regard, both Pater
and Wilde are clearly indebted to the Victorian conception of "character"—the maintenance of a stable, autonomous fund of purposeful
energy—as a leading masculine virtue. This rather surprising affiliation
is typically obscured, however, by a competing rhetoric of selfhood associated with the "culture" that Pater derives from German *Bildung.*
Under this view, the realization of selfhood is attained through a multiplication of "selves"—selves, moreover, which are experienced not as
stepping-stones in some linear ascent (as, for example, in the sequence
of "dead selves" Tennyson contemplates at the outset of *In Memoriam*)
but rather as coexistent, perhaps conflicting, elements of a larger, com-
posite identity. Under this scheme, masculine discipline is figured not
as renunciation but as the simultaneous multiplication and harmoniz-
ing of disparate "selves" into a larger unity. Pater's review of Wilde's
novel criticized it on precisely this point, that it failed to offer an image
of suitably "harmonious development": "A true Epicureanism aims at
a complete though harmonious development of man's entire organism.
To lose the moral sense therefore, for instance, the sense of sin and
righteousness, as Mr. Wilde's hero—his heroes are bent on doing as
speedily, as completely as they can, is to lose, or lower, organization,
to become less complex, to pass from a higher to a lower degree of
development" (*"Dorian Gray"* 59). In arraigning Wilde at the bar of "a
true Epicureanism," Pater acknowledges the affinities between Wilde's
hero and his own Marius. But the failure of "organization" that Pater
identifies is also a central feature of his legacy. The "suspended judgment" with which *Marius* concludes only reaffirms the tension, more
glaring in the "Conclusion," between an ideal of "complete" development and the intervention of any "moral sense" recognizable as a
constraint on conduct. Indeed, the very phrasing of Pater's objection
reveals a more powerful affinity with Wilde: the "moral sense" to which
Pater appeals seems less a regulative principle than one mode of experience among many, without which the "organization" of conscious-

ness is necessarily less complex. As such, the moral sense enforces a thoroughly aestheticized morality; it is one facet of an appropriately refined and manifold taste, or the "tact" Pater celebrates in "Winckelmann."

But "the sense of sin and righteousness" is integral to a more distinctive satisfaction of "Epicureanism," inasmuch as it underwrites the "antinomianism" that Pater savors throughout his writings, particularly in *The Renaissance*. Whatever the qualifications of his later work, Pater's early essays appeal to the moral sense by subtly flouting it. But here we encounter the paradox we have seen in the historical formulations of "Winckelmann": if "the Greek ideal" is in one respect utopian, the (literal) embodiment of liberation from repressive morality, that same repression facilitates an enrichment of the pleasures and possibilities of art. As it renders the experience of art transgressive, an ascetic morality also complicates artistic pleasures, and hence enlarges the possibilities for their "organization." Wilde amplifies this possibility as he elaborates Paterian "antinomianism" into the (characteristically) bolder conflicts and equivocations of "the double life," under which the burden of hostile surveillance also energizes an exhilarating "expansion of consciousness." In Wilde's writings, as in his life, the play of double meanings that so agitated Victorian guardians of manly directness has been developed into the fundamental structure of self-fashioning.

Of course, the structure of the double life is implicit in Pater's rhetoric of secrecy and initiation—as it is, indeed, throughout Victorian preoccupation with secret societies. Pater's rhetoric in "Leonardo da Vinci" obliquely attributes the authority of the critic's "fascination"—a central word in Wilde's social as well as aesthetic vocabulary—to his knowledge of forbidden experience. It is hardly surprising, then, that Wilde should echo this essay of Pater's more than any other single piece of writing. Indeed, Wilde's most sustained apology for Dorian Gray's "scheme of life" tellingly connects the deep moral suspicion that envelops Dorian with a sustained echo of the essay on Leonardo. "He fascinated many," the narrator relates of Dorian; as in Pater's use of the term, the appeal denotes a volatile blend of attraction and suspicion, a "strange and dangerous charm" elicited by Dorian's association with both "whispered scandals" and perfect social form. But, the narrator continues, "Is insincerity such a terrible thing? I think not. It is merely a method by which we can multiply our personalities." "Insincerity" thus understood is a muted version of the double life, which multiplies personality with yet greater force.

Such, at any rate, was Dorian's opinion. He used to wonder at the shallow psychology of those who conceive of the Ego in man as a thing simple, permanent, reliable, and of one essence. To him, man was a being with myriad lives and myriad sensations, a complex multi-form creature that bore within itself strange legacies of thought and passion, and whose very flesh was tainted with the monstrous maladies of the dead. He loved to stroll through the gaunt cold picture-gallery of his country-house and look at the various portraits of those whose blood flowed through his veins. (111)

The trappings of charnel-house Gothic should not obscure Wilde's subtle invocation of a complex and momentous intellectual genealogy to authorize his "new Hedonism." Here as throughout his writings, Wilde recognizes and appropriates Pater's open secret, that Leonardo's portrait is an image of the critic as both artist and artifact, and as such exemplifies the potentially riveting force of "fascination." At the same time, however, Wilde develops in arresting form "the modern idea" that Pater discovers in Leonardo's Gioconda: "the idea of humanity as wrought upon by, and summing up in itself, all modes of thought and life" (*Renaissance* 99). This is the idea of *Universalgeschichte*, broadly understood, but Wilde refracts that idea through Victorian science to yield a theory of cultural evolution that underwrites the imperatives of "Epicureanism." Wilde, that is, recasts Pater's various tropes of tradition and inheritance in emphatically biological terms, so that the "modernity" of Pater's Gioconda becomes a fusion of "legacies" at once cultural and physical, which conflates history and heredity. Culture is thus envisioned as a force not only proved upon the pulses, in Keats's phrase, but flowing within them. Modern science might thus give renewed authority to a form of Platonic *anamnesis*, under which introspection yields encounters with "myriad lives" that are both a collective cultural legacy, as in Leonardo's portrait, and a biological inheritance inscribed in one's very body—the two legacies joined in Dorian's contemplation of the portraits of his ancestors.

Wilde's fantasy owes less to Darwin's theory of evolution than to that of Herbert Spencer, which possesses a teleology conspicuously lacking in Darwin. But Wilde's is not an idiosyncratic fantasy. Pater's criticism of *Dorian Gray* also echoes Spencer's conception of evolution as movement towards progressively more complex "organization"; indeed, the very currency of the word in late-Victorian social discourse is a tribute to Spencer's influence. Why does the model have such appeal? It offers, first of all, a quasi-scientific ground for locating all forms of "otherness" within the self. Eve Kosofsky Sedgwick, who has analyzed this strategy in *The Picture of Dorian Gray*, urges us to see it as above all a mode of circumspection, a means of deflecting attention from the otherness that inheres in same-sex desire (*Epistemology* 159). Yet Wilde's attack on the ideal of a stable, unitary Ego might just as profitably be seen as an effort to subvert all taxonomies, sexual and otherwise, in an extension of Browning's fascination with "the dangerous edge of things."[19] If, moreover, Wilde's "complex multi-form creature" is seen in the larger context of the rise of evolutionary theories of culture, it also represents a claim to cultural authority that not only disarms conventional moral constraints, but promises to repair the rupture of "completeness" and "harmony." In the terms of *Marius the Epicurean*, the idea that all forms of otherness lie within the self offers a means of reconciling the "rival religions" that divide the Epicurean's allegiance between subscription to hierarchic "standards," on the one hand, and a passionate pursuit of "experience," on the other. They are reconciled in the possibility that the observer's very being may embody "culture," inasmuch as it sums up the whole of preceeding intellectual history as an evolutionary inheritance. In the formulation of "The Critic as Artist," "with the development of the critical spirit we shall be able to realize, not merely our own lives, but the collective life of the race, and so make ourselves absolutely modern, in the true meaning of the word modernity" (382). Wilde, one might say, thus offers us the modern observer as the New Gioconda.

But Pater had already created that ideal, and had even labeled it as such, in "The Aesthetic Life." Might the critic's own being, like Leonardo's images, intimate to an observer the informing presence of an exquisite "soul"? As we have seen, this fantasy haunts Pater from the very beginning of his career, in "Diaphaneitè" (1864), where he offers an image of the critic's sensibility embodied in a translucent, crystalline being. In "The Aesthetic Life," written a quarter-century later, Pater locates this triumph in a cloudier and more complex psychology, whose outward presence is shaped by history itself. "The peculiar aesthetic achievement, or possibility" of the present age, Pater argues, lies "precisely in that effect, or quality" of "expression" (26r). By virtue of its decided "intimacy of temper," the introspective modern mind is especially able to apprehend expression in the visible world, where the quality is experienced as a sense of sympathetic "affinities" informing

---

19. This emphasis informs Jonathan Dollimore's reading of Wilde's "transgressive aesthetic" in *Sexual Dissidence.*

that world. But the age's susceptibility to "expression" is registered in
the very countenances of modern observers: "The physiognomical
equivalent of its subtle complexion of mind will be expression, subtlety
of expression in the facial aspect. Nicely balanced contrasts, reflexion,
intricate modification of light and shadow: the mental atmosphere of
the modern world is productive of effects like these, and in them, especially, is the making of expression" (27r). The "making" of expression is thus played out not only in conventional artifacts, but in the
person of the modern beholder, which after all is but one element of
the visible world. We hear again an echo of the inchoate phrenology
that informs so much socio-aesthetic discussion in the 1860s. Thus
Blackwood's of 1864, for example, refers to "the rich variety of expression on the face of a genius, whose nature is so quietly responsive to
every influence" (Cowling 179). Here a romantic notion of "genius,"
in which "expression" registers intensity and variety of feeling, merges
with the Ruskinian gentleman, and thence into Pater's notion of "expression" as an artistic attribute embodied in intricate formal effects.

But Pater gives this rhetoric a more decided historical placement.
The "expressive" countenance is the product of a rich "inwardness"
shaped by the burden of history:

> Achievement and disillusion, fatigue and indefatigable admiration, in-
> defatigable hope, the entire experience of the ages, have told upon the
> heir of them—all that he has learned, rejected, admired, learned that he
> can never know—as we see him in certain of the imaginative productions
> of our time in some choicer creations of French fiction for instance in
> which the whole past world seems in visible effect as the perfect manner,
> so to term it—the perfect attitude towards experience as sustained in the
> early manhood of today. (27r–28r)

In this vision of "the perfect attitude towards experience," Pater's preoccupations in *Marius the Epicurean* are clearly responsive not only to
the aesthetic impoverishment of Victorian England, but also to a haunting sense of belatedness. The governing historical trope, moreover, suggestively captures the Victorian appeal to intellectual authority as
compensation for economic marginality or dispossession. The present-
day "heir" of history's burdens has been "disinherited" of his spiritual
birthright by science (3r), yet through his very belatedness he recovers
"the privilege of the elder brother in becoming a scholar" (16r).
Whereas Kingsley voyages to the West Indies in imagined recuperation
of a lost inheritance, Pater envisions a similar consolation in the recov-

ery of an aesthetic legacy. History offers him compensation not only in its legacy of past art, but by nurturing that intellectual plenitude which, burdensome as it may be, nonetheless has shaped an exquisitely expressive beauty—a beauty inscribed in the very countenance of the age. The structure of compensation is echoed in *Plato and Platonism* (which was written about the same time) where Pater similarly opposes popular wisdom in urging that "what we actually see, see and hear, is more interesting than ever; the nineteenth century as compared with the first, with Plato's days or Homer's; . . . the faces, the persons behind those masks which yet express so much" (156). This development, Pater argues, is in part a function of the rise of analytic thought, which, as it dispels the vivid immediacy of a world "under Homeric conditions," nonetheless enriches the concrete artifact "with the joint perspective, the significance, the expressiveness, of all other things beside" (159). The "scholar," in this view, reproduces the agency of the romantic poet evoked in "Winckelmann": the very act of generalization condenses "double and treble reflexions of the mind upon itself," "breaking" over the object the enrichment of an "artificial light" (*Renaissance* 171). Indeed, Pater's brief apology for generalization condenses his earlier narrative of the passing of ancient Greece as a fortunate fall.

But in "The Aesthetic Life" Pater supplements this appeal with a still more direct consolation. History enriches the visible world not merely by shaping our conceptual apparatus; in Pater's account, the burden of history directly molds the countenance of the modern beholder. History has shaped "the unique the original physiognomic note of our day, as Da Vinci and Reynolds detected the type of theirs . . . all the seriousness of a long survey of experience the twilight hopes and fears resting harmoniously upon the fine firm modelling of cheek and brow and kindling the wholesome lips and eyes to finer motive and light" (30r). The passage seems to describe a representative portrait, to characterize the distinctive "note" defined by the imagination of contemporary artists. But the verb Pater assigns to DaVinci and Reynolds is "detected," and the description explicitly refers to "our modern English youth" (29r). Not the artist's imagination, but the very evolution of consciousness, has shaped this beauty. "Can it be," Pater asks of his "ephebe,"

that centuries of delicate living[,] delicate living as regards things spiritual, delicate thinking, have left his very self his physical presence untouched the human countenance that central residence of all physical beauty . . . ? . . . Have they found no point of contact body and soul, in the last perfection of their delicate power[,] that insane soul (if you will) as all deeply wrought soul seems ever insane in that sane body as the lineaments of a portrait, some exquisite [*anoeos*] there, defining the unique the original physiognomic note of our day. (29r-30r)

With this vision, Pater undermines the Kingsleyan ideal of *mens sana in corpore sano*, savoring the power of "insane soul" to shape and inform the beautifully "sane body." To be sure, the interrogative mood calls attention to a remarkable leap of faith at work in this view of cultural evolution. But this is precisely the quasi-Lamarckian view that Wilde echoes in *Dorian Gray*. And that view in turn recasts an image and a historical scheme that Pater had constructed twenty years earlier—another image of consummate physical sanity informed by "insane" soul: Leonardo's Gioconda.

"The Aesthetic Life" explicitly links the two images in a canceled page heading, "on the new Gioconda = modernity made visible" (12). Although the manuscript at this point is a very rough draft, and the equation is not developed, the context suggests its substance. The new Gioconda, like the original, will incarnate a "modernity" that sums up the mind's preceeding history; the new Gioconda, however, is not the production of an artist. Indeed, for the contemporary artist, Pater argues, the legacy of past art is a potentially paralyzing "great mass of precedent and example"; but "for the aesthetic observer dealing with the product the gain is inestimable" since it ministers directly to his cultivation of a superbly responsive psychological economy (18r). If, then, expression in the modern world embodies the receptive "sensibility" inherent in the age's "intimacy of temper," may not the ephebe himself become its most expressive artifact? This desire comes to imaginative fruition in the idea of a new Gioconda, created when Pater's ephebe transforms himself into modernity made visible, as "the perfect attitude towards experience." History itself thus authorizes "Epicureanism." And it confirms the authority of that program as the most compelling form of creation in the modern age. "The aesthetic observer" has emphatically displaced the conventional artifact as the supreme icon of modernity.

The ideal of "modernity made visible," however, makes the aesthetic embodiment of consciousness a curiously self-effacing gesture: personal identity is subsumed in the "mental atmosphere" of the age at large. But the paradox of a self-effacing portrait is precisely the reward to which Pater's aesthetic critic aspires. That self-effacement is the cul-

mination of Pater's various narratives of education, which seek to identify the aesthete's subjectivity with the intellectual plenitude of
"modernity." There is something of the dandy's logic at work in this
pursuit of a strenuously impersonal subjectivity, as we have seen in *Marius the Epicurean*. The Paterian beholder's "perfect manner," that is,
seems designed to at once attract and resist the gaze of the *profanum
vulgus*. But the critic's modernity also responds to the crisis of critical
authority staked out in the "Preface" to *The Renaissance*. When the
ephebe of "The Aesthetic Life" responds to Pater's challenge, "What
is this to me?" it is history itself that speaks—the very history that has
authored the critic's "subtle complexion of mind." When the critic's
consciousness incarnates history itself, the critic's subjectivity holds the
authority of culture.

It is still not sufficiently emphasized that this most "impressionistic"
of critics articulated a continual yearning to authorize his criticism by
aligning it with a larger order in history. Hence one finds a remarkably
apt description of Paterian education in T. S. Eliot's account of "The
Method of Mr. Pound": "As the present is no more than the present
existence, the present significance, of the entire past, Mr. Pound proceeds by acquiring the entire past; and when the entire past is acquired,
the constituents fall into place and the present is revealed" (1065).
Here is precisely the "modernity" of Pater's Mona Lisa—a debt that
has been obscured by Eliot's fervent repudiation of Pater's example.
Even in "The Place of Pater," however, Eliot's criticism reveals his Paterian affinities. When he objects that Pater "propagated some confusion between life and art which is not wholly irresponsible for some
untidy lives," Eliot pays oblique tribute to dandyism, the font of the
view that life could be judged by the criterion of "tidiness." Of course,
Eliot would hardly accept Pater's quasi-Lamarckian notion of intellectual inheritance as a means of "acquiring the entire past." Nor would
he openly subscribe to the faith that underwrites such histories: the
Platonic notion of *anamnesis*, which would identify an enhanced aesthetic responsiveness with an expansion of selfhood. As Pater puts it in
"The Aesthetic Life," "men become like what they look upon with
inward preference and recognition[,] unconscious resemblances which
seeming accidental are true effects of kinship with the perfection of an
earlier day" (31r).

But just as Pater's Platonic fantasy hints at the element of self-
aggrandizement in Eliot's notion of tradition, so, in turn, Eliot's emphasis on "depersonalization" glosses a more defensive impetus in
Pater's ideal of a self-effacing authority. As soon as Pater puts forth his

version of *anamnesis,* he abruptly qualifies it. "Only," he continues, "along with the maturity of intellectual structure here supposed comes also a fear of being deceived or duped. It is part of his tact his finely educated sense of fitness, to dissemble his true interests, to say less than he really feels, to carry about with him in self-defense through a vulgar age a habit of reserve of [erring?] it may be, this again becoming in its turn but an added means of expression" (31r). This is almost breathtaking in the directness with which it explains Paterian reticence as a defense. There is nothing as explicit as this, I think, in any of Pater's published writings, although the imperative does recall his fantasy of the young Spartan shrinking from "the imperative, inevitable gaze of his fellows, broad, searching, minute" (*Plato and Platonism* 221). The critic's "perfect manner" evidently demands a strenuous self-mastery, in the pursuit of which Pater again appeals to an uneasy conjunction of Tractarian reserve and evolutionary faith. An increasing "maturity of intellectual structure" (a bow to Herbert Spencer) gives rise to a "habit of reserve" (a bow to Newman) in which the inward possession of aesthetic grace is intimated to onlookers as an impersonal "tact"— "the perfect attitude to experience." But like the enigmatic countenance of the Gioconda, this habit reveals a "finely educated sense of fitness" precisely insofar as it *conceals* a more personal identity, the more intimate truths of "what he really feels," or simply dissolves the stable "ego," in Wilde's terms, into the plenitude of "experience itself." Here is the paradox of the Ruskinian gentleman, as of Newman's appeal to a theological economy of truth. But Pater's reserve in this context is more overtly defensive than either of those models. It is motivated not only by fidelity to selfhood or arcane experience, but by "a fear of being deceived or duped." This revelation comes as an abrupt non sequitur in Pater's argument, which seems to expose an informing "soul" less amenable to critical discipline. The logical rupture marks a rupture in the critic's "perfect manner," which reveals an unspecified but evidently powerful sense of personal vulnerability, of depths that must remain secret and forbidden to the observer's gaze.

One might conclude, then, that Paterian reticence ultimately, inadvertently reveals the massive repression required to sustain the critic's "perfect attitude." But I hope that I have suggested a more productive dynamic in Pater's reticence, one further "use of obscurity" that might complement Allon White's valuable study of that topic in modernist fiction. Hostile surveillance might be courted as well as feared: only by acknowledging that possibility can we understand Pater's remarkable influence in the rise of modernism. It was Pater's genius to appropriate a hermeneutic of suspicion—a suspicion that was homophobic, to be sure, but many other things besides—in order to construct new modes of authority in the form of fascination or charisma. Hence his immense influence in late Victorian culture. At the same time, however, this utopian desire in his aestheticism lays claim to social authority by appropriating and thereby reinforcing the Victorian discourse of masculinity. In the process, Pater shows how Victorian revisions of the ideal of the gentleman inevitably reinscribe the dynamic of transgression that they are designed to exclude. "Manliness," in other words, is always passing into "effeminacy" under the pressure of the very dynamic that impels new versions of masculinity: the codification of social authority through the growth of a hermeneutics of suspicion.

But yet—in keeping with the incessant dialectics of Pater's own writings—there remains a more narrowly personal and poignant triumph in Pater's reticence. In "The Aesthetic Life," after describing the physiognomy generated by the age's "subtle complexion of mind," Pater continues, "With the truth of that made visible somewhere, if not the ugliness of the modern world at least the general plainness the conventionality, the dryness of visible things about us may come to seem but a mask a voluntary surrender of superficial and facile decoration that the essential power may tell more directly upon us. For what an interesting period, after all, is this we live in! admitted the ugliness of its material residence how interesting its soul!" (4). It seems peculiar that Pater should dismiss any decoration as merely superficial; after all, "The School of Giorgione" celebrates decoration as a type of all art. But once again a more powerful desire enforces a disjunction between form and content, between an image and its informing "soul." Surely the aesthetic redemption of "plainness" that Pater proposes also speaks to a longing that his own "soul," that exquisitely refined critical sensibility, might be similarly recognised behind his own notorious plainness, that "material residence" that was an object of much comment. Max Beerbohm in "Diminuendo" recalls catching sight in Oxford of "a small, thick, rock-faced man, whose top-hat and gloves of *bright* dogskin struck one of the many discords in that little city of learning or laughter. The serried bristles of his moustachio made for him a false-military air. I think I nearly went down when they told me this was Pater" (59). In James's more curt assessment, shortly after first meeting Pater: "He is far from being as beautiful as his prose." The remark might seem merely catty, the measure of a professional jealousy that reveals more about James than Pater, were it not that the same mingling of surprise, dismay, and rivalry is echoed by so many contempo-

raries after first encountering Pater in person.[20] That chorus, I would
suggest, offers unexpected evidence of Pater's powers of fascination.
After all, Pater had seduced his admirers into expecting that the very
appearance of the author of *The Renaissance* would rival the exquisite
beauty of his prose. The many who expressed surprise upon discovering
his plainness all paid unwitting tribute to the fascination of Pater's
mask.

20. Seiler usefully compiles contemporary reactions, such as that of one obituary writer
    who remarked that Pater's face "was a strange contradiction of what one would have
    assigned to the Apostle of The Renaissance" (169).

Afterword

At the end of chapter 10 of E. M. Forster's novel *Maurice*, Forster's hero comes to a momentous decision: "He would live straight, not because it mattered to anyone now, but for the sake of the game. He would not deceive himself so much. He would not—and this is the test—pretend to care about women when the only sex that attracted him was his own. He loved men and had always loved them" (62). Students in late-twentieth-century America tend to be puzzled, perhaps bemused, at Maurice's resolve to "live straight" by acknowledging that he loves men. The puzzle, they recognize after a moment's perplexity, stems from the fact that "straight" here does not mean "heterosexual"; it means "straightforwardly," directly, openly. The word in this sense grounds Maurice's dangerous avowal of his desires within the complex history that I have tried to sketch in this book. "Straight," that is, appeals to a familiar norm of middle-class manhood, particularly that of the late Victorian public school—a world richly evoked in the appeal, "for the sake of the game." Even as Maurice attempts to break free of respectable norms of masculinity, his new sense of self is constructed, inevitably, out of an existing rhetoric of masculine identity. And within that rhetoric, being "straight" is opposed, not to loving men, but to being guarded, furtive, evasive, deceptive, tangential, oblique, bent—"queer," perhaps.

What we glimpse in Forster's novel, I suggest, is the emergence of our late-twentieth-century idiom of male sexuality from a Victorian discourse of masculine identity—a discourse in which masculinity is centrally bound up with dynamics of communication. One aspect of this continuum is a commonplace: Maurice is "an unspeakable of the Oscar Wilde sort" (159), whose "criminal morbidity" is (of course) the love that dare not speak its name, the sin not to be mentioned among Christians, and so forth. But the force of Wilde's spectacular and wrenching downfall, with all the forms of emblematic closure that have been attached to it, has tended to distort our understanding of Victorian masculinities, by suggesting a misleadingly narrow, rigorous, and persistent association of dissident masculinities with transgressive sexuality. In fact, through much of the culture the indices of "criminal morbidity" are not easy to separate out of a more inclusive and inchoate mistrust of male secrecy as an index of treacherous designs against the social and political order. That hermeneutic of suspicion reinforces in turn the fascination of what it proscribes; the lure of homosocial intimacy will be all the more intense when private fellowship organized around any number of interests—class, occupation, political allegiance, religious belief, sexual object choice—is thought to pose a potential threat to existing structures of authority. Such pervasive suspicion throws into especially sharp relief the far-reaching social power inherent in norms of masculinity, with their authority to define who and what is "manly," and who and what is not. By the same token, however, the subversion of those norms may be taken to reflect an extraordinarily powerful, even charismatic authority in those who are bold enough to risk the stigma of defying them. Hence the remarkably powerful "fascinations" that we have seen in contemporary responses to Newman and Thomas Arnold, Pater and Wilde.

The understanding of masculinity as an ascetic discipline forms an especially powerful continuum between early and late Victorian rhetorics of masculine identity, and between writers who might seem to occupy opposite sides of the (sometimes elusive) boundary dividing normative and transgressive sexualities. In Forster's novel, on the other hand, Maurice's "scandalized, horrified" response to Clive's declaration of love gestures toward a complete rupture with earlier discourses:

> "Durham, you're an Englishman. I'm another. Don't talk nonsense. I'm not offended, because I know you don't mean it, but it's the only subject absolutely beyond the limit as you know, it's the worst crime in the calendar, and you must never mention it again." (59)

"I love you" has the power to disrupt the laws of national identity, social decorum, the legal code, even of language itself. Maurice must repudiate all these powers in order to return another man's love. But such freedom can be won only through a flight into the greenwood of romance, or into the recesses of, as Forster later wistfully put it, "an England where it was still possible to get lost" (254). Maurice can imagine self-fulfillment only as a form of invisibility, an exemption from the burdens of masculine self-fashioning, in a world where there are neither dandies nor desert saints.

Works Cited

Aaron, Daniel. "The 'Inky Curse': Miscegenation in the White American Literary Imagination." *Social Science Information* 22 (1983): 169–90.

Abrams, M. H. "Kant and the Theology of Art." *Notre Dame English Journal* 13 (1981): 75–106.

———. *Natural Supernaturalism: Tradition and Revolution in Romantic Literature.* New York: Norton, 1971.

Adams, James Eli. "The Economies of Authorship: Imagination and Trade in Johnson's *Dryden.*" *SEL* 30 (1990): 467–86.

———. "Gentleman, Dandy, Priest: Manliness and Social Authority in Pater's Aestheticism." *ELH* 59 (1992): 441–66.

[Alison, Archibald.] "Chartists and Universal Suffrage." *Blackwood's English Magazine* 46 (September 1839): 289–303.

Allchin, A. M. *The Silent Rebellion: Anglican Religious Communities, 1845–1900.* London: SCM Press, 1958.

Anderson, Amanda. *Tainted Souls and Painted Faces: The Rhetoric of Fallenness in Victorian Culture.* Ithaca: Cornell University Press, 1993.

Anson, Peter F. *The Call of the Cloister: Religious Communities and Kindred Bodies in the Anglican Communion.* London: SPCK, 1955.

Armstrong, Nancy. *Desire and Domestic Fiction: A Political History of the Novel.* New York: Oxford University Press, 1987.

Arnold, Matthew. *Collected Prose Works.* 11 vols. Ed. R. H. Super. Ann Arbor: University of Michigan Press, 1960–78.

———. *The Poems of Matthew Arnold.* 2d ed. Ed. Kenneth Allott and Miriam Allott. London: Longmans, 1979.

Arnold, Thomas. *Christian Life, Its Course, Its Hindrance, and Its Helps: Sermons, Preached Mostly in the Chapel of Rugby School.* London: B. Fellowes, 1844.

Augustine of Hippo. *Confessions.* Trans. E. B. Pusey. London: Dent, 1907.

Bamford, T. W. *Thomas Arnold.* London: Cresset Press, 1960.

Banton, Michael. *The Idea of Race.* London: Tavistock, 1977.

Barish, Jonas. *The Antitheatrical Prejudice.* Berkeley and Los Angeles: University of California Press, 1981.

Barrie, James. M. *Peter Pan.* In Griffith and Frey 959–1043.

Barrows, Susanna. *Distorting Mirrors: Visions of the Crowd in Late Nineteenth-Century France.* New Haven: Yale University Press, 1981.

Bartley, W. W., III. "Wittgenstein and Homosexuality." *Salmagundi,* no. 58–59 (Fall 1982 Winter 1983): 193–96.

Baudelaire, Charles. *The Painter of Modern Life and Other Essays.* Trans. and ed. Jonathan Mayne. New York: Da Capo, 1985.

Beerbohm, Max. *The Incomparable Max.* New York: Dodd and Mead, 1962.

Bellman, Beryl. "The Paradox of Secrecy." *Human Studies* 4 (1981): 1–24.

Benjamin, Walter. *Illuminations.* Ed. Hannah Arendt. New York: Schocken, 1969.

Bhabha, Homi. "Signs Taken for Wonders: Questions of Ambivalence and Authority under a Tree outside Delhi, May 1817." In Gates 163–84.

Bizup, Joseph. "Walter Pater and the Ruskinian Gentleman." *English Literature in Transition* 38 (1995): 1–19.

Bowen, Desmond. *The Idea of the Victorian Church: A Study of the Church of England, 1833–1889.* Montreal: McGill University Press, 1968.

Bowness, Alan, ed. *The Pre-Raphaelites.* London: Tate Gallery, 1984.

Bradbury, Malcolm, and D. J. Palmer, eds. *Victorian Poetry.* London: Routledge, 1978.

Bradley, Ian. *The Call to Seriousness.* New York: Macmillan, 1976.

Brake, Lauren, and Ian Small, eds. *Pater in the 1990s.* Greensboro, N.C.: ELT Press, 1990.

Brantlinger, Patrick. *Rule of Darkness: British Literature and Imperialism, 1830–1914.* Ithaca: Cornell University Press, 1988.

——. *The Spirit of Reform.* Cambridge: Harvard University Press, 1977.

Brendon, Piers. *Hurrell Froude and the Oxford Movement.* London: Paul Elek, 1974.

Bright, Michael. "English Romanticism and the Oxford Movement." *Journal of the History of Ideas* 40 (1979): 380–404.

Brilioth, Yngve. *The Anglican Revival: Studies in the Oxford Movement.* London: Longmans, Green, 1925.

Brod, Harry, ed. *The Making of Masculinities: The New Men's Studies.* Boston: Unwin Hyman, 1987.

Buckley, Jerome. *The Victorian Temper.* New York: Vintage, 1964.

Buckton, Oliver. "'An Unnatural State': Gender, 'Perversion,' and Newman's *Apologia pro Vita Sua.*" *Victorian Studies* 35 (1991–92): 359–83.

Butler, Judith. *Gender Trouble: Feminism and the Subversion of Identity.* New York: Routledge, 1990.

Camus, Albert. *The Rebel.* Trans. Anthony Bower. New York: Vintage, 1956.

Carlyle, Thomas. "Characteristics." *Caryle's Complete Works,* 14:344–83. Boston: Estes and Lauriat, n.d.

——. *The Collected Letters of Thomas and Jane Welsh Carlyle.* 21 vols. Ed. Charles L. Sanders et al. Durham: Duke University Press, 1970– .

——. *The French Revolution.* 2 vols. in 1. Ed. K. J. Fielding and David Sorenson. New York: Oxford University Press, 1989.

——. *Past and Present.* Ed. Richard Altick. New York: New York University Press, 1978.

——. *Sartor Resartus* and *Heroes and Hero-Worship.* London: Everyman, 1908.

——. *Two Notebooks of Thomas Carlyle.* New York: The Grolier Club, 1896.

Castronovo, David. *The English Gentleman: Images and Ideals in Literature and Society.* New York: Ungar, 1987.

Chadwick, Owen. *The Spirit of the Oxford Movement: Tractarian Essays.* Cambridge: Cambridge University Press, 1990.

Chandos, John. *Boys Together: English Public Schools, 1800–1864.* New Haven: Yale University Press, 1984.

Chauncey, George, Jr. "Christian Brotherhood or Sexual Perversion? Homosexual Identities and the Construction of Sexual Boundaries in the World War One Era." *Journal of Social History* 19 (1985–86): 189–211.

Chitty, Susan. *The Beast and the Monk: A Life of Charles Kingsley.* London: Hodder & Stoughton, 1974.

Christ, Carol. "Victorian Masculinity and the Angel in the House." In Vicinus 146–62.

Church, R. W. *The Oxford Movement: Twelve Years, 1833–1845.* Ed. Geoffrey Best. Chicago: University of Chicago Press, 1970.

Clarke, Norma. "Strenuous Idleness: Thomas Carlyle and the Man of Letters as Hero." In Roper and Tosh 25–43.

Clements, Patricia. *Baudelaire and the English Tradition.* Princeton: Princeton University Press, 1985.

Clough, Arthur Hugh. *Correspondence of Arthur Hugh Clough.* 2 vols. Ed. Frederick L. Mulhauser. Oxford: Clarendon Press, 1957.

Cohen, Ed. *Talk on the Wilde Side.* New York: Routledge, 1993.

Collini, Stefan. *Public Moralists: Political Thought and Intellectual Life in Britain, 1850–1930.* Oxford: Clarendon Press, 1991.

Cominos, Peter T. "Late-Victorian Respectability and the Social System." *International Review of Social History* 7 (1963): 18–48, 216–250.

Conrad, Joseph. *Heart of Darkness.* Ed. Robert Kimbrough. 3d ed. New York: Norton, 1988.

Cott, Nancy. "Passionlessness: An Interpretation of Victorian Sexual Ideology, 1790–1850." *Signs* 4 (1978): 219–36.

Coulson, John, and A. M. Allchin, eds. *The Rediscovery of Newman: An Oxford Symposium.* London: Sheed & Ward, 1967.

[Courthope, W. J.]. "Modern Culture." *Quarterly Review* 136 (October 1874): 205–20.

———. "Wordsworth and Gray." *Quarterly Review* 141 (January 1876): 55–71.

Cowling, Mary. *The Artist as Anthropologist: The Representation of Type and Character in Victorian Art.* Cambridge: Cambridge University Press, 1989.

Craft, Christopher. "'Descend, and Touch, and Enter': Tennyson's Strange Manner of Address." *Genders*, no. 1 (Spring 1988): 83–101.

Culler, A. Dwight. *The Victorian Mirror of History.* New Haven: Yale University Press, 1985.

Curtin, Michael. *Propriety and Position: A Study of Victorian Manners.* New York: Garland, 1987.

D'Aurevilly, Jules Barbey. *Dandyism.* Trans. Douglas Ainslie. New York: PAJ Publications, 1988.

David, Deirdre. *Intellectual Women and Victorian Patriarchy.* Ithaca: Cornell University Press, 1987.

Davidoff, Lenore, and Catherine Hall. *Family Fortunes: Men and Women of the English Middle Class, 1780–1850.* Chicago: University of Chicago Press, 1987.

Dawson, Carl, and and John Pfordresher, eds. *Matthew Arnold: Prose Writings, The Critical Heritage.* London: Routledge & Kegan Paul, 1979.

DeLaura, David J. "Carlyle and Arnold: The Religious Issue." In Fielding and Tarr 127–54.

———. *Hebrew and Hellene in Victorian England: Newman, Arnold, Pater.* Austin: University of Texas Press, 1969.

———. "Ishmael as Prophet: Heroes and Hero-Worship and the Self-Expressive Basis of Carlyle's Thought." *Texas Studies in Language and Literature* 11 (1968–69): 705–32.

———. "O Unforgotten Voice: The Memory of Newman in the Nineteenth Century." *Renascence* 43 (Fall 1990 Winter 1991): 81–104.

———. "Reading Inman Rereading Pater Reading." *Pater Newsletter*, no. 26 (Spring 1991): 2–9.

Deleuze, Gilles. *Coldness and Cruelty.* Trans. Jean McNeil. New York: Zone, 1991.

Dellamora, Richard. *Masculine Desire: The Sexual Politics of Victorian Aestheticism.* Chapel Hill: University of North Carolina Press, 1990.

DeQuincey, Thomas. *The Collected Writings of Thomas DeQuincey.* 19 vols. Ed. David Masson. Edinburgh: Black, 1890.

Dickens, Charles. *Hard Times.* 1854. Ed. George Ford and Sylvere Monod. 2d ed. New York: Norton, 1990.

———. *A Tale of Two Cities.* 1857. New York: New American Library, 1964.

Disraeli, Benjamin. *Coningsby.* 1844. Harmondsworth: Penguin, 1966.

———. *Sybil.* 1845. Harmondsworth: Penguin, 1980.

Dollimore, Jonathan. "Different Desires: Subjectivity and Transgression in Wilde and Gide." *Genders*, no. 2 (Summer 1988): 24–41.

———. *Sexual Dissidence: Augustine to Wilde, Freud to Foucault.* Oxford: Oxford University Press, 1991.

Dowling, Linda. *Hellenism and Homosexuality in Victorian Oxford.* Ithaca: Cornell University Press, 1994.

———. "Pater, Moore, and the Fatal Book." *Prose Studies* 7 (1984): 168–78.

———. "Ruskin's Pied Beauty and the Constitution of a 'Homosexual' Code." *Victorian Newsletter*, no. 75 (Spring 1989): 1–8.

Eagleton, Terry. *Ideology of the Aesthetic.* Oxford: Blackwell, 1990.

Eliot, T. S. "The Method of Mr. Pound." *Athenaeum*, no. 4669 (October 24, 1919): 1065–67.

Faber, Geoffrey. *The Oxford Apostles: A Character Study of the Oxford Movement.* London: Faber & Faber, 1933.

Feldman, Jessica. *Gender on the Divide: The Dandy in Modernist Literature.* Ithaca: Cornell University Press, 1993.

Fielding, K. J., and Roger L. Tarr, eds. *Carlyle Past and Present.* New York: Barnes & Noble, 1976.

Forster, E. M. *Maurice.* 1914. New York: Norton, 1987.

Foucault, Michel. *Discipline and Punish.* New York: Pantheon, 1977.

———. *The History of Sexuality.* Vol. 1, *Introduction.* Trans. Robert Hurley. New York: Pantheon, 1978.

———. *The History of Sexuality.* Vol. 2, *The Use of Pleasure.* Trans. Robert Hurley. New York: Pantheon, 1987.

Freedman, Jonathan. *Professions of Taste: Henry James, British Aestheticism, and Commodity Culture.* Stanford: Stanford University Press, 1990.

Freud, Sigmund. "Medusa's Head." *Sexuality and the Psychology of Love.* Ed. Philip Rieff. New York: Collier, 1963.

[Froude, James Anthony]. *The Nemesis of Faith.* 1849. London: Libris, 1988.

Froude, James Anthony. "The Oxford Counter-Reformation." In *Short Studies on Great Subjects*, 4:151–235. New York: Scribner's, 1885.

———. *Thomas Carlyle: A History of the First Forty Years of His Life, 1795–1835.* 2 vols. London: Macmillan, 1882.

Froude, Richard Hurrell. *Remains of the Late Reverend Richard Hurrell Froude, M.A.* 2 vols. London: J. G. and F. Rivington, 1838.

Gagnier, Regenia. *Idylls of the Marketplace: Oscar Wilde and the Victorian Public.* Stanford: Stanford University Press, 1986.

———. *Subjectivities: A History of Self-Representation in Britain, 1832–1920.* Oxford: Oxford University Press, 1990.

Gallagher, Catherine. "The Duplicity of Doubling in *A Tale of Two Cities.*" *Dickens Studies Annual* 12 (1983): 125–45.

———. *The Industrial Reformation of English Fiction, 1832–1867.* Chicago: University of Chicago Press, 1985.

Gates, Henry Louis, Jr., ed. *"Race," Writing, and Difference.* Chicago: University of Chicago Press, 1986.

Gay, Peter. *The Bourgeois Experience.* Vol. 1, *The Education of the Senses.* New York: Norton, 1983.

———. *The Bourgeois Experience.* Vol. 2, *The Tender Passion.* New York: Norton, 1987.

———. *The Bourgeois Experience.* Vol. 3, *The Cultivation of Hatred.* New York: Norton, 1993.

Gent, Margaret. "'To Flinch from Modern Varnish': The Appeal of the Past to the Victorian Imagination." In Bradbury and Palmer 11–35.

Gilbert, Eliot L. " 'To Awake from History': Carlyle, Thackeray, and *A Tale of Two Cities.*" *Dickens Studies Annual* 12 (1985): 247–65.

Gilmore, David G. *Manhood in the Making: Cultural Concepts of Masculinity.* New Haven: Yale University Press, 1990.

Gilmour, Robin. *The Idea of the Gentleman in the Victorian Novel.* London: George Allen & Unwin, 1981.

Girouard, Mark. *The Return to Camelot: Chivalry and the English Gentleman.* New Haven: Yale University Press, 1981.

Green, Martin. *Dreams of Adventure, Deeds of Empire.* New York: Basic Books, 1979.

[Greg, W. R.]. "English Socialism, and Communistic Associations." *Edinburgh Review*, no. 189 (January 1851): 1–17.

———. "Stanley's *Life of Arnold.*" *Westminster Review* 42 (1844): 363–81.

Greg, W. R. "Kingsley and Carlyle." 1861. In *Literary and Social Judgments.* London: Trubner, 1869.

Griffith, John W., and Charles H. Frey, eds. *Classics of Children's Literature.* 3d ed. New York: Macmillan, 1922.

Griffiths, Eric. "Newman: The Foolishness of Preaching." In Ker and Hill 63–91.

Gubar, Susan. " 'The Blank Page' and the Issues of Female Creativity." In Showalter 292–313.

Haley, Bruce. *The Healthy Body and Victorian Culture.* Cambridge: Harvard University Press, 1977.

Hall, Donald E., ed. *Muscular Christianity: Embodying the Victorian Age.* Cambridge: Cambridge University Press, 1994.

Harpham, Geoffrey Galt. *The Ascetic Imperative in Culture and Criticism.* Chicago: University of Chicago Press, 1987.

Harrington, Henry R. "Charles Kingsley's Fallen Athlete." *Victorian Studies* 21 (1977–78): 73–86.

Hartman, Geoffrey. *Criticism in the Wilderness.* New Haven: Yale University Press, 1980.

——. "Romanticism and Anti-Self-Consciousness." In *After Formalism,* 298–310. New Haven: Yale University Press, 1970.

Hawley, John C., S.J. "Responses to Charles Kingsley's Attacks on Political Economy." *VPR* 9 (1986): 131–36.

Hazlitt, William. "On Effeminacy of Character." *Table Talk.* 1822. London: Dent, 1907.

Heath, Stephen. "Male Feminism." In Jardine and Smith 1–33.

Herbert, Christopher. *Culture and Anomie: Ethnographic Imagination in the Nineteenth Century.* Chicago: University of Chicago Press, 1991.

Hill, Michael. *The Religious Order: A Study of Virtuoso Religion and Its Legitimation in the Nineteenth-Century Church of England.* London: Heinemann, 1973.

Hilliard, David. "UnEnglish and Unmanly: Anglo-Catholicism and Homosexuality." *Victorian Studies* 25 (1981–82): 181–210.

Hilton, Boyd. *The Age of Atonement: The Influence of Evangelicalism on Social and Economic Thought, 1795–1865.* Oxford: Clarendon Press, 1988.

"Historic Fancies, by the Hon. Sydney Smythe." *Fraser's Magazine* 30 (September 1844): 310–21.

Holloway, John. *The Victorian Sage: Studies in Argument.* 1953. Reprint, New York: Norton, 1965.

Honey, J. R. de'S. *Tom Brown's Universe: The Development of the Victorian Public School.* London: Millington, 1977.

Houghton, Walter. *The Victorian Frame of Mind.* New Haven: Yale University Press, 1957.

Hoy, David C., ed. *Foucault: A Critical Reader.* Oxford: Blackwell, 1986.

Hughes, Thomas. *The Manliness of Christ.* Boston: Houghton, Osgood, 1880.

——. *Tom Brown's Schooldays.* 1857. London: J. M. Dent, n.d.

Hutter, Albert. "The Novelist as Resurrectionist: Dickens and the Dilemma of Death." *Dickens Studies Annual* 12 (1983): 1–43.

Hutton, R. H. *Cardinal Newman.* 2d ed. Boston: Houghton Mifflin, 1891.

Hyder, C. K, ed. *Swinburne: The Critical Heritage.* London: Routledge & Kegan Paul, 1970.

Inman, Billie Andrew. "Estrangement and Connection: Walter Pater, Benjamin Jowett, and William M. Hardinge." In Brake and Small 1–20.

——. *Walter Pater's Reading: A Bibliography of His Library Borrowings and Literary References, 1858–1873.* New York: Garland, 1981.

Irving, Washington. *The Life and Voyages of Christopher Columbus.* 2 vols. 1828. New York: Harper Brothers, 1868.

James, Henry. *Letters of Henry James.* 4 vols. Ed. Leon Edel. Cambridge: Harvard University Press, 1974–1982.

Jardine, Alice and Paul A. Smith, eds. *Men in Feminism.* London: Routledge, 1987.

Jay, Martin. "In the Empire of the Gaze." In Hoy 175–204.

Jenkyns, Richard. *Dignity and Decadence: Victorian Art and the Classical Tradition.* Cambridge: Harvard University Press, 1992.

——. *The Victorians and Ancient Greece.* Cambridge: Harvard University Press, 1980.

Ker, Ian. *John Henry Newman: A Biography.* Oxford: Clarendon Press, 1988.

Ker, Ian, and Alan G. Hill, eds. *Newman after a Hundred Years*. Oxford: Clarendon Press, 1990.

Kermode, Frank. *Romantic Image*. London: Fontana, 1971.

Kingsley, Charles. *Health and Education*. New York: Appleton, 1893.

——. *Historical Lectures and Essays*. London: Macmillan, 1880.

——. *Lectures Delivered in America in 1874*. London: Longmans, Green, 1875.

——. *The Life and Works of Charles Kingsley*. 19 vols. London: Macmillan, 1902.

——. *Literary and General Lectures and Essays*. London: Macmillan, 1890.

——. "What, Then, Does Dr. Newman Mean?" In Newman, *Apologia*, ed. DeLaura 310–40.

Kingsley, Charles, and John Henry Newman. *A Correspondence on the Question Whether Dr. Newman Teaches that Truth is No Virtue?* In Newman, *Apologia* (ed. DeLaura) 297–309.

"Kingsley's *Andromeda*." *Saturday Review* 5 (1858): 594–95.

Kinney, James. *Amalgamation! Race, Sex, and Rhetoric in the Nineteenth-Century American Novel*. Westport, Conn.: Greenwood Press, 1985.

Knott, John. *Discourses of Martyrdom in English Literature, 1563–1694*. Cambridge: Cambridge University Press, 1993.

Kucich, John. "The Purity of Violence: *A Tale of Two Cities*." *Dickens Studies Annual* 8 (1980): 119–38.

——. *Repression in Victorian Fiction: Charlotte Brontë, George Eliot, and Charles Dickens*. Berkeley and Los Angeles: University of California Press, 1987.

Landow, George P. *Elegant Jeremiahs: The Sage from Carlyle to Mailer*. Ithaca: Cornell University Press, 1986.

Larson, Magali Sarfatti. *The Rise of Professionalism: A Sociological Analysis*. Berkeley and Los Angeles: University of California Press, 1977.

Lefroy, Edward C. *Undergraduate Oxford: Articles Reprinted from the Oxford and Cambridge Undergraduate Journal, 1876–7*. Oxford: Slatter & Rose, 1878.

Levine, George. *The Boundaries of Fiction: Carlyle, Macaulay, Newman*. Princeton: Princeton University Press, 1968.

Liddon, Henry Parry. *Life of Edward Bouverie Pusey*. 4 vols. London: Longmans, Green, 1893.

Litvak, Joseph. *Caught in the Act*. Berkeley and Los Angeles: University of California Press, 1991.

Litzinger, Boyd, and Donald Smalley, eds. *Browning: The Critical Heritage*. New York: Barnes & Noble, 1970.

Lloyd, Genevieve. *The Man of Reason: "Male" and "Female" in Western Philosophy*. London: Methuen, 1984.

London, Bette. "Mary Shelley, *Frankenstein*, and the Spectacle of Masculinity." *PMLA* 108 (1993): 253–67.

Lorimer, Douglas. *Colour, Class, and the Victorians*. Leicester: Leicester University Press, 1978.

Mack, Edward C. *Public Schools and British Opinion, 1780–1860*. London: Methuen, 1938.

Mack, Edward C., and W.H.G. Armytage. *Thomas Hughes: The Life of the Author of "Tom Brown's Schooldays."* London: Ernest Benn, 1952.

Mangan, J. A. *Athleticism in the Victorian and Edwardian Public School: The Emergence and Consolidation of an Educational Ideology*. London: Falmer Press, 1986.

———. *The Games Ethic and Imperialism: Aspects of the Diffusion of an Ideal.* Harmondsworth: Viking, 1986.

Mangan, J. A., and James Walvin, eds. *Manliness and Masculinity: Middle-Class Masculinity in Britain and American, 1800–1940.* Manchester: Manchester University Press, 1987.

Martin, Robert Bernard. *The Dust of Combat: A Life of Charles Kingsley.* London: Faber & Faber, 1959.

———. *Tennyson: The Unquiet Heart.* London and Oxford: Oxford University Press and Faber & Faber, 1980.

Martineau, James. *Essays, Reviews, and Addresses.* 4 vols. London: Longmans, Green, 1890.

Marx, Karl. *Early Writings.* Ed. T. B. Bottomore. London: C. A. Watts, 1963.

Matthew, H.C.G. "Noetics, Tractarians, and the Reform of the University of Oxford in the Nineteenth Century." *History of Universities* 9 (1990): 195–225.

Maynard, John. *Victorian Discourses of Sexuality and Religion.* Cambridge: Cambridge University Press, 1993.

McCrum, Michael. *Thomas Arnold, Headmaster: A Reassessment.* New York: Oxford University Press, 1989.

McGowan, John. "From Pater to Wilde to Joyce: Modernist Epiphany and the Soulful Self." *Texas Studies in Language and Literature* 32 (1990): 420–26.

Mill, John Stuart. *Collected Works.* 40 vols. Ed. John Robson et al. Toronto: University of Toronto Press, 1964–1992.

Miller, D. A. *The Novel and the Police.* Berkeley and Los Angeles: University of California Press, 1988.

Moers, Ellen. *The Dandy: Brummell to Beerbohm.* 1960. Reprint, Lincoln: University of Nebraska Press, 1978.

Monsman, Gerald. "Old Mortality at Oxford." *Studies in Philology* 67 (1970): 359–89.

Morgan, Thais E. "Reimagining Masculinity in Victorian Criticism: Swinburne and Pater." *Victorian Studies* 36 (1992–93): 315–32.

Mort, Frank. *Dangerous Sexualities: Medico-Moral Politics in England since 1830.* London: Routledge & Kegan Paul, 1987.

Mosse, George L. *Nationalism and Sexuality: Respectability and Abnormal Sexuality in Modern Europe.* New York: Howard Fertig, 1985.

Mozley, Thomas. *Reminiscences, Chiefly of Oriel College and the Oxford Movement.* 2 vols. Boston: Houghton Mifflin, 1882.

Mulvey, Laura. "Visual Pleasure and Narrative Cinema." *Screen* 16, no. 3 (1975): 8–18.

Nelson, Claudia. *Boys Will Be Girls: The Feminine Ethic and British Children's Fiction, 1857–1917.* New Brunswick: Rutgers University Press, 1991.

Newfield, Christopher. "The Politics of Male Suffering: Masochism and Hegemony in the American Renaissance." *differences* 1, no. 3 (1989): 55–87.

Newman, John Henry. *Apologia Pro Vita Sua.* 1864. Ed. David J. DeLaura. New York: Norton, 1969.

———. *The Arians of the Fourth Century.* 1834. 5th ed. London: Pickering, 1883.

———. *Loss and Gain: The Story of a Convert.* 1846. London: Longmans, Green, 1911.

———. *Parochial and Plain Sermons.* 8 vols. London: Longmans, 1838.

———. *Selected Writings.* London: Nonesuch, 1978.

——. *Sermons Bearing on Subjects of the Day.* 1845. London: Longmans, Green, 1898.

Newsome, David. "The Evangelical Sources of Newman's Power." In Coulson and Allchin 11–30.

——. *Godliness and Good Learning: Four Studies in a Victorian Ideal.* London: Cassell, 1961.

Nietzsche, Friedrich. *The Will to Power.* Trans. Walter Kaufmann and R. J. Hollingdale. New York: Vintage, 1968.

Paden, W. D. *Tennyson in Egypt: A Study of the Imagery in His Earlier Work.* 1941. Reprint, New York: Octagon, 1971.

Pater, Walter. "The Aesthetic Life." Houghton Library, Harvard University, bMS Eng 1150(7).

——. *Appreciations: With an Essay on Style.* London: Macmillan, 1910.

——. *Gaston de Latour.* London: Macmillan, 1910.

——. *Greek Studies.* London: Macmillan, 1910.

——. *Marius the Epicurean.* 2 vols. London: Macmillan, 1910.

——. *Miscellaneous Studies.* London: Macmillan, 1910.

——. "The Picture of Dorian Gray." *The Bookman* 1, no. 2 (November 1891): 59–60.

——. *Plato and Platonism.* London: Macmillan, 1910.

——. *The Renaissance: Studies in Art and Poetry. The 1893 Text.* Ed. Donald L. Hill. Berkeley and Los Angeles: University of California Press, 1980.

Pattison, Mark. *Memoirs.* London: Macmillan, 1885.

Perkin, Harold. *The Origins of Modern English Society, 1780–1880.* London: Routledge & Kegan Paul, 1967.

Poirier, Richard. "Pater, Joyce, Eliot." *James Joyce Quarterly* 26 (Fall 1988): 23–38.

Poovey, Mary. *Uneven Developments: The Ideological Work of Gender in Mid-Victorian England.* Chicago: University of Chicago Press, 1988.

Potts, Alex. "Beautiful Bodies and Dying Heroes: Images of Ideal Manhood in the French Revolution." *History Workshop* no. 30 (Autumn 1990): 1–21.

Pratt, Mary Louise. "Scratches on the Face of the Country; or, What Mr. Barrow Saw in the Land of the Bushmen." In Gates 138–62.

[Price, Bonamy]. "The Arians of the Fourth Century." *Edinburgh Review* 63 (April 1836): 44–72.

Reade, Brian, ed. *Sexual Heretics: Male Homosexuality in English Literature from 1850 to 1900.* London: Routledge & Kegan Paul, 1970.

Reader, W. J. *Professional Men: The Rise of the Professional Classes in Nineteenth-Century England.* London: Weidenfeld and Nicholson, 1966.

Reed, John Shelton. " 'A Female Movement': The Feminization of Nineteenth-Century Anglo-Catholicism." *Anglican and Episcopal History* 57 (1988): 199–238.

Reik, Theodor. *Masochism in Modern Man.* Trans. Margaret H. Beigel and Gertrud M. Kruth. New York: Farrar & Rinehart, 1941.

[Rogers, Henry]. "Puseyism, or the Oxford Tractarian School." *Edinburgh Review* 77 (April 1843): 264–96.

——. "The Right of Private Judgment." *Edinburgh Review* 76 (January 1843): 198–217.

Roper, Michael, and John Tosh, eds. *Manful Assertions: Masculinities in Britain since 1800.* London: Routledge, 1991.

Rosen, David. "The Volcano and the Cathedral: Muscular Christianity and the Origins of Primal Masculinity." In D. Hall 17–44.

Rosenberg, John. *Carlyle and the Burden of History.* Oxford: Clarendon Press, 1980.

Rosenberg, Philip. *The Seventh Hero: Carlyle and the Theory of Radical Activism.* Cambridge: Harvard University Press, 1975.

Rothblatt, Sheldon. *Tradition and Change in English Liberal Education: An Essay in History and Culture.* London: Faber & Faber, 1976.

Rowlinson, Matthew. "The Ideological Moment of 'Ulysses.' " *Victorian Poetry* 30 (1992–93): 265–76.

Ruskin, John. *The Collected Works of John Ruskin.* 39 vols. Ed E. T. Cook and Alexander Wedderburn. London: George Allen, 1903.

Sage, Victor. *Horror Fiction in the Protestant Tradition.* London: St. Martin's, 1989.

Sedgwick, Eve Kosofsky. *Between Men.* New York: Columbia University Press, 1985.

——. *Epistemology of the Closet.* Berkeley and Los Angeles: University of California Press, 1992.

Seiler, R. D., ed. *Walter Pater: A Life Remembered.* Calgary: University of Calgary Press, 1987.

Selby, Robin C. *The Principle of Reserve in the Writings of John Henry Cardinal Newman.* Oxford: Oxford University Press, 1975.

Semmel, Bernard. *The Governor Eyre Controversy.* London: Macgibbon & Kee, 1962.

Sennett, Richard. *The Fall of Public Man.* New York: Knopf, 1977.

[Sewell, William]. "Oxford Theology." *Quarterly Review* 63 (March 1839): 525–572.

Shattuck, Joanne, and Michael Woolf, eds. *The Victorian Periodical Press: Samplings and Soundings.* Leicester: Leicester University Press, 1982.

Shaw, Marion. *Alfred Lord Tennyson.* Atlantic Highlands, N.J.: Humanities Press, 1988.

Shaw, W. David. *The Lucid Veil: Poetic Truth in the Victorian Age.* London: Athlone Press, 1987.

Showalter, Elaine, ed. *The New Feminist Criticism.* New York: Pantheon, 1986.

Shuter, William. "The Arrested Narrative of 'Emerald Urthwart.' " *Nineteenth-Century Literature* 45 (1990): 1–25.

Silverman, Kaja. *Male Subjectivity at the Margins.* New York: Routledge, 1992.

Simmel, Georg. *The Sociology of Georg Simmel.* Ed. Kurt H. Wolff. New York: Free Press, 1950.

——. "The Sociology of Secrecy." *American Journal of Sociology* 9 (1905–6): 441–98.

Simon, Brian, and Ian Bradley, eds. *The Victorian Public School: Studies in the Development of an Educational Institution.* Dublin: Gill & Macmillan, 1975.

Sinfield, Alan. *Alfred Tennyson.* Oxford: Basil Blackwell, 1986.

Small, Ian. *Conditions for Criticism: Authority, Knowledge, and Literature in the Late Nineteenth Century.* Oxford: Clarendon Press, 1991.

Smiles, Samuel. *Character.* 1860. Chicago: Belford, Clarke, 1889.

Stallybrass, Peter, and Allon White. *The Politics and Poetics of Transgression.* Ithaca: Cornell University Press, 1986.

Stanley, Arthur Penryn. *Life and Correspondence of Thomas Arnold, D.D.* 1845. New York: Harper Brothers, n.d.

[Stanley, Arthur Penryn]. "The Oxford School." *Edinburgh Review* 153 (April 1884): 305–35.

Stearns, Peter N. *Be a Man! Males in Modern Society.* 2d ed. New York: Holmes & Meier, 1991.

Stein, Richard. *The Ritual of Interpretation: The Fine Arts as Literature in Ruskin, Rossetti, and Pater.* Cambridge: Harvard University Press, 1975.

[Stephen, James]. "The Lives of Whitfield and Froude—Oxford Catholicism." *Edinburgh Review* 67 (July 1838): 500–535.

[Stephen, James Fitzjames]. "Gentlemen." *Cornhill Magazine* 5 (1862): 327–42.

———. *"Tom Brown's School Days." Edinburgh Review* 107 (January 1858): 172–93.

Sussman, Herbert. *Victorian Masculinities.* Cambridge: Cambridge University Press, 1994.

Swinburne, Algernon Charles. *William Blake.* In *The Complete Works of Algernon Charles Swinburne,* ed. Edmund Gosse and Thomas J. Wise, 16:41–350. London: Heinemann, 1926.

Symonds, J. A. *In the Key of Blue.* 1893. New York: AMS Press, 1970.

Tennyson, Alfred, Baron. *The Letters of Alfred Lord Tennyson.* 3 vols. Ed. Cecil Y. Lang and Edgar F. Shannon, Jr. Cambridge: Harvard University Press, 1980–90.

———. *Poems.* Ed. Christopher Ricks. 2d ed. 3 vols. London: Longmans, 1980.

Tennyson, G. B. *Victorian Devotional Poetry: The Tractarian Mode.* Cambridge: Harvard University Press, 1981.

Thompson, E. P. "Time, Work-Discipline, and Industrial Capitalism." *Past and Present* 38 (1971): 56–97.

Thornton, R.J.R. *The Decadent Dilemma.* London: Edwin Arnold, 1983.

Tintner, Adelaide. "Pater in *Portrait of a Lady* and *The Golden Bowl." Henry James Review* 2 (1982): 80–95.

Torgovnick, Marianna. *Gone Primitive: Savage Intellects, Modern Lives.* Chicago: University of Chicago Press, 1990.

Travers, Tim. *Samuel Smiles and the Victorian Work Ethic.* New York: Garland, 1987.

"Treason within the Church." *Fraser's Magazine* 17 (December 1838): 754–58.

Trollope, Anthony. *The Duke's Children.* Oxford: Oxford University Press, 1973.

———. *The Eustace Diamonds.* Oxford: Oxford University Press, 1973.

Tucker, Herbert F., Jr. "From Monomania to Monologue: 'St. Simeon Stylites' and the Rise of the Victorian Dramatic Monologue." *Victorian Poetry* 22 (1984): 121–37.

———. *Tennyson and the Doom of Romanticism.* Cambridge: Harvard University Press, 1988.

Vance, Norman. *The Sinews of the Spirit: The Ideal of Christian Manliness in Victorian Literature and Religious Thought.* Cambridge: Cambridge University Press, 1985.

Vicinus, Martha, ed. *A Widening Sphere: Changing Roles of Victorian Women.* Bloomington: Indiana University Press, 1977.

Viscusi, Robert. *Max Beerbohm, or the Dandy Dante: Rereading with Mirrors.* Baltimore: Johns Hopkins University Press, 1986.

Walsh, Walter. *The Secret History of the Oxford Movement.* 3d ed. London: Swan Sonnenschein, 1898.

Ward, Maisie. *Young Mr. Newman.* London: Sheed & Ward, 1948.

Weber, Max. *From Max Weber: Essays in Sociology.* Trans. and ed. H. H. Gerth and C. Wright Mills. New York: Oxford University Press, 1958.

———. *On Charisma and Institution Building.* Ed. S. N. Eisenstadt. Chicago: University of Chicago Press, 1968.

———. *The Sociology of Religion.* Boston: Beacon Press, 1993.

Wee, C. J. W.-L. "Christian Manliness and National Identity: The Problematic Construction of a Racially 'Pure' Nation." In Hall 66–88.

Weeks, Jeffrey. *Sex, Politics, and Society. The Regulation of Sexuality since 1800.* London: Longmans, 1981.

Welsh, Alexander. *George Eliot and Blackmail.* Cambridge: Harvard University Press, 1985.

White, Allon. *The Uses of Obscurity: The Fiction of Early Modernism.* London: Routledge & Kegan Paul, 1981.

Wiegman, Robyn. "Feminism and Its Mal(e)contents." *Masculinities.* Forthcoming.

Wiener, Martin J. *English Culture and the Decline of the Industrial Spirit, 1850–1980.* Cambridge: Cambridge University Press, 1981.

Wilde, Oscar. *The Artist as Critic.* Ed. Richard Ellmann. Chicago: University of Chicago Press, 1969.

——. *Letters of Oscar Wilde.* Ed. Rupert Hart-Davis. London: Rupert Hart-Davis, 1962.

——. *The Picture of Dorian Gray.* Ed. Donald L. Lawler. New York: Norton, 1988.

Wilkinson, Rupert H. "The Gentleman Ideal and the Maintenance of a Political Elite." *Sociology of Education* 37 (1963–64): 9–26.

——. *Gentlemanly Power: British Leadership and the Public School Tradition.* Oxford: Oxford University Press, 1964.

Willey, Basil. *Nineteenth-Century Studies.* New York: Columbia University Press, 1949.

Williams, Carolyn. *Transfigured World: Walter Pater's Aesthetic Historicism.* Ithaca: Cornell University Press, 1989.

Woodward, Frances. *The Doctor's Disciples: A Study of Four Pupils of Arnold of Rugby.* London: Oxford University Press, 1954.

Woolford, John. "Periodicals and the Practice of Literary Criticism, 1855–1864." In Shattuck and Woolf 109–42.

Wright, Thomas. *The Life of Walter Pater.* 2 vols. London: Everett & Co., 1907.

Yeats, William Butler. *The Autobiography of William Butler Yeats.* New York: Macmillan, 1965.

Zima, Peter. "From Dandyism to Art, or Narcissus Bifrons." *Neohelicon* 12 (1985): 201–38.

Index

Index

249

celibacy; earnestness; Evangelicalism;
gentleman; "manliness"; martyrdom;
masochism; monasticism; repression;
reserve; ritual; soldier

Semmel, Bernard, 126

Sennett, Richard, 12–13, 14n, 191–92

Senior, Nassau, 110

Shairp, J. W., 79

Shakespeare, William, 43, 133, 169

Shaw, Marion, 49–50

Shaw, W. David, 89

Shelley, Percy Bysshe, 60, 133

Shuter, William, 161n, 178

Silverman, Kaja, 11, 142n

Simeon Stylites, Saint, as icon of
asceticism, 37, 42, 48, 51, 107–8

Simmel, Georg, 97, 203–5, 208

Sinfield, Alan, 115

Small, Ian, 194n

Smiles, Samuel, 8, 68, 110, 163, 188

soldier, as model of masculinity, 6, 83,
215–16

Sparta, 215

Spencer, Herbert, 220, 226

Stallybrass, Peter, 111, 121, 128

Stanley, A. P., 17, 64, 76, 81; *Life of
Thomas Arnold*, 65–75, 86n

Stearns, Peter, 5–6, 26, 212

Stein, Richard, 209

Stephen, James, 84

Stephen, James Fitzjames, 69n, 97, 108,
173n, 207

Stowe, Harriet Beecher, 136

Sussman, Herbert, 12, 30, 63

Swinburne, Algernon Charles, 101,
202–3

Symonds, John Addington, 172–73

Temple, Frederick, 90

Tennyson, Alfred, Lord, 25, 109, 112,
133–34, 140 "Anacaona," 117–19, 130;
In Memoriam, 9, 16, 43–51, 104, 141,
147, 218; "Locksley Hall," 111, 115–
18, 125; "The Lotos-Eaters," 59, 104,

116–21, 123–25, 131, 140 "St. Simeon
Stylites," 37–38, 42–44, 52–53

Tennyson, G. B., 80, 89

Tennyson, Hallam, 118

Thackeray, William Makepeace, 55; *Vanity
Fair*, 8, 94–95

Torgovnick, Marianna, 131n

Tosh, John, 3

Tractarianism, 15, 17, 18, 60, 64–65, 74–
106, 108–9, 158–59, 171, 184–86, 206.
See also Newman, John Henry;
priesthood

Tracts for the Times, 87, 92, 100, 102

tradition, 59–60, 88–89, 93–94, 156–62,
169–70, 179–80, 206, 220

Travers, Tim, 163

Trollope, Anthony, 53, 105–6, 195

Tucker, Herbert F., Jr., 37, 42–43, 47

Vance, Norman, 53n, 151

Vaughan, E. T., 76

Viscusi, Joseph, 41n

Walsh, Walter, 87

Weber, Max, 10, 35, 39, 42, 63, 75, 104

Wee, C. J. W.-L., 152

Welsh, Alexander, 14n, 183, 196n, 201

White, Allon, 112, 121, 128, 226

Wiegman, Robyn, 3n

Wilberforce, Samuel, 70n, 105, 209

Wilberforce, William, 44, 91

Wilde, Oscar, 18, 55, 98, 183, 194–95,
209n, 229–30; *The Picture of Dorian Gray*,
194, 204–5, 217–21

Wilkinson, Rupert, 71

Willey, Basil, 66

Williams, Carolyn, 155, 160

Williams, Isaac, 87, 102–3

Winckelmann, Johann, 156–62, 164, 166–
71, 173

Wordsworth, William, 81, 205–6

Wright, Thomas, 209n

Yeats, William Butler, 37, 149–50, 185,
216